THE DESKTOP STUDIO

A GUIDE TO COMPUTER-BASED AUDIO PRODUCTION

EMILE D. MENASCHÉ

HAL•LEONARD®

Hal Leonard Books
An Imprint of Hal Leonard Corporation
New York

Published in 2009 by Hal Leonard Books
An Imprint of Hal Leonard Corporation
7777 West Bluemound Road
Milwaukee, WI 53213

Trade Book Division Editorial Offices
19 West 21st Street, New York, NY 10010
Printed in the United States of America

Book design by Kristina Rolander
Technical Illustrations by Amy Menasché

Library of Congress Cataloging-in-Publication Data is available upon request.

ISBN 978-1-4234-6331-3

www.halleonard.com

For Robert and Bernadette Menasché,
with love from a grateful son,
and for Amy, who still understands.

ACKNOWLEDGMENTS

When I pitched the first version of *The Desktop Studio* back in 2001, I had never before written a full-length book. Yet despite my rookie status and unorthodox approach to teaching computer-based music production—writing about many pieces of software instead of focusing on one application—my publisher at Hal Leonard, John Cerullo, stood behind the idea and supported the book as it slowly found a readership. I thank him for both the initial opportunity and for this chance to update it.

Hal Leonard Senior Editor Rusty Cutchin offered patient and constructive guidance as the book came together, keeping me on track and tapping into his own formidable knowledge of music production to offer advice. Carolyn Keating edited the manuscript, not only catching errors, but also making important suggestions that expanded on my initial points. Her knowledge of recording technology and her sureness with language elevated this book to another level.

The audio professionals who lent their expertise to this book are too numerous to mention, but a special thanks is in order for those who contributed information and tips to this edition: Rich Tozzoli, Jack Freudenheim, Fran Vincent, and the folks at Apogee Electronics.

Thanks to all the companies who lent gear for testing and provided up-to-date software, images, and technical support, including Ableton, Apogee Electronics, Apple, Bias, Cakewalk, Celemony, Digidesign, Euphonix, FXpansion, IK Multimedia, M-Audio, Native Instruments, Propellerhead Software, Roland, Sibelius, Solid State Logic, Sony, Steinberg Media Technologies, Submersible Music, Sweetwater, Toontrack Music, TC Electronic, Universal Audio, and Yamaha. A special shout-out to independent publicists Marsha Vdovin, Sara Griggs, Brian McConnon, and the folks at Giles Communications. Without their generous help, I'd never have had the opportunity to see the big picture.

Thanks to the many writers and editors I work with as a contributor to various magazines, notably Ken Schlager, Mike Levine, and Christopher Scapelliti; you've made me a better writer.

A high five to my colleagues at In Tune Partners, especially contributing writer Jon Chappell (who played a major role in the creation of *The Desktop Studio*'s first edition and offered much advice on this one), visionary CEO Irwin Kornfeld—who constantly pushes me to reach higher—and publisher (and fellow desktop producer/composer) Angelo Biasi.

Thanks to the musical collaborators who keep my exploration of music technology more about music than technology, including my mates in Speak the Language, Bob Hoffmann and Tom DeMartino; filmmakers James Spione and John G. Young; and Douglas C. Lane, John Montalto, and Monica Zane.

An extra-special thanks to my family for putting up with conversations about sample rates and hard-drive rotation speeds. And yes, now that the book is done, I'm getting all that gear—and all those boxes—out of the house!

Finally, thanks to the readers of the first edition of *The Desktop Studio*, whose enthusiasm made it possible to create this update. I love to hear from you—you teach me more than I can ever convey on these pages. As we enter the second decade of the new century, it's easier than ever to stay in touch. Please join the dialog at thedesktopstudio.blogspot.com.

TABLE OF CONTENTS

CHAPTER 4: AN OVERVIEW OF SOFTWARE-BASED PRODUCTION

PART II: WORKING WITH AUDIO

CHAPTER 5: AN INTRODUCTION TO HARD DISK AUDIO

APPENDICES

INTRODUCTION

I'll never forget my first music computer. A gray box that my dad had bought for keeping the books, it was nicely equipped for its day, boasting an 8 MHz processor (capable of reaching a screaming 12 MHz in "turbo" mode), 640K of RAM, and a whopping 40 MB internal hard drive.

After hours, this staid business machine became an important part of my recording studio. It was loaded with a DOS-based sequencer, Voyetra's Sequencer Plus, which offered multitrack MIDI recording, matrix-style MIDI editing, and the ability to synchronize to an external tape deck. Eventually, I added an 8-track analog reel-to-reel tape recorder and a DAT machine to the system, and started living my lifelong dream of having my own (albeit modest) recording studio.

The technology of 2-track hard disk recording emerged not long after I assembled that first rig. Suddenly, I could record actual audio—not to tape, but to my computer. Better yet, I could edit the audio after I recorded it. I ran out and bought a huge 200 MB (yes, that's *mega*bytes) hard drive and got busy dumping my mixes into the computer. They needed the editing.

Funny as it sounds now, that was a powerful system at the time (the speed and memory capacity specifications of those old machines look like typos when viewed today), and I used it to produce a lot of projects, including my first album and my first film score. But as much as I liked working with MIDI and editing my mixes, I dreamed of a time when I could record *everything* on my computer—audio and MIDI—in a multitrack environment.

Today, all of the tools I wished for are readily available. But the reality has gone way beyond the scope of my imagination. Nowadays, integrated software that offers multitrack audio, MIDI, automated mixing, effects plug-ins, waveform editing, and other advanced features is commonplace. Computer-based mixers boast features once reserved for the most expensive automated mixing consoles. Software instruments deliver sounds that rival—and outstrip—their hardware counterparts. Even programs designed for hobbyists—like Apple's GarageBand—boast capabilities way beyond the professional recording studios of yesteryear.

Unfortunately, it's easy to be overwhelmed by the sheer volume and complexity of the software and hardware that make up the desktop studio environment. The biggest complaint most people have is that the computer gets in the way of their creativity; its sheer power is seen as an obstacle. Time has a way of changing technology, but one consistent question I hear from first-timers (and some veterans) is, *How do I decide what pieces I need to achieve my musical goals?*

Software and hardware developers seem determined to make answering the above question harder and harder. They keep blurring the lines between traditional production techniques — like recording and mixing — and such creative disciplines as composing, arranging, and performing. In a desktop studio environment, you're often doing all of the above at the same time. Is Propellerhead's program Record — brand-new as this book goes to press — a variation on the traditional DAW? Or is it simply a way to add a missing element (audio recording) to the company's suite of musical instruments, Reason? Does it even matter? Probably not. What is important is whether you're able to produce satisfying music when you open the program.

As computer musicians, we enter a creative relationship with our machine that's not unlike the bond a guitarist, violinist, horn player, or drummer forms with his or her instrument. There's no ideal setup for all players. Ultimately, you have to find the right fit for yourself.

The Desktop Studio's purpose is to make that task easier by offering an overview of the tools and techniques available to computer-based musicians. And you'll find that, despite some differences in terminology and a few unique features here and there, just about every application in each category equips you with the same essential tools — and yet they're far from interchangeable. Think of it as the difference between classic electric guitars like the Gibson Les Paul and the Fender Stratocaster. Any guitarist who favors one can surely adapt to the other — they both have six strings, are tuned the same way, offer multiple sounds from their electronics, and so on. But each has its own tone, feel, look, and general vibe that appeals to some players more than others in a very personal way. The distinction between two pieces of music software can be just as subjective — and no less valid.

* * *

While the first edition of *The Desktop Studio* addressed the issues outlined above, the music business has undergone several major changes since this book first appeared in 2002.

First, music distribution has now almost completely shifted from the sale of tangible objects like CDs to the virtual world of downloads. Years ago, a mix engineer's ultimate test of a song was how well it translated to a car stereo; today, many fans listen to music on computers or portable players like the iPod or Zune. Thanks to broadband Internet connections and the popularity of "viral" sites such as YouTube, Twitter, and others, artists now compete for

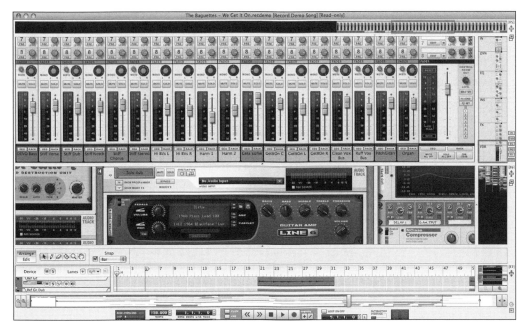

Music software is constantly evolving. Just as this book was going to the printer, Propellerhead Software debuted Record, the company's take on the DAW concept; read more about this and other developments at thedesktopstudio.blogspot.com.

audiences online instead of onstage. Artists are "discovered" on social networking sites like MySpace and Facebook—sometimes before ever playing a live show.

Second, increases in computer power have made laptops, once marginally effective for music, viable in the studio and for live performance. In addition, small, portable digital recorders (which can interact with computers) have become useful tools for capturing ideas. Many can even operate as audio interfaces and sound generators. Apple's iPhone has become a recording device, synthesizer, beatbox, tuner, and more. The desktop studio is no longer confined to a desk.

Third, the distinction between computer platforms has almost disappeared. Windows and Mac OX users enjoy virtually the same choices in audio interfaces, software instruments, and DAWs (though the latter is the one area where key products remain platform specific). Linux has also become a viable environment for making music.

Finally, the size and affordability of storage has revolutionized the way musicians can store their work. Today's machines make it possible to record more tracks than ever before, assemble vast collections of samples and loop, and work with digital video without ever leaving the desktop environment. Remember that 200 MB hard drive I mentioned earlier? It cost hundreds of dollars more than the 2-*tera*byte drive I have on my desk—which literally holds a million times more data!

But the question remains: Is the music we make with our fast and vast systems better than the work we did with the old gear? If not, what are the roadblocks? By getting a handle on the principles of desktop recording, you can make informed choices and build a system that suits you both objectively *and* subjectively. And once that system is in place, you'll have a head start in mastering the tools that can turn your ideas into tangible recordings.

This book won't replace your owner's manuals, but it should help you know what to look for inside them. As the saying goes, "If you want the right answer, ask the right question."

—Emile Menasché, July 2009

PART I THE BASICS

CHAPTER 1:   SYSTEM REQUIREMENTS

IN THIS CHAPTER ▪ THE KEY COMPONENTS OF THE DESKTOP STUDIO
▪ OPERATING SYSTEMS
▪ HARDWARE CONSIDERATIONS
▪ YOUR COMPUTER'S COMPONENTS

It's obvious, but we'll say it anyway: the computer is at the heart of the desktop studio. No matter what kind of hardware and software you use, its performance is only as good as the computer allows it to be.

▪ THE KEY COMPONENTS OF THE DESKTOP STUDIO

If you pay attention to the ads on TV that depict a population of happy computer producers living in a multimedia paradise, you'd think that every computer is an audio powerhouse right out of the box. Unfortunately, although many modern computers are designed with multimedia in mind, professional-quality audio is not the primary concern of most computer vendors. Computers are general-purpose tools: they must function in the number-crunching world of databases and word processors, spreadsheets, and e-mail. For the computer builder, audio is usually an afterthought.

Still, the typical consumer or business-oriented computer can offer a basic platform upon which to build a complete audio system. Yet with thousands of models and variations to choose from (not to mention the constant changes in technology that turn today's state-of-the-art dream machines into tomorrow's obsolete "doorstops"), it would be difficult to make concrete recommendations as to brand, model, or type.

There are, however, a number of factors that can influence a computer's performance in the desktop studio. These are the system requirements you'll find on every box of software or computer hardware. They tell you the minimum and recommended configurations for your computer. Keep in mind that software manufacturers can be a little optimistic when it comes to "minimum" system requirements; you might want to look at the "recommended" requirements as a baseline for setting up your computer.

▪ OPERATING SYSTEMS

Every computer needs an operating system (or OS) to function. And it goes without saying that your music hardware and software needs to be compatible with your operating system. The two most popular operating systems are Windows and Mac, but the open-source OS Linux has also developed a devoted following for music, especially with folks who like to tinker with their systems.

WINDOWS

Apple computers once dominated the pro audio arena. Today Microsoft Windows has become a popular alternative among pros—and an even more common choice for home studios. This is good news for the majority of users out there—Windows is far and away the most predominant computer platform in the world.

Thanks to Windows' massive user base, there is plenty of hardware and software to choose from. Windows has always been popular for entry-level and intermediate audio products—lower-cost units that appeal to first-timers. These days, there is also plenty of higher-end hardware and software available for Windows.

Keep in mind that Windows has a number of different versions, however, and audio products are not universally compatible among them. As I write this, Windows Vista has been out for more than a year, and yet has not completely displaced Windows XP, which did a lot to make Windows credible with pro audio users. By the time you read this, Vista may become the audio professional's choice, but one thing is certain; as operating systems evolve, software and hardware may take time to catch up. Make sure your OS is compatible with your product before you buy.

MAC

In the early days of computer music, Apple got the jump on DOS-based systems (the forerunners of today's Windows machines). Major audio programs such as Pro Tools, Digital Performer, and Opcode Studio Vision were all Mac only. The pro audio community followed the software, and the Mac became the dominant machine in studio circles.

Windows has made enormous strides as an audio platform, but the Mac still enjoys wide support, especially for intermediate and high-end applications. The Unix-based OS X completely changed the Mac and has helped revive Apple Computer's popularity. It's a powerful platform for all kinds of creative computing, and Apple made a major commitment to audio and video production by developing programs like GarageBand, iMovie, Final Cut Pro/Studio, and Soundtrack, as well as purchasing Logic from the German software developer Emagic, turning that already deep program into one of the most powerful on the market.

But, like Windows, Apple's OS is revised regularly (I'm writing this using OS X 10.5), and audio software and hardware is not always compatible with a new OS upon its release. This is doubly significant for Mac users because—as of this writing—Apple computers aren't backward compatible with earlier versions of OS X; if you buy a new machine and your music software is not yet compatible with the OS that shipped with it, you can't simply "downgrade" to the previous version and run the music software. You have to wait, or use an older machine.

LINUX

Linux is an open-source operating system, which means that users can get it for free—or at minimal cost—and can use it as they see fit. Like the Mac OS, it's based on Unix, but the two platforms are not cross-compatible.

Part of the culture of using Linux is shared development, so most Linux music software is either free or shareware. On the plus side, there's a ton of stuff available, mostly for download, so Linux users can experiment with unique tools without having to fork over hundreds of dollars for commercial software. On the minus side, commercial companies have the budgets to develop cutting-edge technology, so those wanting to stay ahead of the curve may not find what they're looking for in Linux. But even if your main machine is equipped with a commercial OS and software, Linux might be a fun way to keep an older machine running.

CHOOSING A PLATFORM

If you're shopping for a machine, you must balance Windows' advantage in cost and availability against the Mac's traditional edge in ease of use. Having used both for years, I can say that Windows machines can match Macs in many performance areas, but can also be a little harder to configure for audio.

The cost of a Mac notwithstanding, it's an outstanding audio machine, supported by a mature and elegant range of software. However, many of the applications on people's must-have lists are *only* available for Windows. And having a Windows machine makes it easier to share files with the rest of the Windows world, which, in addition to holding sway over business circles, makes up the majority of the music-making public. If that sounds like a hedge, well, that's why I have a Mac and a Windows machine, as well as a MacBook Pro that can run Windows using either Apple's Boot Camp or my preferred utility, Parallels Desktop.

Many of the leading audio and MIDI applications, including Steinberg's Cubase and Nuendo, Digidesign's Pro Tools, Ableton's Live, and Propellerhead Software's Reason, are **cross-platform** (meaning that there are both Mac and Windows versions available). Almost all plug-ins and software instruments—including those from leading companies like IK Multimedia, Waves, Arturia, Spectrasonics, Native Instruments, Steinberg, and others—work equally well on Macs and PCs.

A number of popular programs also remain firmly associated with a single platform. The most popular Windows-only vendors include Sony Creative Software (Acid, Sound Forge, and Vegas), Cakewalk (Sonar and the extended family of Cakewalk sequencers—though the company's Dimension software instrument, Dimension Pro, is cross-platform), Magix (Samplitude), and Adobe (Audition). On the Mac-only side, there's Apple's Logic Studio, GarageBand, and Soundtrack; the Bias Peak family; and MOTU's popular digital audio sequencer Digital Performer (though like Cakewalk, MOTU makes software instruments that cross over to the other OS).

Linux users have their own software to choose from. Linux is compatible with VST plug-ins, a format that also works with Mac and Windows.

Hardware is also tied into the operating system. Most of the leading MIDI interfaces support both platforms; on the audio side it's more of a mixed bag. While the majority of audio interfaces that support Macs also support Windows, there are still a few Windows-only interfaces on the market—though this has become less common with OS X's maturity.

STAYING CURRENT

While each new operating system is meant to squeeze more performance out of your computer, an OS upgrade is not always good news for desktop music production. After a new OS release, vendors must rewrite their hardware drivers. And even when these drivers become available, unforeseen problems can arise.

The vendors eventually catch up, but as one developer told me, "Musicians are always a couple of years behind the computer technology curve. They get something that works and want to stick with it." So a word of caution: *Always* check that your hardware and software are compatible with the latest version of your operating system.

Most of the pro musicians I know stick with what's working until they have to make the switch. By that time, they've already learned about the new operating system—perhaps by equipping a spare computer with it. Home users don't always have that luxury, but it may be worth keeping your old computer configured until you've worked the bugs out of the new operating system. (With the low cost of hard drives, users with one machine can do the following as relatively cheap insurance: Keep a spare boot drive configured with the old OS and software before you install a new OS on your computer. Starting up from the drive with the old system will allow the computer to operate as it did before the upgrade.)

■ HARDWARE CONSIDERATIONS

Software performance depends on hardware capability, so your choice of hardware is critical for music applications. The good news is that even a relatively modest system by today's standards can deliver outstanding audio performance. But, like many things in life, as capabilities improve, so do expectations. Performance that's blazing today will seem poky tomorrow.

DESKTOPS

Desktop computers are the most common computer models for audio production. Not only are they less expensive than similarly equipped laptops, but they also offer more robust performance and greater expandability. You have a wider choice of audio interfaces and other hardware at your disposal.

More important, the hard drive—one of the most critical components in a computer-based studio—is faster on a desktop. You can also mount multiple drives in a single chassis. The ability to house multiple drives can be critical for audio applications; most experts recommend using one drive for the computer's operating system and applications and a separate drive for audio files.

Desktop computers can often run two—and with an expansion card, more—video displays. A large, wide display is a great asset when working with complex music software, and is especially useful if you are running multiple applications simultaneously or doing something like programming a software instrument at the same time you are working on a multitrack arrangement.

The drawback of a typical desktop system is its lack of portability, though there are models designed specifically for music that can be mounted in the same 19-inch racks as other audio gear, and other kits will let you retrofit a computer to a rack (see **Fig. 1.1**). If you need to take your computer studio on the road, you'll have to haul the computer, the video monitor, and all your peripherals. Of course, with today's flat-panel monitors, this is less of a chore than it was in the days of heavy CRT displays, but it's still a consideration.

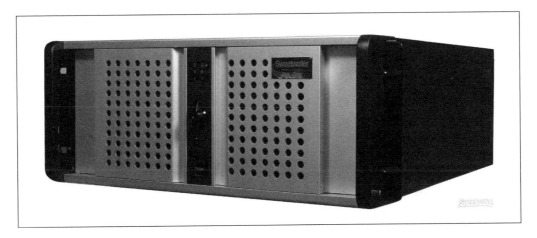

Fig. 1.1

Sweetwater's Custom Computing Creation Station Rack Plus is a "turnkey" computer system pre-configured for audio.

LAPTOPS

Laptops are getting faster and lighter every day—two factors that make them ideal companions for the musician on the go. The traditional limitation of laptops—expandability—has been largely overcome with the development of USB and FireWire MIDI and audio interfaces.

Laptops may not offer the raw processing power or hard-drive muscle of their desktop counterparts, but they make up for it in convenience. You can compensate for their main limitation—hard drive speed and capacity—by adding an external portable drive. Like desktops, audio-friendly laptops are also available as complete "turnkey" systems.

Some of the newer laptops now boast hard drives that are as fast as the drives that were offered on speedy desktops just a few years ago. On the downside, a typical laptop can only house one internal drive, which means you'll need to add an external hard drive if you want to use a separate drive for audio—which is highly recommended. But with high-speed, high-capacity portable hard drives easily available and affordable, this is less of a drawback than it was a few years ago.

Laptops still tend to be limited in terms of the amount of RAM they can accommodate, though this capacity continues to go up. (My MacBook Pro, for example has 4 GB of RAM—double the maximum capacity of the computer it replaced.)

Many laptops also offer expansion slots that can be used to add peripherals, including high-speed audio interfaces, additional FireWire or USB connections, and even high-speed SATA hard drive connections. The two types of expansion slots available are the older PCMCIA and the newer (as of this writing) ExpressCard format (see **Fig. 1.2**). Be sure when adding such peripherals that they work with your device, however. I've had the experience of audio losing sync when working with an ExpressCard expander that wasn't equipped to deal with the clocking issues of audio traveling across its FireWire bus. (Oddly enough, it worked fine over USB—an object lesson in how you must check a component carefully before adding it to your system.)

Fig. 1.2

An ExpressCard expander lets laptop users add high-speed peripherals.

ALL-IN-ONES

Some desktops, like Apple's iMac, are all-in-one systems. Like laptops, they have built-in monitors and limited expandability, but are larger (and more affordable). Serious pro audio users may frown upon these computers' lack of internal hard drive expansion and comparatively low onboard RAM—but their relative affordability makes them appealing for home users.

However, because FireWire and USB devices have become so popular among audio hardware manufacturers, you can equip an all-in-one for music production pretty easily.

■ YOUR COMPUTER'S COMPONENTS

The most important factors affecting computer performance are processor type, speed, and RAM. Other considerations, like the bus speed of the motherboard and the capabilities of the video display card, can also come into play.

Fig. 1.3

The interior of the Sweetwater Creation Station Rack XT audio PC. These custom-built machines use high-quality components—from motherboards to fans to drives and RAM—to optimize performance for audio recording while reducing ambient noise.

MOTHERBOARD

The **motherboard** (or **logic board,** if you're a Mac user) is a computer system's foundation. Most of the operating components of the computer—the processor, hard drives, RAM, video, communication ports, and expansion cards—are mounted on or connected to the motherboard.

The bus speed of the motherboard affects system performance. More important, the motherboard's chipset can cause conflicts with some hardware. For example, some sound cards, such as those used in Digidesign Pro Tools HD systems, will work with either Apple PCI Power Macs *or* the newer PCIe format found on Mac Pros and many PCs. The same scenario can happen any time a manufacturer releases a hardware upgrade.

PROCESSOR TYPE AND SPEED

The processor, or **CPU**, speed is one of the sexiest computer stats. The first computer music rigs had processors running at 8 MHz. How times have changed. The 3 GHz barrier was broken long ago, and the trend will only continue toward faster processors.

Just as important, many of today's machines have *multi-core* processors—single chips that behave like two or more CPUs. As I write this, eight-core machines are at the top end of the performance scale, and are known for their blazing speed. Of course, people used to consider the 20 MHz Intel 386 chip "blazing" in its day—and it was, when you consider that the software written for it wasn't that demanding by today's standards.

In theory, the more cores you have, the better your computer will be able to handle processor-intensive tasks like playing software instruments and processing audio effects in real time. And this is true—if the software and the operating system are written to take advantage of multi-core architecture. Not all of it is.

No matter how many cores you have, computers with faster processors cost more than their slower counterparts. Sometimes a mere 0.2 GHz difference in processor speed can raise the price of a computer by few hundred bucks. Is the performance worth the cost? Yes—but not always.

"Faster is better" might work well on the showroom floor, but processor speed is not the be-all and end-all of audio performance. Different types of chips may be rated at the same—or similar—speed, but may perform differently. For example, a machine built around Intel's lower-cost Celeron chip won't be as fast as one based on the Pentium or Core 2 Duo. More advanced chips not only have faster processors, but also utilize a larger *cache*—a kind of quick-access memory that stores frequently used data to help reduce the time it takes for the processor to access the computer's RAM. Without getting into too much detail, let's just say that a bigger, faster cache is a good thing.

Aside from general performance, CPU speed mainly affects a software program's ability to process audio in real time. A fast processor will allow you to run more real-time plug-ins. Some other operations, like the computer's ability to communicate with the disk drive, are also aided by a faster CPU.

But while a fast processor in and of itself doesn't necessarily mean a computer will be an audio speed machine, machines that are equipped with the fastest CPUs also tend to have other high-performance parts, like fast hard drives, fast logic/motherboards, high RAM capacity, etc. So to answer the question "Is the performance worth the cost?" all other factors being equal, you may not want to spend more on the CPU: invest in more RAM instead. But if the faster CPU comes on a machine with more RAM and a faster hard drive, then go for it.

EXPANSION SLOTS

There are two ways to add components to a computer: by connecting peripherals to built-in ports (such as USB and FireWire connections) or by connecting hardware via the computer's expansion slots.

Most desktop computers have expansion slots built onto the logic/motherboard. The most common formats on desktops are PCI (Peripheral Component Interconnect), PCI-X (X meaning "extended"), and the newer PCIe (E is for "express"). PCI and PCI-X use the same basic parallel architecture, but PCIe uses a smaller and faster serial architecture, so the two are *not* compatible. Some PC motherboards offer both types of expansion slot—which is great when you want to combine older and newer hardware. From the later G5 models on, Apple desktops feature PCIe slots. One reason the now obsolete G5 is still being used in many recording studios is that the new machines won't accommodate the PCI-format Pro Tools systems that are still in place.

Older types of slots—such as **ISA** (PC) and NuBus (found on older Macs)—have become rare and are no longer widely supported.

One unfortunate trend in computer design seems to be the reduction in the number of slots in newer machines. Look for a system with at least three slots: one for an audio sound card; another for a SCSI or FireWire interface; and a third for a video card, additional audio card (such as a DSP expander card), digital video input, or display card for a second monitor.

The absence of PCI slots is less of a problem today than it was a few years ago, thanks to FireWire and USB, which support audio interfaces, video input and output, and storage devices. Because you can chain FireWire devices together (and connect USB devices to a hub), you can add a number of peripherals to the same computer port.

RAM

Random Access Memory (**RAM**) is one of the most vital factors in computer performance. More RAM is *always* better. RAM is especially critical for multitrack audio because it serves as a buffer between the hard drive and the audio engine. More RAM allows the software to run more tracks (and more effects) at the same time.

RAM is also important when you're running multiple applications. Unlike other software, audio production applications don't run well under **virtual memory** (a technology that uses the hard drive to increase apparent RAM performance). In fact, many audio programs won't work *at all* if virtual memory is turned on. Buy as much physical RAM as you can afford. Think of 2 GB as a baseline for good multitrack performance.

HARD DRIVES

The hard drive in a desktop recording system has two important jobs. In addition to storing your system software, applications, and documents, it is also your recording medium. It will need to store vast amounts of data—and access it quickly.

For best performance, dedicate a separate high-performance drive to audio. This is even more imperative if you're working with audio and video at the same time.

Like processor speed, disk capacity is one of those stats that is often played up in brochures. And, because audio files are large, capacity is important. But if you're working with multitrack audio, disk speed and seek time are also important considerations, as is the throughput speed of the hard drive's interface. All three factor into the system's ability to read the tracks off the disk in time and intact.

Because choosing a hard drive **interface** is the first decision you need to make when selecting a hard drive, we'll review the different types available. Your computer can connect to hard drives via four types of interface: SCSI, IDE, FireWire, or USB.

IDE

IDE drives include Ultra DMA, IDE ATA/66, ATA/100, ATA/133, and SATA (Serial ATA), and are the standard for internal drive connections in most off-the-shelf computers. If your computer is compatible with these high-throughput IDE variants, you should be okay. These drives are much less costly on a per-megabyte basis than SCSI drives. Look for a drive that spins at a rate of at least 7,200 rpm and has an average seek time of less than nine milliseconds (ms).

SCSI

SCSI (Small Computer System Interface), once the only type of drive you could use with a Mac, used to be considered the cutting edge of hard disk performance. Today, the SATA interface is starting to take over, but SCSI drives are still used on high-e servers. There are actually several varieties of SCSI interfaces, and their differences lie in their **throughput**, or how quickly data can travel through the bus.

Standard SCSI, at 5 MB per second, is pretty slow by today's standards. Wide (20 MB/sec), Ultra (40 MB/sec), and Ultra Wide (80 MB/sec) are better suited to multitrack audio. If you're also planning to work with video, go for the fastest interface and drive you can afford.

SCSI drives can either be internally mounted or housed in external cases and connected to the computer with a cable, which means that they're also portable. Unless your computer is pre-equipped with a SCSI interface, you'll have to factor an interface card into the cost of the drive. Fortunately, SCSI devices can be chained together, allowing you to attach between seven and 15 drives to one SCSI card.

In addition to the cost, the SCSI card will take up one PCI slot in your machine, which could be an issue if you want to add lots of other peripherals. SCSI-to-USB and SCSI-to-FireWire converters exist, but these stopgaps won't give you maximum performance.

FIREWIRE

FireWire is a high-speed data-transfer protocol found on audio interfaces, digital video cameras, CD burners, and hard drives, among others. As of now, there are two types: FireWire 400 (400 Megabits per second) and FireWire 800 (800 Mb/s).

External FireWire drives can offer performance similar to the faster IDE-type formats, and have become extremely popular for audio and video production. FireWire ports come standard on all Apple desktop and laptop computers, as well as on many Windows machines. You can also retrofit FireWire to your system with an expansion card.

External FireWire drives are great for audio. For recording, look for a drive that spins at 7,200 rpm or higher. If you're using the FireWire drive exclusively for archiving and backup, you can go with a more affordable 5,400 rpm unit.

For audio applications, the case the drive comes in can be as important as the drive itself. Some external cases can be noisy—as in, "Holy turbine, Batman, that thing is loud!" noisy. The main culprit is the fan, which keeps the drive from overheating. Some models made for media production offer greater ventilation and quieter cooling; they cost more, but are worth the expense if you plan to record acoustic instruments in the same room as the drive.

Some FireWire drives can run on power supplied by the computer's FireWire bus—very handy when you're using a laptop on the go.

You can also mount a bare IDE drive in an external FireWire housing by using a commercially available mounting kit. Some of these kits allow you to swap drives within the chassis—cartridge style—essentially giving you high-capacity, high-speed performance in a cost-effective, removable unit.

USB

USB 1.1 drives are affordable and portable, but their performance is not generally considered to be up to the standards required for multitrack digital audio above four tracks. You can use USB to connect your computer to a **CD burner**, as well as to removable drives that you use for backup. **USB 2.0** offers speed more in line with FireWire and can support older USB 1.1 devices. My personal experience is that USB works well for storing audio for playback—things like sample libraries—but is less robust for multitrack recording. As with FireWire, some

USB drives can be directly powered by the computer. There are a number of portable devices, like Western Digital's wallet-sized My Passport (see **Fig. 1.4**), that are ideal for musicians on the go.

Fig. 1.4

Portable, bus-powered drives like WD's My Passport can store content such as sample libraries, backup song files, and more.

OTHER TYPES OF DRIVES

As technology develops, smaller storage devices, such as USB thumb drives and SD cards, are increasing in capacity. As I write this, thumb drives, which simply plug into a free USB slot, are too slow for audio recording, though they can be handy for transferring files.

SD cards have become popular in many computer peripherals, such as digital cameras, phones, video cameras, and portable audio recorders. These and other types of compact storage require a reader (some computers have them built in) to work with a computer. They offer amazingly high capacity for their size, and while they're not recommended for multitrack recording from the computer, they're great for transferring audio from a portable recorder and sharing files between computers.

All things being equal—such as interface and capacity—the performance of a removable drive isn't as sharp as that of a fixed drive. Removables can also be more error-prone: a removable might make a good second drive or backup, but it isn't recommended as a primary audio drive.

CD/DVD BURNERS

A CD burner is one of the most useful components in your system. It offers an avenue for distributing your music (allowing you to create your own audio CDs and video DVDs). It also serves as a tool for backing up your data files (one CD-R can hold up to 700 MB of data; a DVD can hold more than 4 GB).

Many of the latest computers offer built-in CD/DVD burners, and these will work well for both audio and data storage. You can also retrofit a CD/DVD burner for your system. You'll find burners with IDE, SCSI, FireWire, and USB interfaces.

One important note: By "CD/DVD burner," we're referring to peripherals that attach to your computer. Stand-alone audio CD/video DVD recorders that connect to your system via audio and video cables aren't used for data. These function more like traditional tape machines.

ADVANCED STORAGE OPTIONS

A **RAID** (Redundant Array of Independent Drives) gangs a number of hard disks into a high-speed modular system that behaves as one unit. A RAID can connect to your system via SCSI, SATA, or FireWire. Because standard drives offer such high capacity, a RAID system may be overkill for today's music applications.

Magneto-optical (MO) drives offer high capacity, reasonable speed, removable media, and great durability, making them a viable medium for audio backup. Many pros swear by MO drives because they're virtually indestructible, but on a cost-per-megabyte basis, solutions like FireWire might be more attractive.

Tape drives can't be used for recording audio, but they do provide high-capacity data backup to a relatively affordable medium.

VIDEO MONITOR AND DISPLAY CARDS

You might consider your video monitor to be an afterthought for an audio system. But consider this: music production software is data intensive, and there's a lot to look at onscreen. A typical session involves editing, recording, and mixing—and often all three activities at once. A high-resolution, 17-inch or larger monitor is recommended. Video resolution determines the number of pixels the monitor can display on the screen: the lower the resolution, the smaller the screen area.

Another factor is the card that sends signal to the display. Video displays tax system resources, and can slow performance. A high-performance video card with at least 32 MB of video RAM can improve performance of screen redraws and overall system speed.

Because screen space is at such a premium, you might want to consider a dual monitor setup, which is great in a music environment because it lets you look at your track editor on one screen and your mixer on another. To do so, you may need to add a second video card, or purchase a card that supports two monitor outputs.

Beware of conflicts between the video card and your music applications and hardware. Check your music vendor's website for information on potential conflicts.

COMMUNICATION PORTS

Communication ports allow your computer to interface with any number of peripherals, including standard computer hardware like printers, scanners, and modems, as well as studio gear such as MIDI and audio interfaces.

We've already discussed USB and FireWire as interfaces for disk drives and CD burners. But both interfaces can be used for other important peripherals as well. FireWire can connect directly to many digital video (DV) cameras, as well as a range of video digitizers. More important, it's beginning to gain support for audio interfaces. We discuss these in *Chapter 2: Gearing Up for Music.*

USB is widely used for connecting MIDI and audio interfaces, video digitizers, and other peripherals—including MIDI keyboard controllers, mixing control surfaces, joysticks, and other input devices. Although USB devices can't be daisy-chained like FireWire, a USB hub allows you to connect multiple devices to one USB port.

Serial ports are no longer available on some computers (such as current Macs), but they can play a role in the desktop studio as a connection for MIDI interfaces. Older pre-USB interfaces still exist, and offer excellent performance. In fact, some users feel that serial is more reliable for MIDI than USB. USB-to-serial converters can connect a serial interface to a USB-only computer, but like most converters, reliability can be spotty.

Parallel ports are used for connecting printers.

Ethernet is a high-speed networking protocol. You can use Ethernet to connect your computer (and some hard disk recorders) to other computers in your studio (in a network), and to gain high-speed access to the Internet.

Thanks to the increasing speed of Ethernet connections, networking is becoming more viable in audio circles. Some applications feature databases that manage files stored over a network.

Wireless connections are standard on many computers. A wireless network allows you to store masses of data on remote drives, access remote printers, and go on the Internet while keeping your main audio machine lean and portable. But even fast consumer-priced wireless networking can be too slow for real-time audio recording—at least it was in early 2009. But perhaps the day will come soon when an affordable wireless network will be fast enough for high-performance audio and video production.

Bluetooth is another popular wireless connection. While it's most widely used for phones, it can also be used for connecting peripherals like QWERTY keyboards and printers.

INPUT DEVICES

Okay, so you probably don't spend hours poring over catalogs for keyboards and mice. But these two devices will have a major influence on your computer/music experience. After all, you'll spend a huge percentage of your studio hours touching them.

For music, you don't necessarily need the most advanced QWERTY keyboard—you won't be typing all that much—but you will want one with a full complement of function keys. Wireless keyboards can be especially handy in a home studio because they allow you to stand away from the computer while recording.

Also, consider getting a separate keyboard just for music, and labeling its keys to show the keyboard shortcuts of your favorite application. Commercial products such as KB Covers' keyboard covers (see **Fig. 1.5**) and Editors Keys' keyboard skins let you view popular shortcuts—which, as we'll learn, can be true to their name when you're working in the complex world of computer-based music creation. You can also buy custom, prelabeled keyboards for popular applications from dealers such as Sweetwater, though these can get a little pricey and cannot easily be reconfigured for use with other applications.

Fig. 1.5

An overlay that labels the keyboard can make it much easier to master complex music software.

As for mice, I recommend getting both a conventional mouse and a trackball/track pad—and alternating between the two when you can. Mice require room to move and can be a pain in the neck if you're working on a cluttered desk, but overusing a trackball or track pad can cause problems in your fingers (I speak from painful personal experience).

In either case, look for a mouse with multiple buttons. Apple computers notoriously come with one-button mice, but the operating system does support multi-button mice, even those designed for Windows. I have a couple of Microsoft mice and a trackball that work well with my Macs; the extra buttons can be assigned to functions like the Control, Command, and Option keys, which saves me lots of time when accessing commands, etc.

Finally, you might opt for an input device designed specifically for media use. Since these fall under the category of "controllers," we'll examine them later in the book.

◼ MOVING ON

Once you have your basic computer system in place, you're ready to start adding the studio tools that will transform your gray (or graphite) box into a recording and production powerhouse. That's all coming in Chapter 2.

SHOULD YOU BUY USED?

When I'm not futzing around on my computer—actually, even when I *am* futzing around on my computer—I'm a guitarist. And like others of my breed, I love old gear. I have a 35-year-old Telecaster that I use all the time, a 27-year-old Strat, a 40-year-old amp, effects boxes from the '80s, and lots of other stuff that's been through the wars and has lived to tell the tale. None of this gear is what I'd call vintage in the "added value" sense. They're all good, working pieces, many purchased at a bargain. Why am I telling you all this? Because like a lot of us, I love a deal, and there are few things cheaper than used computer gear. And hey: if it worked for making records a few years ago, what's to say an old Pro Tools TDM system can't still produce the goods?

Nothing.

So, should you buy one on eBay?

I wouldn't.

And I say this from experience. A couple of years ago, I decided to get an Apple G5 on eBay because it seemed to be the last machine that would still be compatible with the software and hardware I had at the time. Intel Macs had spelled doom for some of my stuff. I shopped for a while and started bidding. I won a machine that looked perfect (I won't bore you with the specs).

But when it arrived, I noticed a bunch of little things didn't match the ad. The machine was loaded with software that I soon suspected was pirated. Extras that were supposed to come with it were missing. The guy who sold me the machine responded to my queries, but his name did not match that of the seller. Yet I had the machine in hand, and I had a project to do that was too demanding for my old gear, so I went with it.

Then I realized that the new machine's PCIe expansion format didn't match my PCI card. I should have known better, but in my excitement, I didn't bother to check and find out that Apple changed expansion bus formats before it went with the Intel processors. So my PowerCore plug-in card would not work on the new machine. Unlike the stuff I mentioned previously, however, this was all about my own lack of research. The seller hadn't misrepresented the PCIe slots. I couldn't very well return the machine for that.

Then, however, another problem arose. The computer's power supply died. I learned that this had been a problem with this model and Apple would fix the machine for me. But, in the process of getting the repair done, I again found out that there was something fishy about the G5. The name on the bill of sale did not match the serial number. I spent a long time on tech support. Apple was helpful, but I was getting worried. Finally, once the power supply was fixed, Apple told me the FireWire ports were now no good. This would be a $700 repair.

So my bargain machine was broken before I could complete the job I bought it for, had cost me a lot of very valuable time, and now would cost a big chunk of change to repair. I went through eBay and was able to negotiate a settlement with the seller. The machine ended up being used for journalism, but never again for music. It was a very painful and expensive lesson about used computer gear.

Unlike guitars and amps, digital electronics are almost impossible for lay people to repair. Worse, as models disappear, parts become scarce. Manufacturers really don't want to support their old hardware. The marketplace is designed to get us to buy new machines every couple of years. New software constantly pushes the processing power of the latest machines. Old machines can barely run it.

If you do buy an old machine, I suggest you get a turnkey system, meaning that the computer comes with hardware that can run on it. As for software: it may or may not be legal to buy installed software from a private seller. Ideally, you'll want to transfer the license to the software, but we all know people don't always *own* the license to software on their computers. Either way, don't expect much tech support from the software vendors.

CHAPTER 2:   GEARING UP FOR MUSIC

IN THIS CHAPTER
- AUDIO SYSTEMS
- AUDIO INTERFACES
- MIDI INTERFACES
- VIDEO INTERFACES
- SETTING UP YOUR SYSTEM

In Chapter 1 we examined the computer and some of its peripherals. To complete the picture, let's take a look at the hardware tools you need to transform your computer from a well-mannered business or home entertainment machine into a full-blown production system.

The key to setting up a workable, stable computer for the desktop studio depends less on the individual components in your system and more on how well they integrate. The expression "the whole is greater than the sum of its parts" is dead-on when it comes to computers. Another worthy cliché is, "a chain is only as strong as its weakest link." As you're assembling your gear, keep the entire system in mind, and never add a component without understanding how it will fit with all the others.

AUDIO SYSTEMS

The audio system, which governs the way the computer records and processes the audio signal, is one of the most central decisions you'll confront as you put together your desktop studio. In a nutshell, what type of system to get boils down to two choices: **native**, which costs less and is compatible with a wider field of hardware and software, or **DSP** (digital signal processing), which is more expensive, but boasts more robust performance. Of course, as with all things computer-driven, there are a few options in between.

NATIVE SYSTEMS

Native systems are by far the most popular option among home, semi-professional, and even professional computer recordists. "Native" means that the software relies on the computer's processing power for audio. The computer's own CPU, in addition to handling normal computer operations, will also be responsible for routing audio to the interface and powering real-time plug-ins and software instruments. Sonar, Logic, GarageBand, Digital Performer, Cubase, Nuendo, Reason, Live, Fruity Loops, and Pro Tools LE/M-Powered are all examples of native programs (though, as we'll see shortly, there's a difference between the Pro Tools products and the others).

The advantage of a native setup is that its capabilities can grow as the power of your computer increases. A speedy processor—or multiple speedy processors—is essential for getting maximum performance from a native system. As we've seen over the years, computers continue to get faster. Performance on native systems is plenty powerful as I write this and will only continue to improve as chip makers develop speedier CPUs with more processing cores.

In addition to costing less than hardware-based solutions, native systems enjoy wide compatibility and support from a majority of hardware and software manufacturers. Therefore, you can mix and match software and hardware from a variety of vendors. Mac users will find that competing products such as Steinberg's Cubase, Apple's Logic, Ableton's Live, and MOTU's Digital Performer can all address many of the same audio interfaces—or work quite well with the computer's built-in audio. On the Windows side, the story is similar, as Cubase, Live, Sony Creative Software's Acid and Cakewalk's Sonar will all work with any interface you choose. As long as the interface has its driver correctly installed in the computer, you're in business.

The same holds true for third-party plug-ins. Most native effects and software instruments are compatible with a long list of host applications.

The disadvantage is that whatever software and hardware you choose to use will have to work well with your specific computer system. When hardware and software come from different manufacturers, there are more variables at play—and therefore more potential problems.

Another potential disadvantage of the native approach is **latency**—the amount of time it takes the audio engine to process an incoming signal and route it to an output. The very nature of digital audio—converting a signal from analog to digital, processing it, and converting it back to analog for output—generates latency.

Low latency offers the best performance for real-time recording. High latency creates an audible delay between the input signal and the output. This delay makes it difficult to monitor an incoming signal directly through the audio engine. At its lowest (or fastest), it's barely noticeable, but latency of, say, 20 ms or more can get annoying when you're trying to play music and monitor through the computer's audio system. We'll discuss latency and ways of working around it in *Chapter 5: An Introduction to Hard Disk Audio.*

When native systems first appeared, latency was their biggest drawback. Today, most systems let you reduce latency to a reasonable level, but at a cost: the settings that reduce latency put more strain on the computer's processor. And although processors continue to get faster, the software has also become more complex, using up the CPU's resources. The type of audio interface—and the way it's connected to the computer—can also determine the amount of latency. FireWire and USB interfaces tend to have higher latency than interfaces connected to PCI, PCIe, PMCIA, and ExpressBus expansion slots.

Because native, real-time plug-ins rely on the computer's processor, they can use up your computer's CPU resources very quickly. Overloading the processor won't hurt your computer, but it can cause inconsistent performance, audio dropouts, distortion, and even system crashes. Few things are as frustrating as being in the middle of recording a take only to have the audio stop and the dreaded "System Overload" warning appear. A faster processor can help solve these problems, but they won't completely go away, as long as the computer's processor has to do double duty.

EXTERNAL DSP SYSTEMS

Instead of relying solely on the computer's built-in CPU, external DSP systems employ add-on expansion cards that specialize in audio signal processing. These continue to be the standard in professional applications, though this is beginning to change with the steady growth of professional-quality native applications. Pro Tools HD is the best-known DSP-based system. The advantage of a DSP-based system is consistency and stability: because the CPU does less of the number crunching, you can run a DSP system on a slower computer without fear of dropouts and crashes. DSP systems have traditionally boasted much lower latency in audio throughput, resulting in better performance than their native counterparts for tracking.

Digidesign's Pro Tools (see **Fig. 2.1**) is the reigning standard in desktop audio production, and will remain an important platform for years to come. It has also basically cornered the market when it comes to DSP computer audio.

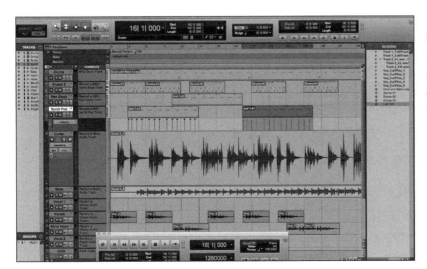

Fig. 2.1

Pro Tools HD uses specialized audio processing hardware.

The disadvantages of DSP-based systems are cost (they're much more expensive than native systems) and a lack of flexibility. The hardware and software are proprietary, meaning that you have a limited number of applications to choose from. For example, Pro Tools software works *only* with Digidesign hardware. On the positive side, Digidesign hardware can work with a variety of third-party applications, including native audio programs such as Cubase, Logic, Digital Performer, Nuendo, and others.

Digidesign *does* make native versions of Pro Tools, which work almost the same way as the HD version, but which cost far less. But they still require special hardware to run: Pro Tools LE works with Digidesign interfaces including the M-Powered software series and the 003. Pro Tools M-Powered software—sold by Digidesign's corporate sibling M-Audio—works with a variety of M-Audio interfaces.

HYBRID SYSTEMS

Hybrid systems—which combine a native application with a hardware DSP device, such as TC Electronics' PowerCore products, Universal Audio's UAD-1 and UAD-2, and Solid State Logic's Duende—give you the best of both worlds: the processing power of a DSP system in a format that's compatible with a wide range of native applications. DSP devices are available either as expansion cards or as FireWire devices that can work with either a desktop or a laptop—and can be integrated into an existing native audio system.

Powered plug-in systems come in a variety of configurations, from portable products costing a few hundred dollars, like the PowerCore Compact and the UAD-2 Solo/Laptop, to larger systems costing thousands, like the PowerCore 6000, Duende, and UAD-2 Quad Omni.

All of these systems offer a number of plug-in effects that operate in the same way as the host application's native plug-ins, but don't tax the CPU as much because the audio processing is handled by the device. Think of it as outsourcing for audio. Note that these DSP devices do nothing to improve latency (in fact, some can actually *increase* latency), but they take some of the load off your processor, freeing up your system resources to run both native and DSP plug-ins simultaneously.

Another important note about DSP cards is that they will only work with the effects written specifically for them. You can't, for example, use the PowerCore to accelerate the reverb effect that comes with Logic or to power Native Instruments' Guitar Rig. But you *can* use a PowerCore reverb, compressor, or EQ on the same track as one of those effects processors.

▪ AUDIO INTERFACES

Next to your computer, the most important piece of hardware in your studio is the audio interface, the device that converts an analog audio signal into a digital format, routes it to your software, and then sends it back to your speakers or headphones for monitoring.

Audio interfaces come in a wide array of types and price points. There are a number of important factors to consider when choosing one for your studio.

FEATURES TO CONSIDER

INPUTS AND OUTPUTS (I/O)

One of the most important steps in choosing an audio interface is determining the number and type of audio inputs and outputs (**I/O** for short) that you need.

Inputs are connections that bring audio into your computer. **Outputs** send audio from the computer out to the rest of your studio system. Inputs and outputs fall into two basic categories:

- **Analog** An analog input can connect to an analog sound source, such as the output of a tape recorder, guitar preamp, microphone preamp, or analog mixing board. Analog outputs can connect to mixing boards, tape decks, effects devices, monitor speakers, and headphones. In order for analog connections to work with the computer, your interface must convert the signal from analog to digital (and, on output, back from digital to analog). This is known as **AD/DA** conversion. We'll talk more about A/D and D/A conversion in *Part II: Working with Audio.*

- **Digital** These inputs and outputs interface with digital gear such as digital mixers, effects devices with digital I/O, digital mixdown decks, and outboard A/D converters. Unlike analog inputs, digital inputs perform no A/D conversion. You can't send an analog signal to a digital I/O device, or vice versa.

Many interfaces offer both analog and digital I/O, and can process both at the same time.

The number of inputs and outputs you'll need depends largely on your production style and on the capabilities of the rest of your studio gear. For example, if you work alone and never record more than two tracks of audio at a time (say, guitar and vocals, or the output of a stereo tape recorder), then a 2-in/2-out interface should suffice. But if you plan to multitrack a full band live, mic up a drum kit, or create surround-sound mixes, a minimal system would start at eight channels of I/O and go up from there. See **Table 2.1** on page 26 for a quick look at some recommended configurations.

Note, however, that interface I/O and track count are *not* the same thing. The number of tracks you have to work with depends on the capabilities of your software and system resources. You can easily create a 24-track (or larger) production using a 2-in/2-out interface.

SYSTEM COMPATIBILITY

Your audio interface *must* be compatible with your computer platform *and* operating system. Today, almost all audio interfaces are cross-platform (capable of working with both Windows and Mac systems).

APPLICATION	CD BURNING/ MUSIC ARCHIVING	VIDEO POST PRODUCTION	REMIXING	MULTITRACK RECORDING	INTERNET DISTRIBUTION
Audio Interface	16-bit or better stereo I/O (built-in is OK)	24-bit stereo I/O	24-bit stereo or multitrack with analog and digital I/O	24-bit multitrack with analog and digital I/O	16-bit or better stereo I/O (built-in is OK)
Video Interface with TV monitoroutput, FireWire (IEEE 1394) port with link to D/V camera	N/A	Full-frame digitizer	Optional	Optional	Optional
Software	Mastering software (opt.)	Video capture software	Multitrack loop construction software	Multitrack sequencer	Web browser
	Wave editor	Video editing software, Wave editor	Wave editor	Wave editor	Wave editor
	CD burning software	DVD burning software	CD burning software	CD burning software	Format converter
			Software instruments/ Effects plug-ins	Software instruments/ Effects plug-ins	FTP software (opt.)
			MIDI Editor/ Librarian (opt.)	MIDI Editor/ Librarian (opt.)	
				Score/notation software (opt.)	
Accessories	Turntable/preamp	Videotape deck	MIDI interface	MIDI interface	High-speed modem
		Television monitor	Mixing console	Mixing console	
			MIDI modules	MIDI modules	
	CD burner	DVD-RW burner	CD burner	CD burner	
	Monitor speakers	Monitor speakers	Monitor speakers	Monitor speakers	
			Sampler	Sampler	
			Loop/sound library	Sample library	
			Outboard effects	Outboard effects	
				Microphone(s), microphone preamp(s)	
Computer Reqs.	Stock machine	Fast processor	Fast processor	Fast processor	
		2 GB+ RAM	2 GB+ RAM	2 GB+ RAM	
		Dedicated high-speed hard drive for video	Dedicated high-speed hard drive for audio (opt.)	Dedicated high-speed hard drive for audio (opt.)	
		Dual monitor display card (opt.)	Dual monitor display card (opt.)	Dual monitor display card (opt.)	
			Expansion slots for audio I/O	Expansion slots for audio I/O	
Comments	For archiving, a minimal system will do. If you're using the machine as a "mixdown" deck in a high-resolution audio system, go for a 24-bit card	If you're using this as part of a multitrack recording rig, consider separate drives for system, audio, and video	Beat-matching/loop construction features are becoming more common in standard sequencers. Special effects are especially useful here	A good set of audio effects plug-ins will allow you to mix your project entirely on the computer. You can combine standard multitrack techniques with loop construction	Internet studio application lets you interface your multitrack software with other users online, allowing you to produce (as well as share) projects with people around the world

Table 2.1

However, there's another factor to consider: system upgrades. It is vital that your interface work with the same version of the operating system you have installed on your computer. An interface that works with Windows XP, for example, may not work with Windows Vista or whatever succeeds it (for more on operating systems, see Chapter 1). Each time Microsoft or Apple upgrades its operating system, interface manufacturers may need to upgrade their drivers to keep up. What's a "driver"? Glad you asked.

THE DRIVER

In addition to working with your operating system, an audio interface must communicate with your music software. This is done through a piece of software called a *driver*, which acts as a bridge between your software and the interface. The appropriate driver must be installed before your software can work with your interface.

Fortunately, an interface may have any number of compatible drivers, allowing it to work with a variety of software. The most popular driver types include the following:

- **Built-in** All computers offer some type of built-in sound that can be addressed on the operating system level. System drivers (like Core Audio on the Mac, **MME** on Windows, and ALSA in Linux) can address the basic sound input and output that comes standard with your computer. In most cases, audio software can use these drivers, as can third-party interfaces. Built-in audio used to have less robust performance than other audio systems, but today, it can offer excellent results. In fact, on the Mac side, most native formats use Core Audio, allowing you to switch freely among third-party hardware interfaces and the Mac's internal audio.

- **ASIO** Developed by Steinberg as part of its native VST (Virtual Studio Technology) system, ASIO (Audio Streaming Input and Output) drivers enjoy wide compatibility across both Mac and Windows platforms. There are two types of ASIO drivers: ASIO 1.0 offers basic compatibility, while ASIO 2.0 provides extended features and improved performance. ASIO provides multichannel I/O and is the de facto industry standard for native applications.

- **WDM** The latest audio protocol for Windows, WDM (Wavelength-Division Multiplexing) delivers improved performance compared to standard Windows drivers like MME by offering low-latency audio throughput. Cakewalk's Sonar and a number of other audio interfaces support WDM.

- **TDM and DAE** These drivers support Digidesign hardware. While they're primarily designed for use with the Pro Tools family of products, several native software applications, such as Logic, Digital Performer, and Peak, can address TDM (Time-Division Multiplexing) systems directly. Digidesign interfaces are also accessible via ASIO, but without the DSP processing power of TDM.

For best performance, always use the latest driver with your software (unless the vendor calls for an older version). It's always a good policy to check both the software vendor's and the interface manufacturer's websites for the latest compatibility information.

BUILT-IN AUDIO

The most basic audio system you can have is the one built into the computer. This can vary in quality from adequate to abysmal, depending on the specific hardware your manufacturer has chosen.

While built-in audio can work for basic music production and recording, even the best built-in systems lack the advanced features that are common in third-party audio interfaces, such as high-resolution throughput, digital inputs, and multichannel I/O.

An important consideration with a built-in audio interface is **full-duplex** operation. This allows you to hear playback while you record a new signal into the system. Without full-duplex support, it's pretty difficult to perform common audio operations such as overdubbing. Some built-in systems, such as those found on the latest Apple computers, have output but no input. You can play a signal back, but can't record without adding additional hardware.

PCI INTERFACES

A PCI audio interface—also known as a **sound card**—resides inside your computer and is mounted (you guessed it) in a PCI slot.

Audio connections to and from the computer may reside on the card itself, or on a satellite unit called a **breakout box**, which is connected to the PCI card by a special cable. The advantage of the breakout box is that it can be situated away from the computer and near your other audio gear. Some breakout boxes offer additional features, such as headphone outputs, microphone preamps, and word-clock inputs, which can come in very handy in a larger studio configuration.

PCI cards offers top-shelf performance, in part because they connect directly to the computer's motherboard and can take advantage of the speed of the system bus. On the down side, you must open your computer to install a PCI card.

In order to install a PCI interface, the computer needs to have an available PCI slot. Other peripherals, including video and SCSI interfaces, Ethernet cards, and add-on modems, use PCI slots, as do audio DSP cards and expanders. Unfortunately, the number of available PCI slots can be limited—even on a relatively well-equipped desktop machine. Worse, laptops lack PCI slots altogether, as do consumer desktops, such as the iMac G4.

PCMCIA INTERFACES

A **PCMCIA slot** is a standard expansion bay for laptops, which, because of the dimensions of their cases, don't have PCI slots. The high-speed PCMCIA connection gives a laptop many of the same advantages as the PCI slots on a desktop computer—fast data access and throughput. In addition to audio interfaces, you can find PCMCIA-to-PCI bridge interfaces, which allow a laptop to connect to an external PCI chassis via a PCMCIA card. This would be the only way to use PCI audio systems (such as Pro Tools TDM) with a laptop.

USB AND FIREWIRE (IEEE 1394) INTERFACES

At one time, the PCI slot was the only way to bring professional-quality audio into a computer. These days, fast peripheral connections such as USB and FireWire serve as viable alternatives. This is good news if your computer lacks PCI slots (as laptops do), but many of these interfaces perform so well that they're worth consideration for use with machines that have PCI slots.

If you have both a laptop *and* a desktop computer, FireWire and USB are especially appealing: you can connect the interface to your desktop when you're working in your studio, and to your laptop when you want to take your music on the road.

USB and FireWire are similar in that they're **hot-swappable**, meaning that you can connect devices while the computer is on. Each device can also connect to the computer via a **hub**, which can be very convenient when you need to interact with multiple USB or FireWire devices such as digital video cameras, hard drives, and CD burners.

As we discussed in Chapter 1, FireWire is faster than USB, and is considered the better choice for multichannel I/O devices, such as the 8-in/8-out MOTU 896 Mk3 (see **Fig. 2.2**) and the Apogee Ensemble. You'll also find FireWire control surface/interfaces, like the M-Audio Pro Control and Digi 003, as well as audio mixers with FireWire built-in, like the Yamaha 01v96.

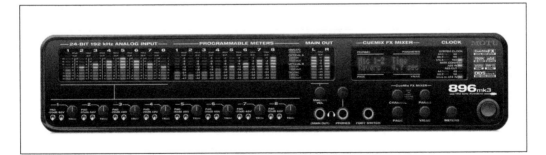

Fig. 2.2
The MOTU 896 Mk3

USB is more widely supported, and works well for 2-in/2-out and 2-in/multichannel-out interfaces. USB is also used for MIDI I/O, and some interfaces, such as the Tascam US-428, combine USB audio and MIDI. As of this writing, all of the USB and FireWire devices currently available are for native audio systems only. DSP-based systems (such as Pro Tools TDM) are still the exclusive domain of the PCI card.

Roger Robindoré is head tech at Apogee Electronics, a company that makes high-end A/D converters and other pro digital audio devices, as well as USB and FireWire interfaces. He says to watch out for three things when using an audio interface on an external bus.

- On the FireWire bus: "The FireWire bus is a great format, but it is possible to overload it without any sort of warning from the computer. Therefore, it's best to recognize these limitations and take care with just how many devices one connects. We've tested the connection of Ensemble [a multichannel FireWire audio interface for Apple computers], a hard drive, and a DSP processor on one FireWire bus, and this is pushing the limit, depending on the Mac used."

- On connecting hardware: "We don't specify a certain cabling order of devices, but depending on the device, unmounting it may remove the devices connected to it. Sometimes there's a bit of experimentation involved if one is connecting an audio interface and a DSP processor [such as the PowerCore]."

- On interfacing: "Clock configuration of digital devices is a bit like musical ensembles; the larger number of devices (or performers) that must work together, the greater the necessity for a master clock (or conductor). With this analogy in mind, it's easier to imagine what's necessary to make digital devices work together. Choose one device as a master, and distribute its clock as directly as possible to all the other devices. Our Big Ben Master Clock [and other such devices] does this quite well."

For more on master clocking, see Chapter 14.

MIDI Interfaces

MIDI, or Musical Instrument Digital Interface, is a control language that allows compatible devices to communicate with each other. With MIDI, you can use one device (known as a master, or **controller**) to operate another (called a slave). Each MIDI cable can carry 16 channels of information. The most common MIDI application is to have a keyboard controller driving one or more sound modules. The keyboard generates the note information (called a message) and the slaves make the sound.

Your computer can play a central role in a MIDI production studio by running sequencers and patch editors (we'll examine their uses in depth in *Part III: Working with MIDI*). But, as with audio, before you can use MIDI with a computer, you must set up a MIDI interface.

BASIC MIDI INTERFACES

With MIDI, the role of master and slave can change, depending on the situation. For example, in a basic computer MIDI system, a keyboard synthesizer can act as the controller while you record MIDI data into a software sequencer. When the sequencer plays the data back, however, the keyboard becomes the slave—its internal sounds are triggered by the sequencer.

The interface acts as a conduit for MIDI signals traveling to and from your computer. Interfaces generally connect to the computer via USB or a serial port, though some FireWire audio devices also include MIDI I/O, and therefore double as MIDI interfaces. Some PC game/sound cards (such as the Creative Technology SoundBlaster family) also offer built-in MIDI support. Today, almost all keyboard controllers—and some drum and guitar controllers—can connect directly to a computer via USB.

MIDI interfaces come in sizes ranging from basic 1-in/1-out devices (see **Fig. 2.3**) to compact multiport devices (see **Fig. 2.4**) to rack-mountable, multiport units with synchronization features that can be ganged together to form a huge MIDI cabling system (see **Fig. 2.5**). These larger devices are less common today than they were a few years ago. The emergence of software instruments (see Chapter 12) has reduced the number of MIDI modules in a typical studio.

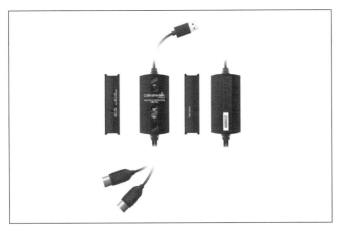

Fig. 2.3

MIDI interfaces with single ports for MIDI in and out are limited to 16 channels

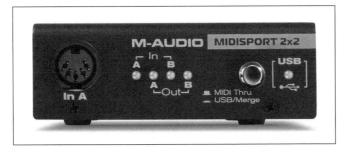

Fig. 2.4

M-Audio's MIDISPORT 2 x 2 can handle 32 MIDI channels.

Fig. 2.5

MOTU's 8 x 8 MIDI Timepiece AV can route more than 128 MIDI channels at one time while providing advanced synchronization features.

Whether it's a controller, a sound module, or both, every MIDI-capable device in your studio must make a data connection to your system via its **MIDI port**. There are separate ports for receiving (MIDI In) and transmitting (MIDI Out) MIDI data. Many devices also feature a third port, called MIDI Thru, which repeats any signal at that device's MIDI input. MIDI Thru can be used to daisy-chain multiple devices to a single MIDI port. Some of the more advanced controller keyboards on the market have multiple MIDI ports, in essence acting as multiport interfaces that can connect other MIDI modules to the computer system, or address these modules directly.

UNDERSTANDING MIDI CHANNELS

As you connect your MIDI gear, it's important to understand how the MIDI protocol works, so that you can send MIDI messages to the correct devices in your studio. Unlike an analog audio cable, which transmits one channel of audio (or, if it's a stereo cable, two channels), each **MIDI port** can transmit *16* MIDI channels. Each MIDI channel is an independent data stream. A device set up to receive on channel 1 will ignore everything assigned to channel 2, and so on.

CONTROLLERS, SEQUENCERS, AND SLAVES

MIDI systems typically consist of three types of devices: controllers, sequencers, and slaves.

A *controller* transmits **MIDI messages**. This is most often a keyboard, but other controllers include guitar synthesizers, wind controllers, and percussion pads.

A *sequencer* records, routes, and plays back MIDI data.

A *slave* receives MIDI data. Slaves can include sound modules, such as synthesizers, samplers, and drum machines, as well as MIDI-compatible effects devices and mixers. A keyboard controller, if it is capable of producing sounds, may also act as a slave.

MULTICHANNEL MIDI

Because many MIDI modules are *multitimbral*—capable of playing more than one channel at a time—16 MIDI channels can be used up quickly. A **multiport** MIDI interface (**Fig. 2.4**) lets you expand the number of available MIDI channels by offering independent MIDI data streams, each capable of playing up to 16 channels.

ADDING AN INTERFACE TO YOUR SYSTEM

Modern Mac and Windows computers make it easy to install a MIDI interface for basic routing. In fact, if the interface is **class compliant**, all you have to do is plug it into a USB port, and it should work.

Yet if you want to take advantage of advanced features such as multichannel operation and address more than one application at a time, you may need to install additional drivers, which are usually supplied with the MIDI interface. (Although the necessary drivers can be found in the interface's installation CD, you should still go online to download the most recent driver for your operating system.)

Fig. 2.6 shows Apple's OS X Audio MIDI Setup, which allows me to see all the interfaces I have—even those not actively connected to the computer—and graphically configure them to route MIDI data between the computer and my MIDI sound modules.

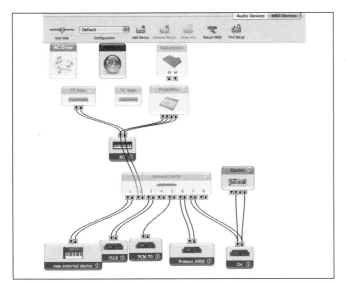

Fig. 2.6

Apple's OS X Audio MIDI Setup

Once you configure your studio, you'll be able to access each component in your MIDI system by name—much easier than having to remember port numbers and channel designations.

In Windows, there is no central routing station. All available MIDI ports will appear within your music software, and you can configure them from there.

TESTING THE SYSTEM

Troubleshooting MIDI can be a little daunting; after all, you're dealing with a chain of gear, and problems can occur anywhere in the chain. For example, you might blame the MIDI connections for the fact that you're not hearing the output of a synth module, only to find that the module's volume is turned down. If your MIDI software provides a MIDI monitor screen (see **Fig. 2.7**), you can use it to check MIDI connections. The MIDI monitor can tell you if MIDI information is being received by the system. Some monitors offer more detailed information—such as the type and channel number of the information coming in.

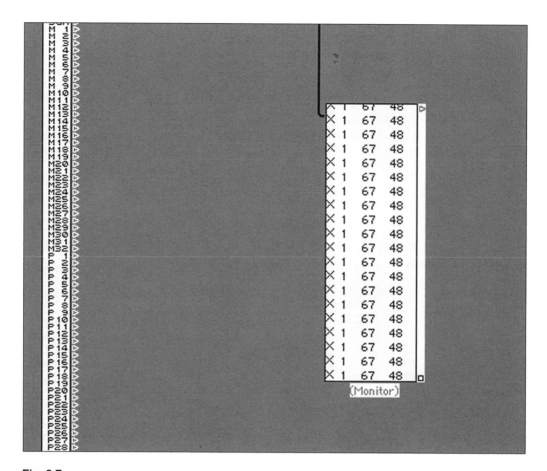

Fig. 2.7

A MIDI monitor can help troubleshoot MIDI connections.

ADVANCED ROUTING

Your MIDI interface can also act as a patchbay, routing MIDI information from one port to a number of different destinations. You can use this capability to layer the sounds of multiple MIDI modules together (also known as stacking). You can also set up your interfaces to route MIDI signals even when the computer is turned off, which is handy if you just want to jam without having to power up your whole system.

▪ VIDEO INTERFACES

Audio for video is one of the fastest-growing desktop studio industries. The computer's ability to quickly locate and mark different sections of a project is especially well suited for video work. A digital video interface allows you to transfer video into your computer, where it can be stored as a video file, then be imported into your audio and MIDI software and be synchronized with your music.

Like audio interfaces, there are PCI, FireWire, and USB video interfaces. Some of the more elaborate models offer onboard DSP that allows you to add complex video effects and **render**, or write, any edited video files quickly. But for general musical use, a more modest video capture device will work fine. Look for one that can capture **full-frame** video—up to 30 frames per second (30 fps)—and can import CD-quality (16-bit, 44.1 kHz) or better audio. A video interface that can output digital video to a separate TV monitor is also a plus. We'll discuss audio for video in greater depth in *Chapter 14: Synchronization and Working with Video*.

■ SETTING UP YOUR SYSTEM

Desktop studios come in a variety of sizes and configurations, and there's no "right" way to set up your system. The most important feature your studio can have is compatibility—with you. It must suit your style and fit your goals. If you're starting from scratch, you can build a system from the ground up to do just that. However, if you're like most of us, you won't be building your desktop studio in a vacuum; instead, you'll be adding to an already existing arsenal of audio tools.

THE INTEGRATION BETWEEN NEW AND EXISTING EQUIPMENT

Unless you're completely new to the audio production game, you probably have some gear lying around already: MIDI controllers, tape recorders, digital effects units, a mixing board, etc. If you're upgrading from an older computer production system, you may also have sound cards and MIDI interfaces that you'll want to add to your new computer.

Check the compatibility of any legacy hardware or software with your new system. The simplest incompatibility can sink you. If, for example, you have an older computer that can only host a couple of gigabytes of RAM, you may not be able to use newer software. And what if your motherboard has PCI slots, but your hardware is in the PCIe format? Or you have USB 1.0 and need USB 2.0 for that outboard audio interface? These are all important considerations to keep in mind as you build your system.

DEFINING YOUR GOALS

Every time a new computer catalog comes out or I see a new piece of software, my heart starts beating a little more quickly. I put down my guitar and think about how many tracks I'll be able to mix in real time with a new computer, and how cool my next project will sound with the latest plug-ins. There's nothing wrong with that, but sometimes it's easy to lose sight of the more important picture—the music and the performance.

Understanding your goals will help you build a system that will work now, and grow as your needs change. If you're hoping to catalog a bunch of LPs (extra credit for those of you who remember what those are) and burn them onto CD, your needs will differ from someone who wants to add sound to video projects, or someone hoping to produce and remix dance music, or a band trying to record an album. And of course, there are probably a lot of readers who are looking at this list and thinking, "I want to do all those things—and more!" Fortunately, the manufacturers have the "and more!" part pretty well covered.

COMMON APPLICATIONS

Figs. 2.8–2.11 shows some basic hardware and software setups for a number of applications. You can mix and match components from any of these applications in your system.

Because desktop studios are **modular**—made up of a number of interchangeable components—you can add elements as your needs grow. The fact that many of the tools you're going to use are software-based makes things even easier. For example, your multitrack sequencer, waveform editor, and loop-construction software may well be compatible with the same software plug-ins and hardware audio interface. These software applications may link together so that you can operate them as a complete system.

EXAMPLE SETUPS

The computer might be the central component in the desktop studio, but it's still only one part of a larger audio system. There are no hard-and-fast rules about how to set up a computer with other audio gear. In fact, how you cable everything together is one of the first ways you can exercise your creativity. Still, there are some basic configurations that can serve as a starting point for setting up your ideal system (see **Figs. 2.8 – 2.11**).

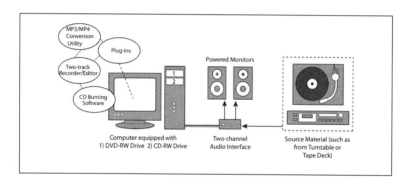

Fig. 2.8

A basic system for digital archiving of existing recordings.

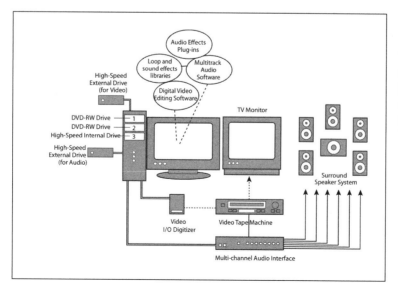

Fig. 2.9

This video editing system can handle both predigitized video and material that's on videotape.

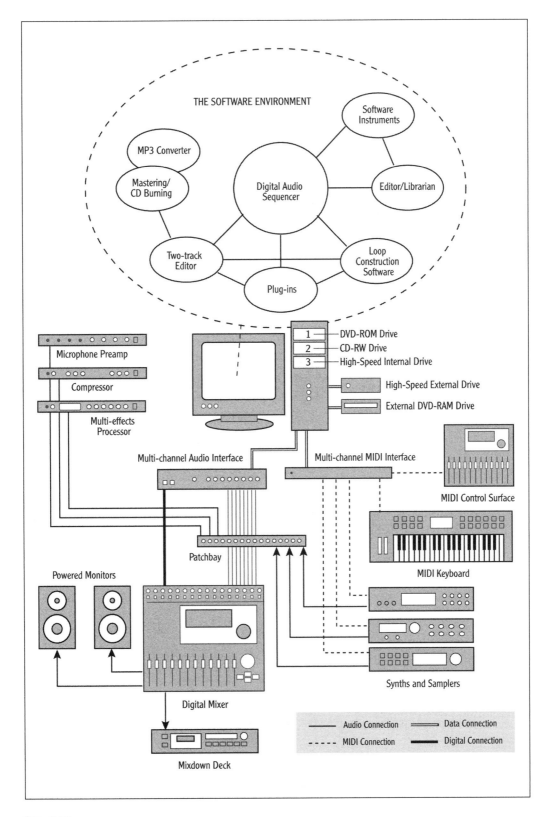

Fig. 2.10

A comprehensive audio production system integrates a range of hardware devices and software applications.

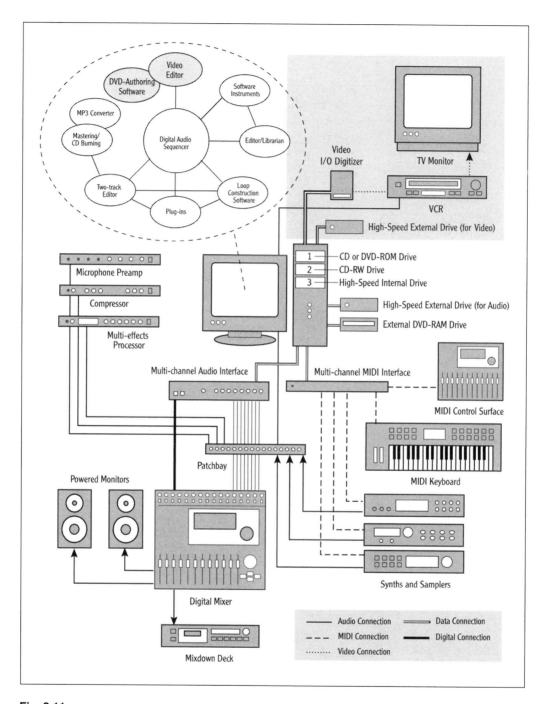

Fig. 2.11

With a video digitizer (or DV camera) added, this system can cover almost any kind of production.

A COMFORTABLE WORKSPACE

You're going to be spending many hours in your studio, so it had better be comfortable. One of the nice things about a desktop studio is that you can place all of your controls within arm's reach. But there's a flipside—the studio can get very cramped.

Start with a table that's a comfortable height. You'll need good sightlines to your monitor and comfortable access to your keyboard, mouse, and any other control devices, such as MIDI keyboards and mixing surfaces.

When you're setting up your system, bear in mind that you'll be doing two types of monitoring: visual (via your computer screen) and auditory (via your monitor speakers). You must decide which devices will sit in your ideal monitoring position, or sweet spot. **Fig. 2.12** and **Fig. 2.13** show two example setups.

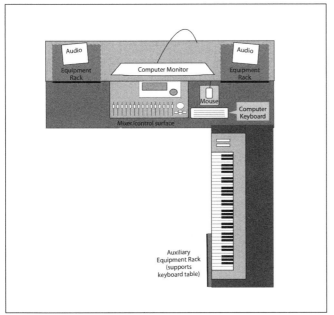

Fig. 2.12

Arranging your gear in an L shape gives you room to move—especially nice if you play guitar or bass.

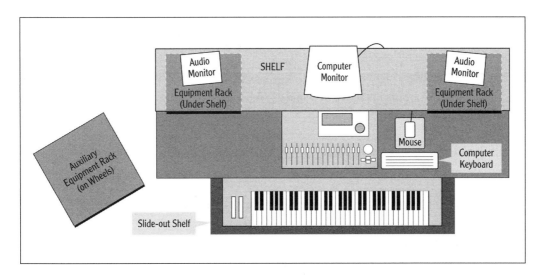

Fig. 2.13

With both keyboard and mix control surfaces in easy reach, this setup can be very efficient for composing.

INSTALLING COMPONENTS

Setting up a desktop studio can be intimidating for the uninitiated. The biggest psychological hurdle some of us have is opening up the computer and installing hardware inside it. Fortunately, as long as you follow your manufacturer's guidelines and observe a few precautions, it's not the ordeal you may envision.

Since computer case design varies so widely from manufacturer to manufacturer, we'll stick to a few general tips that should help you through the process.

INSTALLATION TIPS

- **Back up your hard disk before you open your computer.** In truth, you're unlikely to lose any of your work if you take precautions, but why take a chance? It's a good idea to keep your backups current at all times.

- **Unplug everything before opening up the computer.** Disconnect all peripherals and power cables unless otherwise instructed in your computer's documentation. Wait a few minutes before touching anything, as voltage can still be stored in the computer's components even after it is unplugged.

- **Work in a well-lit, stable environment.** Small parts can fall into a computer, and it's no fun trying to find them when you're stretched out on the floor under your synthesizers, mixing boards, and audio cables. Also, when installing PCI cards and RAM, you may need to exert considerable force to seat them. A solid table or workbench is the ideal working environment.

- **Eliminate static.** Static electricity can damage computer components. You can wear a special "ground strap" to protect against static. You can also get rid of a static charge on your person by touching a grounded or metal device.

- **Use a magnetic screwdriver.** Computer screws are small, and will fall away from you at the least opportune times. A magnetic screwdriver can hold the screw when your free hand can't.

- **Keep all parts in a safe place.** This is a good idea under any circumstances, but is even more vital when working with computers. Did I mention that the screws are small?

- **When installing RAM and expansion cards, push firmly and carefully.** Line the card up precisely with its slot, and don't be afraid to exert the pressure needed to get the card all the way in. If the card doesn't mount on the first try, unseat it and try again. Sometimes, it takes a really good push.

- **Screw expansion cards firmly in place.** This keeps the card stable. Otherwise, pressure can move the card out of its slot, damaging your system.

- **When installing hard drives, make sure the connections are secure and the jumpers are set correctly.** Hard drives and other storage devices have an ID setting that lets the system identify them. These and other settings are often made with tiny hardware connectors called **jumpers**. Follow the manufacturer's instructions and keep any extra jumpers safe—you never know when you might need them. Hard drive connections include the interface for the drive and the power supply. Don't forget the power supply.

- **Replace the computer cover and install any driver software.** You computer should automatically recognize upgraded RAM, but other kinds of hardware installations involve some software setup. Have the latest drivers on hand before you start installing the software. (*Hint:* Check the appropriate websites for the latest drivers before you take your computer apart. This way, their installers will already be on your computer when you're ready to configure your system.) If you're installing disk drives, they may need to be formatted before your system will recognize them (some drives come preformatted).

- **Check your work.** I like to test new components before I put the computer back in its original location. This way, if there are problems, I don't have to crawl back under my racks in order to fix them.

If you're installing external gear, such as FireWire and USB audio interfaces and storage devices, or USB MIDI interfaces, you don't need to venture inside the computer. But you'll still need to install driver software. As always, download the latest version.

MAKING CONNECTIONS

In order to integrate your desktop studio with other recording equipment, you'll need to make a number of different connections. These fall into two categories:

- **Data connections** include connections between the computer and any audio, MIDI, or video interfaces, and MIDI connections between the MIDI interface and your MIDI gear.

- **Audio connections** include analog and digital audio connections between your audio interface, mixer, sound modules, and monitoring system.

AUDIO CONNECTORS

Audio connectors come in many types (see **Fig. 2.14**). Analog connectors can be unbalanced (two-conductor) or balanced (three-conductor). Which connections you'll make depends on your gear. In all likelihood, your studio will feature a mix of balanced and unbalanced lines. Your gear's documentation will detail which connections you need to make.

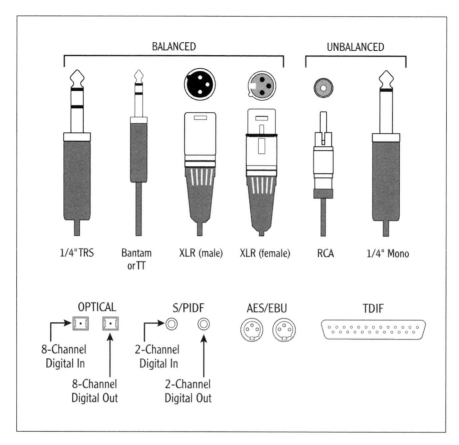

Fig. 2.14

Common audio connectors

Unbalanced connectors are common on consumer and semi-professional gear. They can be noisier than balanced lines on longer cable runs and generally have a lower line-level output (–10 dBV) than balanced circuits.

Balanced connectors are standard in professional audio gear and are becoming more common in desktop studio applications. Balanced lines feature separate wires for positive, negative, and ground, thereby reducing the possibility of noise in the system over long cable runs. Balanced cables also have a higher line-level output (+4 dBu) than their unbalanced counterparts.

Use high-quality audio cables. Computers and monitors can generate noise that may be picked up by cheap cables. And why would you want to negate the investment you make in a good audio interface by feeding it lousy signal through a cheap cable?

DIGITAL AUDIO CONNECTIONS

Desktop recording is by definition a digital medium, and many computer sound cards feature digital as well as analog connections. There are several formats for digital I/O:

- **S/PDIF (Sony/Philips Digital Interface):** A very common stereo digital interface found on semi-professional and consumer digital gear. Uses either an RCA or optical-type connector.

- **AES/EBU:** A stereo digital interface used on professional audio gear. Uses a three-conductor XLR connector.

- **ADAT or Lightpipe:** An 8-channel digital connection over an optical cable.

- **TDIF (Tascam Digital Interface):** An 8-channel digital connection with a 25-pin D-sub connector.

▓ Moving On

Now that you have your hardware muscle in order, you're ready to start adding some brains to your outfit—in the form of software. *Chapter 3: Software at a Glance* offers a thumbnail sketch of the most important applications that make up the desktop studio, while the succeeding chapters will take us deeper into each one.

CHAPTER 3:   SOFTWARE AT A GLANCE

A traditional recording studio is a system of interrelated components: multitrack recorder, mixing board, effects processors, outboard preamps, and mixdown deck. Back in the day, a well-equipped studio would have included a hardware sequencer for recording MIDI, plus various other music-making tools: instruments, microphones, drum machines, and more.

▓ THE DIGITAL AUDIO WORKSTATION CONCEPT

The desktop studio is capable of combining almost all of the traditional studio tools detailed above into one centralized system of software components. This concept is known as the digital audio workstation (DAW), an integrated software environment that allows you to record, edit, process, mix, and distribute your music.

A DAW can consist of one all-inclusive software application — that's the most common use of the term — or can be made up of individual software elements. Most serious computer music makers opt for a combination of both. One central application, such as a digital audio sequencer, will handle the bulk of the work, while supporting software will be called in for specific tasks (like effects processing or waveform editing).

Some of the most popular support applications are listed below:

- **Audio plug-ins** provide audio effects processing, such as reverb, compression, and delay.

- **Software instruments** provide synthesizers, samplers, and drum machines.

- **Waveform editors** let you edit audio files at the sample level to optimize sound quality.

- **Loop construction/beat-matching software** lets you manipulate the tempo and pitch of audio files.

- **MIDI editor/librarians** allow you to store and edit all the MIDI setups in your studio, and to download and upload these setups to and from your MIDI devices.

- **Mastering software** helps you prepare your mixes for final output to CD or other media.

- **CD and DVD authoring software** lets you create CDs of your audio and back up your data files.

- **File conversion software** lets you convert your mixes to Internet-friendly formats, such as MP3.

- **Internet software** lets you share your music with others online.

- **System and driver software** connect the pieces together.

You may find that many of these tools are built into your DAW; for example, when Apple acquired the program Logic, the company added the beat- and pitch-stretching capabilities of GarageBand to Logic's feature set. Many programs, including Logic, Live, Cubase, Digital Performer, and Sonar, now come with an ever-growing collection of software instruments, virtual drum machines, and effects. The trend in software development is to continuously add features, often "borrowing" ideas from popular stand-alone programs. Even the most "traditional" of the production DAWs, Pro Tools, now has a host of software instruments, as well as music creation and loop production features.

But whether they're components within a package or independent pieces of software, these applications all play an important role in the desktop studio.

■ MULTITRACK RECORDERS AND SEQUENCERS

The combination of sequencing and nonlinear audio recording is the foundation of desktop audio. Because you can edit nonlinear audio in much the same way you can manipulate sequencer data, the two types of recording can live side by side.

The first program of this type to be available on computers was Opcode System's StudioVision, which used Pro Tools hardware and allowed audio to be recorded alongside MIDI. It's been over 20 years since the release of StudioVision, and there's a whole generation of recordists who've never used anything but a computer to record music. But for those of us who remember tape, it's still a bit of a treat to be able to drag a piece of audio from one part of a song to another.

The degree of integration between audio and MIDI has increased within this category, but there are some major differences in how the leading programs handle these two different chores. Digidesign's Pro Tools, for example, began life as an audio program, and its features still emphasize audio over MIDI production (though its MIDI capabilities continue to improve). Logic, Steinberg's Cubase, Cakewalk's Sonar, and MOTU's Digital Performer evolved from MIDI sequencers, and so combine some deep and highly developed MIDI tools with a healthy audio feature set.

Wherever the balance lies within a piece of software, a DAW has two primary tasks: multitrack audio recording and MIDI sequencing.

MULTITRACK RECORDING

The multitrack audio recorder is at the heart of the DAW concept, and most computer audio systems are built around this application. Multitrack audio recorders that include MIDI recording and playback are often called *digital audio sequencers* because they allow sequencer-type editing of audio material.

Multitrack audio recording (sometimes referred to as "sound-on-sound recording") got its start in the days of analog tape, when audio was recorded on physical sections of the tape (a track). A multitrack lets you record and play back two or more separate tracks at the same time.

A multitrack recorder's most important feature is its ability to overdub, or record new material, alongside previously recorded material *without erasing that previously recorded material*. This lets you add additional parts to previously recorded instruments and record alternative takes of important parts, like lead vocals and guitar solos.

Most computer-based multitracks take this concept further by offering what are called **virtual tracks**. This is a great feature to use—but a tricky one to explain. But bear with me and I'll have a go: On a multitrack tape recorder, a track is a single entity. It can contain audio, but every time you record new audio on that track, you record over the old audio, erasing it. So, if track 8 has a guitar solo you want to do over, you have two choices: record another one on track 9, or erase the one on track 8 and try again. A virtual track works differently, letting you record many versions of track 8, without erasing the original. Track 8 can still only play one of these versions at a time, but you can switch freely among them. Even better, you can edit among them, or even copy one of the extra track 8 recordings to any other track in your project. Make sense? I hope so, because it will come up time and again throughout this book.

In studio jargon, combining the best parts of a performance is called "comping." One of the latest trends in multitrack audio software is the *comp track*, which is like a single container containing a number of virtual tracks. The comp track concept lets you see all of the virtual tracks for a particular part at once and select pieces of them quickly. We'll address this feature in depth in Chapters 4, 5, and 6.

SEQUENCING

Most computer musicians use the term *sequencer* to describe any piece of software that can record MIDI data, even if the program can also record audio. In fact, most software sequencers today can handle both audio and MIDI. Digital Performer, Sonar, Cubase, and Logic (see **Fig. 3.1**) are among the programs that started life as MIDI sequencers.

Fig. 3.1

Apple Logic Pro

The term *sequencer* originally referred to hardware devices designed to record electronic impulses, which would in turn trigger sounds on a synthesizer or drum machine. These impulses were recorded in a series—a "sequence," as it were.

A MIDI sequencer (or a digital audio sequencer's MIDI component) records data called *messages*. These messages are used to control the sounds made by other devices. They act as triggers, but generate no sounds of their own. Note messages, for example, merely tell your MIDI sound-generating devices what notes to play, and when. The sound generator can then be set to any tone, at any volume, that you like.

The sequencer's greatest appeal lies in its ability to alter a performance after it has already been recorded. You can change a song's tempo or key, or go inside the music to change an individual note's pitch, timing, and other attributes. MIDI sequencers can trigger external devices that are connected to the computer, or play software instruments that reside inside the computer itself.

New developments in audio software are making this kind of note-to-note editing possible on audio recordings as well.

In addition to the sequencers found in DAWs, you'll also find sequencers that are built into software instruments (such as Propellerhead's Reason and Image Line Software's FL Studio), which specialize in playing sounds resident in their respective programs, but which do not trigger any external sound modules.

■ LOOP-CONSTRUCTION SOFTWARE

Loop construction tools have revolutionized audio production. Designed to eliminate the tedium of *beat-matching* (editing audio loops so they can match a specific tempo), these tools quickly caught on with producers of beat-driven genres like hip hop, electronic, house, etc. Unlike conventional audio recording, in which the tempo of an audio file is fixed, loop construction allows you to manipulate the tempo of an audio file after it has been recorded—without affecting other attributes, such as pitch.

Sony's Acid (see **Fig. 3.2**) and Cakewalk's Sonar were early multitrack recorders that featured time stretching and pitch manipulation of previously recorded material, but this capability is now available in a wide range of programs.

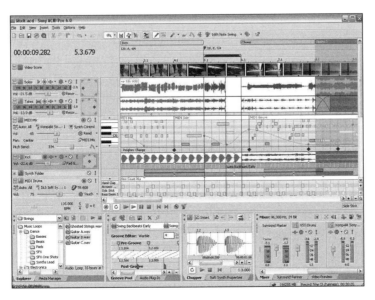

Fig. 3.2

Sony Acid loop construction and multitrack recording software

Propellerhead's ReCycle is another useful loop-construction tool that divides an audio file into segments that can be triggered individually, in effect allowing the file to play back at any tempo.

2-TRACK RECORDERS AND WAVEFORM EDITORS

2-track recording and waveform editing software, such as Bias Peak (see **Fig. 3.3**) work with digital audio at its most basic level: the sample. These programs are useful for recording mixes, culling previously recorded material from CD, preparing previously recorded audio files for distribution, or mastering and editing audio files in fine detail.

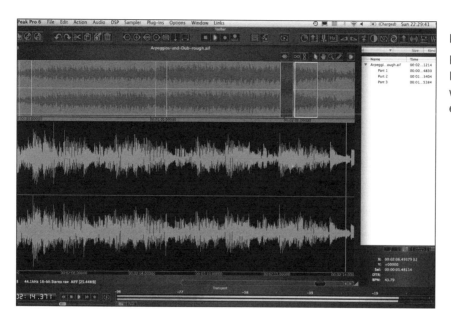

Fig. 3.3

Bias Peak Pro 6 waveform editor

Where a sequencer offers plenty of large-scale editing tools, a waveform editor takes you inside an audio file with exacting precision, letting you tackle problems that would be impossible to address in the broader sequencer environment. In fact, the sample-accurate waveform editor plays such a vital role in modern audio production that this feature is now included as an internal component within many multitrack digital-audio programs. Many waveform editors include CD burning and mastering tools to help you prepare your audio files for distribution.

EDITOR/LIBRARIANS

One of the best things about modern synthesizers, samplers, effects, and other MIDI devices is their ability to store sounds in memory for later recall. Unfortunately, most of these devices hold so many sounds in memory that it's hard to keep track of them. That perfect orchestral pad that you created last week does you no good if you can't find it today. A MIDI editor/ librarian lets you alter, store, and organize the settings of your MIDI devices.

An editor program lets you manipulate the parameters of your synthesizer and other devices via MIDI. You can alter an existing sound or develop new tones from scratch, all from the comfort of your computer.

Librarian software lets you transfer System Exclusive (SysEx) data between your MIDI devices and your computer. You can catalog and organize your data by criteria that you specify. You can group sounds by type, such as orchestral, percussion, or analog synth; or you can group all the sounds you used on a specific project together into one library. You can organize and arrange all the sounds for one device and create a database that lets you search through all the sounds of all your devices to find just what's called for.

While you may find instrument-specific editor/librarians on the market, a universal editor/librarian, such as Sound Quest's MIDI Quest (**Fig. 3.4**) and MOTU's Unisyn, give you access to many different MIDI instruments in one central application.

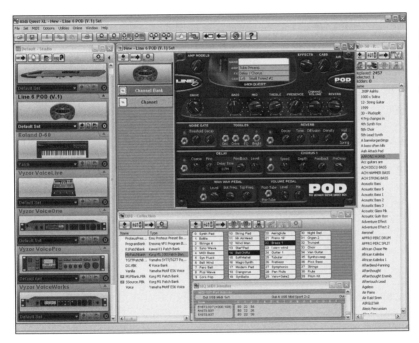

Fig. 3.4

Sound Quest MIDI Quest universal editor/librarian

▌ PLUG-INS AND EFFECTS

A *plug-in* is any program that can work within another piece of software (or host) and enhance its performance. In audio, the term "plug-in" generally refers to signal processors, or effects, although soft synths and samplers can also function as plug-ins.

A signal processor is any device that alters an existing sound. Common audio effects include reverb, delay, chorus, equalization, compression, and gating. Because software is relatively inexpensive to design and upgrade, you'll also find a range of experimental and unusual effects that are less common in hardware devices.

Plug-ins can work in real time (which means that they affect the audio as it plays back, but don't alter the actual audio file) or on the file level (the plug-in permanently changes the original audio file).

Most DAWs are bundled with a collection of plug-ins. Third-party developers such as IK Multimedia, Waves, Cycling '74, TC Electronic (see **Fig. 3.5**), and Mac DSP make plug-ins that can be integrated into a host application. There are a number of plug-in types and formats, some of which require special hardware to function. We examine them in *Chapter 11: Software Signal Processors.*

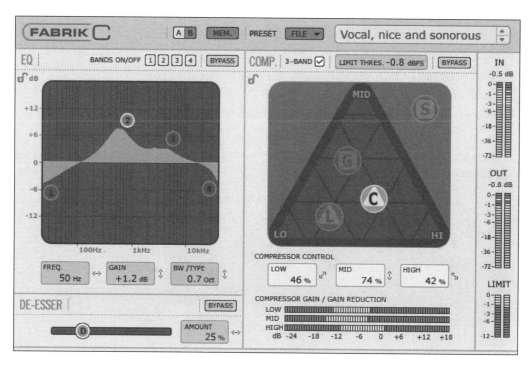

Fig. 3.5

TC Electronic's Fabrik effects plug-in

Software Instruments

One of the most exciting computer music developments in recent years has been the software-based instrument, or soft synth. A soft synth (see **Fig. 3.6**) is a software model of a hardware synthesizer. Like its hardware counterpart, it can generate sounds when triggered by a sequencer or MIDI keyboard. Many soft synths have built-in sequencers and drum machines, which allow them to produce sound without the use of external software.

Fig. 3.6

Native Instruments Elektrik Piano software instrument

Soft synths function in two ways: as stand-alone devices (where you can play their sounds directly without opening any additional software), and as plug-ins that operate within host software, such as a digital audio sequencer.

VIDEO CAPTURE AND EDITING

Video has become an integral part of desktop audio. Most production software, sequencers, and waveform editors can import and play back pre-existing digital video files. However, few of these programs actually let you capture and edit the video yourself. To do this, you'll need video capture and editing software such as Sony's Vegas, Pinnacle Systems' Pinnacle Studio, or Apple's Final Cut Pro, Final Cut Express (see **Fig. 3.7**) or iMovie.

Fig. 3.7

Apple Final Cut Express

NOTATION

Notation software lets you create finished printed manuscripts of your music. You'll find basic notation components in most music production software. You can even edit your sequencer data from the music notation. Detailed scores, however, require specialized software. Since this book is focused on production, we won't address this category. However, some of the leading notation packages include Sibelius Software's Sibelius 5 (see **Fig. 3.8** and MakeMusic's Finale.

Fig. 3.8

Sibelius 5

▣ UTILITIES

Utility software comprises a great range of functionality, some with features you'll also find in more conventional software like waveform editors and production packages. These applications include format conversion for audio and sampler files, audio encoders, file-compression software (used to save storage memory when making backups), CD-burning software, and useful little tools like delay-time calculators, session organizers, and more.

General computer-care utilities are also important in desktop production. Disk maintenance and troubleshooting tools are vital if you plan on recording to your hard drive. The most important of these is a disk-optimizing utility that can defragment your drive. Other useful tools include backup, file-tracking, and database software; a Web browser; and FTP software (see **Fig. 3.9**), which allows you to transfer files over the Internet.

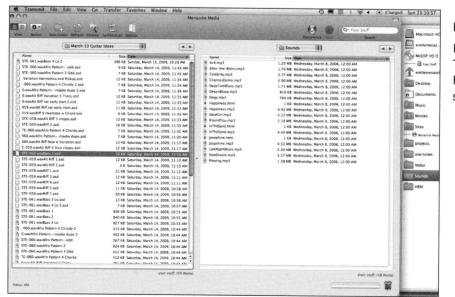

Fig. 3.9

Panic
Transmit
FTP
software

We'll examine each of these applications throughout the rest of the book. Note that we call them applications instead of programs, because many of the leading desktop studio production packages include at least a few of these component applications. Fortunately, whether your DAW has all these features built in, or you're assembling a system consisting of several compatible programs, the functions — recording, editing and preparing audio, and MIDI — are universal. Once you understand each of these applications, you'll be ready to take command of the desktop studio.

■ INSTALLATION TIPS

Software installation may seem like one of those straightforward tasks that no one really thinks about, but installing music software can be a little more demanding than loading up the typical business application.

Follow installation instructions carefully. Music software can be sensitive to system conflicts, is demanding on resources such as memory, and may require that you make special settings on your computer for optimal performance.

Keep all documents. You need to hang on to your manual, registration materials, and any cards or discs that contain serial numbers and access codes.

Keep the original discs safe. You need your original disc to reinstall the software in the event of a disaster, and the software may require you to insert it from time to time as a form of copy protection.

Stay up-to-date. One of the beauties of software is that it's always being updated. Scan the Internet on a regular basis for updates, and always use the latest revision of your software (unless there's a specific reason not to, such as a conflict between a particular revision and your computer hardware).

Prepare your computer. First, as we'll see later in this book, many applications now come with extra *content* material: loops, samples, instrument sounds, etc. This means that, while the program itself might take up a few hundred megabytes of space, the content might take up several gigabytes. You need to have room for all of that stuff. And because most operating systems use the system drive for virtual memory, you must be careful not to use too much of that drive's capacity; doing so will slow performance.

Check compatibility. Music software applications often interact with one another — for example, through the use of ReWire and effects plug-ins (see Chapters 11 and 12). You need to know how the new software will work with the existing programs on your computer. An upgrade in your sequencer, for example, may mean that you need to upgrade a plug-in to maintain compatibility. The same holds true — and is even more important — when it comes to the software's compatibility with your current operating system and hardware. Don't ever assume that just because the software is new that it works with the latest computer. It should, but it may not. Check!

Authorization considerations. Music software uses two main kinds of authorization in order to prevent illegal distribution. The first method authorizes a specific system or hard drive to run the application. Usually, you're given a serial number and use a code (sometimes called a "question and response code") to authorize your machine. On launching the software, you'll be asked for the authorization code, and if you've not yet obtained it, you are sent to a secure website to get it. The good thing about this system is that, once authorized, you don't need to worry about launching your software. It also makes it easy to upgrade a demo version of an application you may have downloaded to a fully authorized version; just pay the manufacture and they send you the code. The disadvantage is that your software can only run on the computer(s) it's authorized for (I use the plural because you usually get two or three authorizations with a single purchase). And if something happens to your computer—like a hard disk crash—you lose that authorization and must request another from the manufacturer.

The other option is via a *hardware key*. Here, a USB key, sometimes known as a "dongle," is encoded with the authorization code. You can use your software on any computer, provided you have your dongle. The disadvantage is that losing the dongle is like losing the software! Another annoyance is that dongles require USB ports, which you may want to use for other devices. (You can, of course, use a USB hub to increase the number of USB ports available on your system.)

The most popular type of dongle is the iLok, a format used by many different manufacturers. A single iLok key (see **Fig. 3.10**) can hold many authorizations.

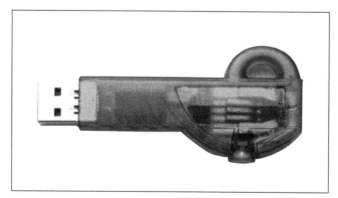

Fig. 3.10

An iLok key lets users easily transfer software authorizations from computer to computer.

▓ MOVING ON

Now that you have your software installed, you're ready to put it through its paces. *Chapter 4: An Overview of Software-Based Production* lays out some of the concepts that are at the heart of the desktop studio.

CHAPTER 4: AN OVERVIEW OF SOFTWARE-BASED PRODUCTION

We're going to cover specific arranging and editing techniques throughout this book, but first, let's look at a few concepts that are central to the desktop-studio environment.

THINKING AT RANDOM

The term *random access* refers to the way a computer looks for data, but it's also an important metaphor for how you can create and arrange your work. One of the toughest things to grasp when you're new to computer-based production is the freedom that random-access technology allows. When you separate the parts of your project into distinct and self-contained elements, you're no longer restricted to the structural constraints you'd find in a linear medium.

For example, let's say you're working on a song that consists of an intro, verse, bridge, chorus, solo, and outro. You can record the song linearly (in the order that the parts appear) or you can focus on one part—say the chorus—leaving the others for later. More important, you can restructure the song—for example, moving the chorus to the beginning to replace the intro, removing the bridge, adding a verse after the chorus, and using the outro section as a bridge between the solo and a series of choruses at the end. The new structure would look like this: chorus, verse, chorus, verse, solo, outro, chorus, chorus.

A computer lets you save and recall multiple versions of the same project. This gives you the freedom to make major structural changes without losing the original idea.

You can also import elements from other projects into your current one. For example, if you recorded a guitar riff as part of an instrumental piece, you can import it into a second, independent project and build a completely new arrangement around it, this one with vocals. This ability to share parts among projects can be taken even further when you work with pre-recorded material provided by others—either in commercial libraries or through personal collaboration.

THE ONSCREEN OVERVIEW

One of the biggest advantages to working with a computer is the way it lets you visualize your work on a central screen. Whether your software calls it the Tracks, Arrange, or Edit window, the central screen's functionality is almost universal. For consistency, we'll call it the **Arrange window** throughout the book, unless we are referring to the window in a specific piece of software.

The Arrange window gives you an **overview** of your project and lets you arrange and edit its various elements in the context of the whole. Think of it as the nerve center of your production studio—the jumping-off point for your recording, editing, and mixing activities. You'll probably spend 90 percent of your working time here.

Figs. 4.1–4.6 show the Arrange/Edit windows of some of the most popular DAWs. As you can see, though the names vary, they convey much of the same information. Tracks are shown along the left side; time is shown across the top. Individual audio and MIDI segments are displayed on a grid.

Think of the left side of the window as the "information station." In addition to displaying the content of each track, this is where you can control track parameters such as audio routing, MIDI routing, record-ready status, and solo and mute status.

Fig. 4.1

Pro Tools

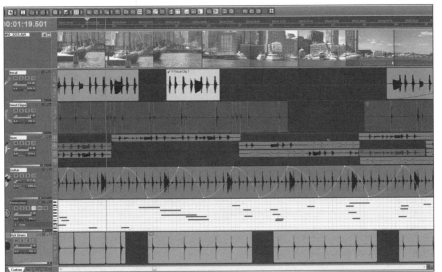

Fig. 4.2

Sonar

Fig. 4.3

Logic

Fig. 4.4

Cubase

Fig. 4.5

Live

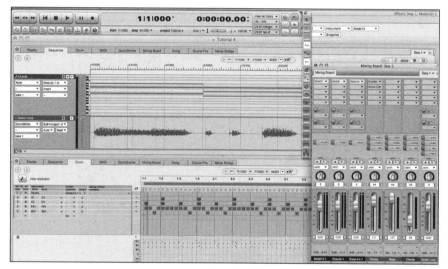

Fig. 4.6

Digital Performer

One important thing to keep in mind is that there's no physical connection between the track assignment and the audio or MIDI data on it. Therefore, you can move material from the grid onto a different track simply by dragging it. Conversely, you can usually reassign the audio channel or MIDI destination of the track without touching the audio or MIDI regions. **Fig. 4.7** and **Fig. 4.8** show this in action.

OVERVIEW OF THE OVERVIEW

The Arrange window gives you an instant overview of how and where the elements of your project fit together. You can see individual parts in the context of the larger project.

In **Fig. 4.8**, we see an arrangement that includes audio and MIDI tracks. Each track is made up of individual segments that contain MIDI or audio data.

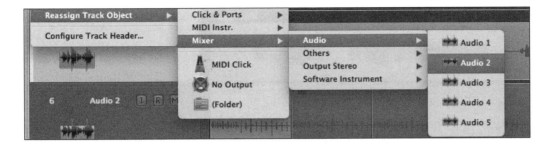

Fig. 4.7

Reassigning the audio routing of a track, shown here in Logic, lets you send the audio to a different set of effects processors, buses, or interface outputs.

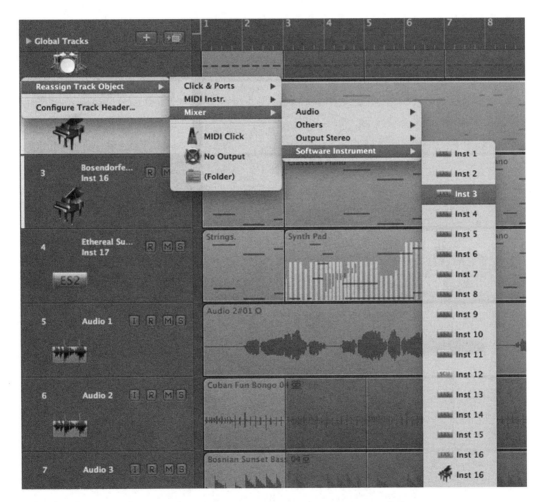

Fig. 4.8

Reassigning the MIDI destination of a track lets you use the material recorded on it to trigger a different MIDI instrument than the one originally used to record it.

TRACKS, OBJECTS, SEGMENTS, AND REGIONS

A *region* (sometimes referred to as a "**segment**" or "object") is the basic unit of computer-based recording. Regions are generally used for *nondestructive* editing—editing that doesn't permanently change the underlying data. An audio region, for example, draws on the content of an audio file, but can be edited without affecting the source file. MIDI tracks can also be divided into regions, which can be moved and edited as blocks. Editing MIDI regions is slightly different than editing audio regions, because you can make more detailed edits *within* a region. For example, if you want to move the MIDI part for a song's chorus back by, say, four bars, you'd do this on the regional level. If you want to change one note *within* that chorus's part, you do it on an individual note level by going inside that region.

TIP

Once a part is divided into regions, there are many ways to rearrange the pieces. The ability to copy a section and use it more than once in an arrangement is central to many styles of desktop production—in fact, it's the basis for most loop-based production. One important decision to make when copying regions is whether to make an independent copy or to use an "alias"-type copy. This is especially important when working with MIDI regions. With a "real" copy, any alterations you make in the copy will have no effect on the original—and vice versa. With an alias, any changes you make to one version will appear in all copies derived from that region. So, let's say you want to extend a song's ending by repeating the chorus: if you simply make an alias of the original chorus and repeat it, the second time around it will sound exactly as it did the first time. If, however, you want to create a slight variation—say, by changing the voicing of the last chord—you would need to make a new copy. **Fig. 4.9** and **Fig. 4.10** show this in action.

Fig. 4.9

When regions section "aliases," any changes you make in the original (the leftmost in this image) will affect the contents of the copies.

Fig. 4.10

By making a "real" copy of a region (far right), you can change its contents without affecting the original source region (far left).

TIMELINE

The **timeline**, shown in **Fig. 4.11**, shows where each element in a project occurs in relation to time. You can view time in a number of formats, including Bars/Beats/Ticks (subdivisions of the beat), Minutes/Seconds, and **SMPTE** time code, which is used in film and video production.

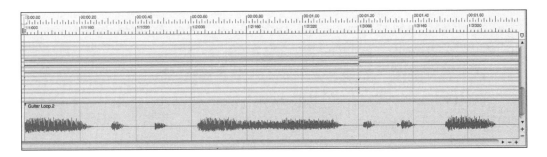

Fig. 4.11

Digital Performer's timeline is typical of those found in DAWs. Here, we see time in both minutes/seconds/frames (top line) and in bars and beats.

When you're using the Bars/Beats/Ticks display, the song's tempo and time signature will influence when an event will actually occur. So, if the song's tempo is 120 bpm and the time signature is 4/4, an event at measure 30 will occur one minute after the first beat. Change the tempo to 100 bpm, and measure 30 now comes up at 1:15.

Most DAWs allow you to see both types of time simultaneously, and many allow you to choose which type of timekeeping will be used for the complete project or for individual tracks within the project. We'll explore these different ways of treating time in the sections on working with loops and on audio for video.

The timeline may also show navigational elements, such as:

- **Markers** and **location points**, which help you to identify specific parts of your project and get to them instantly.

- Loop boundaries, which let you identify a section of music for repeated playback.

- **Punch-in** and punch-out locations, for setting up automatic recording.

- Tempo and time signature.

- Thumbnails of any video synced to the project.

THE GRID

The **grid** refers to the way the Arrange window interacts with the timeline. You can restrict your edits so that they adhere, or *snap*, to the grid. For example, if the grid value is set to a bar (or whole note), you will be able to move an edit selection only by one-bar increments. If you set the snap value to a quarter note, you can edit in quarter-note steps.

Grid resolutions can get very fine—you can position your segments by very small musical values (64th-note triplets, 128th notes, and smaller), SMPTE time values (hours, minutes, seconds, and frames), or even by individual samples (which, at a sample rate of 96 kHz, means 1/96,000th of a second!). Most applications also allow you to *snap to markers,* meaning you can place a pointer or marker in a specific location and then drag regions—or even individual MIDI events—to it quickly.

TRACKS AND REGIONS

Unlike a conventional tape recorder, where the track and its contents are one entity, desktop production tools provide a more flexible approach. Tracks are lanes that can contain material, but the material itself is separate from the tracks. It can be copied, moved to other tracks, muted, and rearranged.

With all that flexibility, staying organized is absolutely essential. You can name the tracks themselves *and* also name the individual segments that populate those tracks. For example, **Fig. 4.12** shows a track called "Bass," and includes segments called "Bass Hit," "Bass Chorus," and "Bass Verse."

TIP

When recording, most applications will automatically assign a track's name to the regions—and associated audio files—recorded within it. If you take a second to name a track before you start recording, it can help you stay organized. It's a lot easier to tell what's on "Bass DI" (what I'd call a bass part recorded via direct input) than it is to tell what's on "Audio 4." You can make your recording sessions even more efficient by creating templates containing common settings and using one of those each time you start a new session.

Color is another useful tool for identifying the elements in your project. Most programs allow you to assign colors to tracks or to individual elements within a track. For example, you could use color to distinguish multiple takes of the same part, or to identify various sections of an arrangement. Color can be especially handy when you're recording several takes of a multitrack source, such as a drum kit. In most cases, each drum in the kit will be assigned to its own track, but the sound from any one drum may be picked up by the microphones recording the other drum tracks. Because of this, you will usually want to edit the drum tracks from each take as a group, so that the kick drum and the corresponding snare, cymbals, etc., are heard together. If you assign one color to all the drum tracks in each take, it's easy to identify which tracks (and corresponding edit regions) belong together. From there, you could use the "blue" take for the verses, the "red" take for the choruses, and so on.

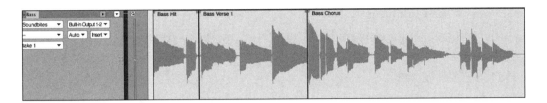

Fig. 4.12

One track can contain several different regions.

Fig. 4.13

A typical DAW transport module is modeled after controls found on a tape recorder.

NAVIGATION

Of the great advantages of a desktop studio is the ease with which you can move around a project. While most DAWs still pay homage to the tape machine by including virtual transport buttons, there are other alternatives that can be more efficient.

TAPE-STYLE TRANSPORT

The **transport** bar, like the one shown in **Fig. 4.13**, is the primary vehicle for getting around a session. It duplicates the controls found on old-school tape recorders, with separate buttons for Play, Record, Fast Forward, Rewind, Stop, and Pause.

Software transports also boast some options not available on physical tape recorders. The transport's locator functions let you specify and store sections of your project for instant access. The cycle/looping tools let you specify sections of your project for repeated playback, as well as set the boundaries for punch-in and punch-out recording. The Return-to-Zero function (usually engaged by hitting Stop twice) takes you back to the beginning of the project, or to the start of a cycle or a loop.

The transport also has a counter, which shows you the current song position in whatever time format you've elected to work in. You can change locations by simply typing values into the counter. If you're working with musical time, you type in the bar, beat, and any subdivisions of the beat. In SMPTE time, you type in the hours, minutes, seconds, and frames.

The transport bar can either be built into a window or appear as a separate pop-up window you can show or hide as needed. While it may seem old-fashioned, the transport bar is especially useful when you're working away from the timeline-equipped Arrange and Edit windows. When working in the Mix window, or when editing parameters on, say, a software instrument, the transport bar can be the most efficient way to get around.

THE PLAYHEAD

The *playhead* (see **Fig. 4.14**) is the vertical line that runs perpendicular to the timeline. It's named after the stationary head that tape passes over on a tape recorder. As the song plays, the playhead moves along the timeline, seeming to trigger the regions as it passes over them. You'll see the playhead in the main Edit/Arrange window as well as individual audio and MIDI edit windows.

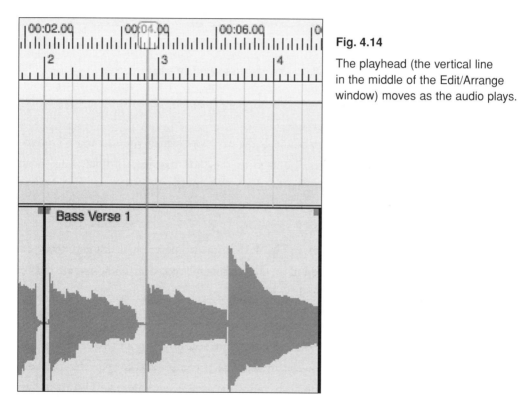

Fig. 4.14

The playhead (the vertical line in the middle of the Edit/Arrange window) moves as the audio plays.

You can drag the playhead to move to a new location, or reposition it by clicking on the desired location in the timeline—very handy when you're eyeballing regions for editing.

The playhead can also be used to set up edit points. For example, you can use the playhead's position to define a marker, or determine a place to split one or more regions.

In some situations, the playhead can be used to "scrub" audio; i.e., to drag the playhead manually over a region to hear the audio in slow motion. This is useful for finding edit points.

LOCATORS AND MARKERS

Locators and markers (see **Fig. 4.15**) are extremely useful navigational tools. You can position these in key parts of your project. Clicking on a locator or marker will transport you to the appropriate place instantly. You can create markers for important sections of an arrangement (e.g., chorus, solo, breakdown), or for specific locations, such as film cues or edit points.

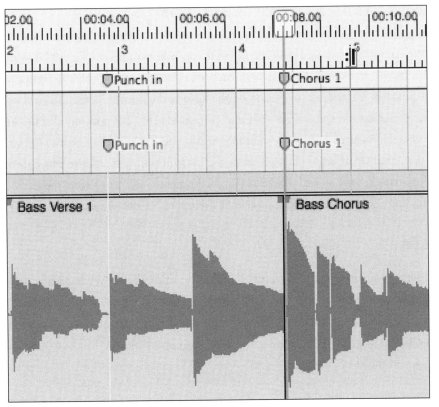

Fig. 4.15

Markers and locators provide instant access to key points in a project.

Markers can be named and moved around, and some programs, such as Pro Tools, let you use markers to set up edit boundaries and store them for later recall (see **Fig. 4.16**).

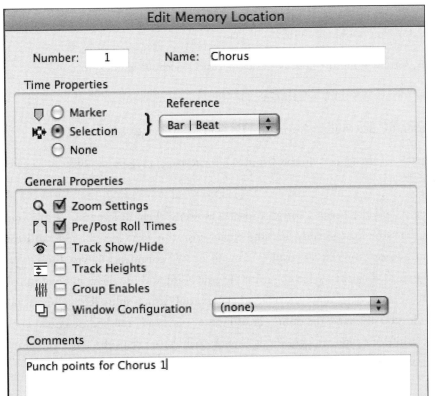

Fig. 4.16

Using markers to store edit boundaries in Pro Tools.

QWERTY KEYBOARDS AND EXTERNAL CONTROLLERS

Mousing around the screen is not always the fastest way to operate your software's transport. Fortunately, your computer keyboard—or an external controller connected via MIDI—can serve as the "hardware" transport controls, with each component on the software transport assigned to an equivalent physical key or button on the keyboard/controller (the most common example of which is using the spacebar to start and stop playback). But you can also use key commands for more specialized tasks—for example, using one key combination to play only the selected region, another to begin playback from the last edit point, another to move to the next or previous marker, and so on. The exact key commands can vary from program to program, and finding them requires a little time with the respective owner's manuals.

TOOL SETS

Tools—icon-driven commands that determine the function of the cursor while editing—are another distinguishing element of desktop production. The tools you'll use are numerous and varied. Specific programs offer different tools, and almost all programs make tools available on a contextual basis; that is, MIDI editing tools are only available for MIDI tracks, and audio tools for audio tracks.

The most common tools include the:

- **Pointer** or **Grabber**, for selecting, copying, and moving objects.

- **Scissors**, or Splitter, for separating objects.

- **Joiner**, or Glue, for merging objects.

- **Eyeglass**, for zooming in and out of objects.

- **Trimmer**, for changing the boundaries of an object without altering its content.

- **Scrubber** (or Speaker), for auditioning specific regions or events.

- Loop cursor, for determining how often a region will be repeated.

- Time Stretcher (often based on the Trimmer), for resizing a region to conform to a new tempo.

Here's one area where the various software packages show their differences. While most software offers the same functionality, the implementation can vary. For example, **splitting** one region into two or more pieces requires a menu or key command in Pro Tools—you place the playhead, or drag the cursor, to create the edit point and use the command to split the region. Cubase and Logic, however, offer a Scissors tool, which splits the region as soon as you click on it (you also have the option of using the "playhead" method described above for Pro Tools). While one type of operation isn't necessarily better than the other, one might better suit your working style.

The behavior of the cursor—or the tool it represents—may change depending on context. This concept, sometimes called the **smart cursor**, is used by a number of programs, and can be alternately timesaving and confusing. Often, the cursor's position within a region will determine what tool it becomes. For example, when the cursor is in the lower left corner of a region, it might act as a Trimmer tool, capable of changing the region's boundaries. Move the cursor up to the top center of the region, and it becomes a Grabber, letting you move the region in the timeline. Move it to the upper right corner, and it becomes a Looper, letting you draw alias-type copies that will repeat the region's contents (see **Fig. 4.17**).

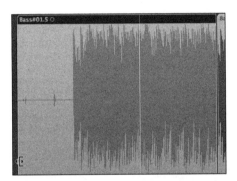

Fig. 4.17

"Smart cursor" tools change depending on the cursor's position relative to the material you're editing. Here, the cursor has become a "loop" tool that can be dragged to repeat regions.

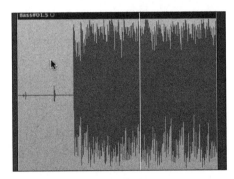

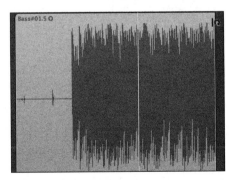

The advantage of the smart cursor is that it saves you time—you don't need to keep selecting different tools from the menu. The disadvantage is that the cursor's function can change on the subtlest movement, so you might find yourself performing an undesired edit while trying to do something else. You really have to practice positioning the cursor accurately to keep it in the correct editing zone.

TIP

Zooming in for a closer look at a region can give you more control over a smart cursor's behavior. When you're zoomed out too far, even the slightest movement relative to the region can change the cursor's behavior.

HOT KEYS

One of the best ways to get to know your software and increase your speed and efficiency is to learn the **hot keys,** or **key equivalents,** of most editing commands. Hot keys are keyboard assignments that replace menu and mouse actions. You can use hot keys to open windows, make edits, select editing tools, navigate your project, and more. Most programs allow you to assign your own hot keys to different functions, and some—such as Logic—offer extended features that have no menu equivalent but can be assigned to hot keys.

TIP

Often, you can program your own set of keyboard commands—especially useful if you're using more than one DAW regularly, because you can assign most of the same keyboard commands to each program. Also, commercially available QWERTY keyboards and overlays can display the keyboard commands so that you don't have to memorize them.

TAKING A CLOSER LOOK

The way you wish to view a project at any given time will change depending on the task at hand. The *macro* view—where you zoom out to see the whole arrangement at once—can give you an overview of all the tracks in your project. This kind of contextual view is especially useful when you're recording, or when you want to see how the entire arrangement fits together.

The *micro* view can show you precisely how individual elements are positioned. Zooming in for a close look is necessary when you want to make fine-resolution edits to your regions, and is especially important when you're cutting or cropping audio waveforms.

You can zoom in on your data in two different ways. Horizontal zooming (see **Fig. 4.18**) affects how you see your data over time. Vertical zooming (see **Fig. 4.19**) "opens up" your track to show you more precisely what's inside. Many DAWs let you change the zoom level for individual tracks or the entire project.

You may find yourself switching between micro and macro zooms quite often—for example, after zooming in to perform a detailed trim on a region, you'll likely want to zoom out to locate the next edit point. This can get a little tedious. Fortunately, most DAWs let you store zoom and other display settings for instant recall.

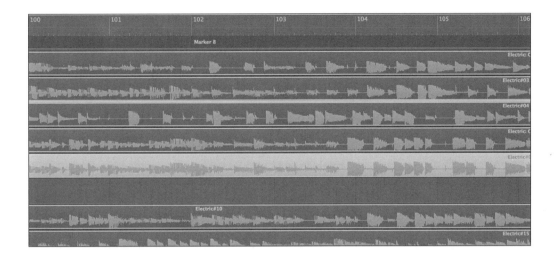

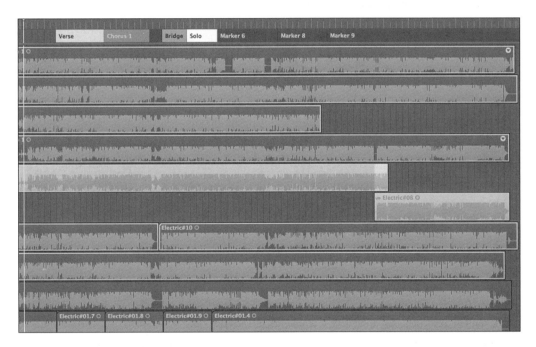

Fig. 4.18

Horizontal zoom

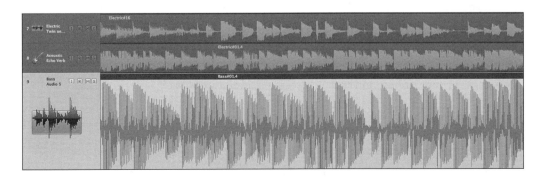

Fig. 4.19

Vertical zoom

■ LINKING TO EDITORS

Part of the Arrange window's role as the central nervous system of your project is providing easy access to other features and editors. With most DAWs, you can select and double-click an object from within the Arrange/Edit window, and the software is smart enough to launch the appropriate editor. These include waveform editors for audio, and matrix (or piano roll), event, score, and controller editors for MIDI. Each of these will be examined in detail in upcoming chapters.

■ OTHER RECURRING THEMES

The following factors play an important role in the mechanics of desktop production. We'll examine each in context throughout the book.

TEMPO AND TIME SIGNATURE

The tempo and time signature of a project are important because they determine the grid values that come into play in song arranging and audio and MIDI editing. A few years ago, one could have said that tempo would determine the playback speed of a MIDI region, but not an audio region. This distinction is no longer as prevalent; some types of audio files or regions can follow a song's tempo, and all of the major DAWs allow this kind of time manipulation to some degree. We'll examine these relationships in detail in Chapters 5–9.

ASSIGNING

Assigning is another key term that describes the way your software processes an object, instrument, or track. To *assign* is to create a virtual pathway for an object in your project (hey, that rhymes!). You can assign audio tracks to mixer channels, assign the hardware input from your audio interface to a recorder track, assign MIDI tracks to software instruments or outputs on an interface, and assign mixer channels to audio outputs, internal buses, or internal effects.

UNDO

One of the great advantages of working with a computer is the ability to undo your mistakes. Simple undo takes you back one command. An *undo history*, or multiple undo, allows you to look back on your project and make corrections several steps back.

TIP

Note that each time you save a project, you're likely wiping out its undo history. If you're embarking on a complex operation, save a copy of the project first so you can go back to your original if necessary.

MENUS AND SUBMENUS

Menus are common to all software, and would hardly bear mentioning were it not for the fact that many of the top audio and MIDI programs are laden with submenus—menus within specific windows. One of the first things you should do when learning a new piece of software is explore these submenus. You'll find important commands hidden there. I wish I had a dollar for every time I went hunting for a command that was buried in an unexplored submenu.

MOVING ON

Now that we've covered some of the basic terrain, it's time to venture a little further. Chapters 5–7 will introduce you to audio recording, arranging, and editing. Chapters 8 and 9 focus on MIDI, while Chapter 10 and beyond will help you put the finishing touches on your project.

PART II WORKING WITH AUDIO

CHAPTER 5: AN INTRODUCTION TO HARD DISK AUDIO

IN THIS CHAPTER
- HOW THE COMPUTER HANDLES AUDIO
- PREPARING TO RECORD AUDIO
- INPUT MONITORING
- 2-TRACK RECORDING
- MULTITRACK RECORDING

When **hard disk recording** was first developed in the late 1980s, it was seen as an alternative to old-fashioned tape-editing techniques, which required an engineer (hopefully one with a steady hand) to cut a physical piece of magnetic audio tape with a razor blade and then splice sections together. This editing was by its very nature destructive. The advent of the hard disk recorder meant that pre-existing recordings could be transferred into a computer, edited nondestructively, and then output back to a tape-based medium, such as digital audio tape (**DAT**).

But as hard drives became larger and faster, the hard disk became the medium of choice for many types of audio production, including 2-track recording, multitrack recording, loop construction, and audio for video. In fact, many projects include all of these elements. Still, the editing tools and techniques developed in those early hard disk programs remain staples of modern audio production.

▓ HOW THE COMPUTER HANDLES AUDIO

A tape recorder—be it digital or analog, audio or video—handles material in an absolute and linear fashion. When you record your cousin's violin recital at the beginning of a piece of blank tape, the material will remain there, with the performance unfolding just as it was originally played, forever (or until it degrades or someone records over it).

Many handheld digital recorders work along similar lines. The audio that goes into them can't be altered, at least with the recorder's controls. The only difference is that instead of being located on a fixed piece of tape, each recording is captured into its own audio file, and the user can choose among the files at random.

A nonlinear hard disk system starts out by recording a performance as it unfolds, just like tape. But after the recording is captured on disk, the audio can be manipulated in a number of ways, in exacting detail. Sections of the performance can be moved in time, erased, repeated, and reordered to create something completely new. If I spoke the words: "Not sense make, does this phrase" into a tape recorder, you might listen back and think you were talking to Yoda. But with a hard disk recorder, I could easily alter it to say, "This phrase does not make sense." Which, of course, it now does, creating a paradox that should keep those of you studying philosophy amused for several seconds.

The most important thing to remember, though, is that *all edits can be accomplished while leaving the original recording intact.* This is the cornerstone of modern audio production.

They key to understanding how this works is understanding the relationship between an audio file (which is the nearest equivalent to an absolute, linear tape recording) and an audio region (which is a section of an audio file that can be edited nondestructively).

Note: Much of what we're about to discuss applies to stand-alone hard disk recorders and portable digital multitrack devices as well as to computer-based recorders. I mention that now because portable digital recorders can be integrated into your main computer system, so you may want to consider the file type and recording resolution of any recordings you make on the portable if you plan to import that material into your computer for later editing or other use.

AUDIO FILE FORMATS

Any time you record audio to disk—be it to a traditional hard drive or a portable format such as an SD card—you create a file on that disk. Audio files can be in a number of different **formats**. The most common formats for multitrack recording are **AIFF**, **SD2** (also referred to as SDII), and **WAV**.

These formats are *uncompressed*, meaning that the recorded signal is stored at full resolution and frequency response, and therefore offer the best possible sound quality. They're also quite large. Three factors determine the size of a file (in terms of bytes used on a hard disk): **bit depth** (usually 16- or 24-bit); **sample rate** (44.1 kHz, 48 kHz, 88.2 kHz, and 96 kHz, but sometimes 192 kHz and even higher); and number of **channels** (all things being equal, mono files are half the size of stereo files). **Fig. 5.1** details typical file sizes.

BIT DEPTH	SAMPLE RATE	MB PER MINUTE (MONO)	MB PER MINUTE (STEREO)
16	44.1 kHz	5.0	10.1
16	48 kHz	5.5	11.0
24	44.1 kHz	7.6	15.1
24	48 kHz	8.25	16.5
24	96 kHz	16.5	33.0

Fig. 5.1

Bit Depth, Sample Rate, and File Size: The two right-hand columns show how much disk space is used up by one minute of recording (mono or stereo).

Some recorders—especially portables and "consumer"-oriented computer programs—also let you record directly to *compressed* formats such as MP3. These formats—in which some of the data in the file is reduced so that the file uses less storage space—don't sound as good as uncompressed files, but are very useful for capturing ideas without using much disk space. (An MP3 can be 1/10th the size—or smaller—of a WAV or AIFF file of the same length.) Many modern DAWs can open MP3s. Sometimes, the program must first convert the MP3 to an uncompressed format. Note that while this new file will be larger, there will be *no* improvement in sound quality, since the source file is compressed and therefore sonically inferior.

HOW REGIONS RELATE TO FILES

Whenever you record an audio file, your software creates an object that represents that file, called a *region*. The first region always consists of the whole file; later, you can create smaller regions that consist of parts of the file.

Unlike an audio file, a region takes up very little disk space. It just serves as a representation of the file that can be addressed by your software. Regions can be assembled and put in any order. Removing the regions does not alter or erase the original audio file. The computer stores both files for safekeeping. Every region you create from an audio file is stored for later recall.

Most editing operations are done on the region level. These are *nondestructive*. Editing operations that are done on the file level, however, are *destructive*, because they change the original audio file to create something new. We'll examine both in detail in *Chapter 6: Audio Editing and Assembling*.

THE PLAYLIST

The order in which regions play back can be thought of as a *playlist* (though not all programs use that terminology). You can assemble playlists consisting of regions from the same file, or regions taken from different audio files, as shown in **Fig. 5.2** and **Fig. 5.3**.

Fig. 5.2

Two regions made of material from the same audio file.

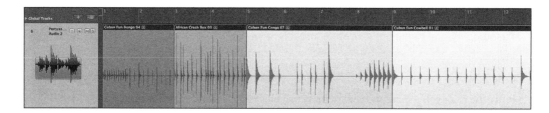

Fig. 5.3

One track containing regions from four different audio files.

When you arrange regions in a multitrack DAW's Edit or Arrange window, you're essentially creating a playlist for each track.

When you assemble finished mixes to create the running order of a CD, you're also creating a playlist.

▓ PREPARING TO RECORD AUDIO

The recording bug can hit you in a moment of inspiration, and—thanks to their editing capabilities—computers are great for off-the-cuff stuff. But before you jump onto the Record button with both feet, you should prepare your computer and your software by following a few simple steps.

OPTIMIZING YOUR RECORDING DISK

Since your hard disk is your recording medium, it needs to be running at peak performance at all times. Disk **fragmentation** is among the biggest problems in audio performance (computer performance in general, actually). A fragmented hard disk is slow and error prone. Other disk-related problems, like corrupt files and viruses, may also cause problems. This is one reason to use a separate disk for audio. A good defragmenting utility—especially if you're operating in the Windows world—can keep your drive clean and fast. (**Note:** Mac OS X handles defragmentation as part of normal system operation, and Apple recommends not using a defragmenting utility on drives formatted for use with OS X.)

CONFIGURING YOUR AUDIO INTERFACE

The type of audio interface you use and the settings you make on that interface play an important role in the quality of your recordings. While some interfaces can be configured within the DAW itself, others use specific software (or have onboard hardware controls) to determine crucial settings such as bit depth and resolution—which govern sound quality—and buffer size, which governs performance and latency.

TIP

It may sound obvious, but make sure the interface is turned on and connected. If you have a built-in interface, or are using one that's attached to the computer via an expansion slot built into the mother/logicboard, there's probably nothing to do there. But interfaces that attach via FireWire or USB can get unplugged pretty easily—even if it appears the plug is in place. Sometimes, only a slight movement of the plug can cause the computer to lose its software connection to the device—something that can happen quite easily if you're using a laptop. So double-check that the interface is plugged in, turned on, and recognized by the computer before launching your DAW. If it's not, you may need to reboot the system to reestablish the connection.

SETTING THE SAMPLE RATE AND RESOLUTION

Okay—your disk is in tip-top shape, your interface is on, and you've launched your audio recording software. The next step is to decide on a sample rate and resolution. These settings will determine what types of audio files will be compatible with your project.

Although some software can handle audio files of varying resolutions simultaneously, sample rate is another matter. For almost all applications, the sample rate of all audio files *must* match. If they don't, some of the audio files will play at the wrong speed and pitch (if they play at all).

There is no *correct* setting here. Most of the time, it's best to use the highest resolution your system offers. This is largely determined by your audio interface's A/D conversion and digital input capabilities (see Chapter 2). If you're using an outboard A/D converter to send a digital signal to the audio interface, make sure the interface is set to "slave" to the external converter's clock. This will allow the external device to determine the sample rate.

If your project includes files culled from an audio CD, you can save disk space by recording at the CD resolution of 16-bit, 44.1 kHz. Spoken word and dialog, which doesn't require the frequency response or **dynamic range** of most music, can also be recorded at a lower resolution. But if you're using mics to capture acoustic instruments, consider using 24-bit/48 kHz resolution or better. The extra bit depth will make an audible improvement in the recording. With hard drives now so large and affordable, there's little reason to choose a format that offers a smaller file size in exchange for lesser audio quality.

DECIDING WHEN TO USE MONO AND STEREO TRACKS

A typical audio DAW can handle both mono and stereo tracks. If you're dealing with a mono signal, such as a bass track, always use a mono track. Feeding a mono signal to a stereo track can waste disk space (a stereo track is twice as large as a mono track) and can also leave you with a recording that's out of balance, where one side contains all of the audio information, and the other just silence (or worse, noise). **Fig. 5.4** shows what can happen if you assign a mono input to a stereo track.

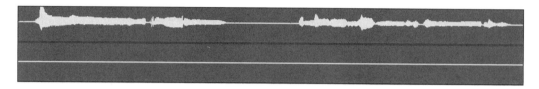

Fig. 5.4

When you assign a mono source to a stereo track, you run the risk of printing one side with audio, and one side with silence.

If you're working with a stereo source, you must decide whether to combine both sides into one stereo track (see **Fig. 5.5**) or split them into two mono tracks (see **Fig. 5.6**). This will have no effect on the amount of disk space used—the one stereo file will be about the same size as the two mono files. If you expect to process both sides of the stereo field in the same way when you mix, it makes sense to use one stereo track, as this will make it easier to edit the track. If you think you might use different processing on each side of the stereo field, however, splitting the recording into two mono tracks is the way to go. For example, to record room ambience using a matching pair of mics, I'd opt for a stereo track nine times out of 10. To record a stereo acoustic guitar part with one type of mic pointing at the neck and another pointing at the body, I'd use two mono tracks.

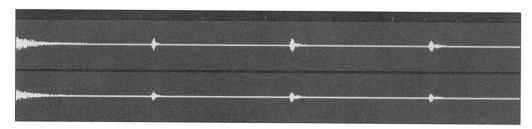

Fig. 5.5

A stereo track

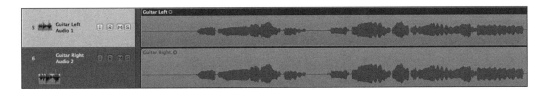

Fig. 5.6
Two mono tracks used for the same source.

TIP

If you do go the "dual mono" route, make sure that both tracks are record-enabled and assigned to different inputs in the audio interface!

NAMING AND LOCATING YOUR AUDIO FILES

This sounds obvious, but the name and location of an audio file is crucial; you can't hear it if you can't find it. Most software recorders will use a default location and file name, but these names aren't generally very descriptive. Get into the habit of creating a separate folder for every project. This folder should contain the audio and other data files. If you're dealing with many files, try organizing them into subfolders. In addition to keeping things organized, this makes it easier to back them up.

TIP

Most DAWs can automatically gather all the elements of a project and save them into one folder. In some programs, like Pro Tools and Digital Performer, this is done as soon as you begin a new project; the program creates a folder with the project name, and creates subfolders within it for audio and other types of files. In other programs, you may need to set this up manually using a command such as "Save as Project..." under the File menu.

PREALLOCATING DISK SPACE

The practice of preallocating disk space—setting aside disk space for recording—is less critical with today's fast drives, but doing so can still improve performance. If you know how long your recording is going to be, specify the preallocation amount. One advantage of preallocation: you can leave the room during the recording process. When the recording time reaches the preallocated limit, the recorder will stop. If you're working alone and going outside the control room to, say, overdub an acoustic guitar part, this can be handy.

GETTING SIGNAL INTO YOUR COMPUTER

Input routing is one of the most basic elements of recording—and can also be one of the biggest sources of aggravation. The more variables your system has in terms of input and output routing, the more closely you'll have to pay attention to signal flow.

Step 1: This is obvious: Connect an audio source to your interface's audio input. Remember that analog outputs should connect to analog inputs, and digital outputs should connect to digital inputs.

Step 2: Set up your software for recording. The process for doing this varies from program to program. On some, you may need to activate each hardware input, as shown in **Fig. 5.7**.

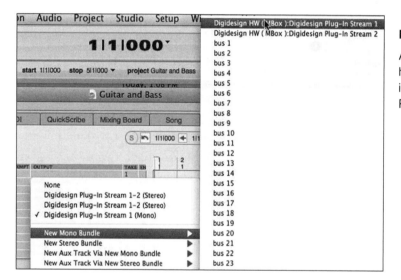

Fig. 5.7

Activating a hardware input in Digital Performer.

Step 3: Choose which input will route signal to the track. This is usually done from either the Edit/Arrange window or from the Mixer window, as shown in **Fig. 5.8**.

Step 4: Record-enable the track(s). Record-enable is a quick way of saying, "put the track into Record." A red light will flash when the track is record-enabled.

With most systems, you must record-enable, or *arm*, a track before you can hear any audio through it. There are exceptions to this, which we'll address in the section on input monitoring.

UNDERSTANDING THE SIGNAL CHAIN

Two phrases that audio engineers like to use are **_signal flow_** and *signal chain*. These describe the path an audio signal takes on its way to your gear and—ultimately—your ears.

Signal chain and level setting go hand in hand. Each element in the signal chain has an effect on the overall **gain**, or **signal level**. Some devices, like preamps, boost gain. You'll need to do this, for example, to raise a microphone's output to a level that your audio system can work with.

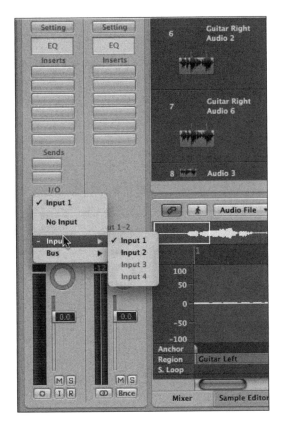

Fig. 5.8

Assigning audio inputs to a track in Logic.

Other elements in the signal chain reduce gain. Compressors and limiters do this, and are often used to prevent the kind of signal overload that can produce distortion. Some computer-audio interfaces include built-in microphone preamps, but many others have no gain controls of their own. With these, you set the input levels with outboard gear. Some interfaces let you change level settings via special control software (see **Fig. 5.9**).

SETTING AND CHECKING INPUT LEVELS

One of the key elements of recording audio is getting the proper signal level into your recorder. This is especially true with a digital recording system: if the signal is too **hot** (or high), it will cause *clipping*, an ugly distortion that can ruin your track. A signal that is too low is also bad. Not only does

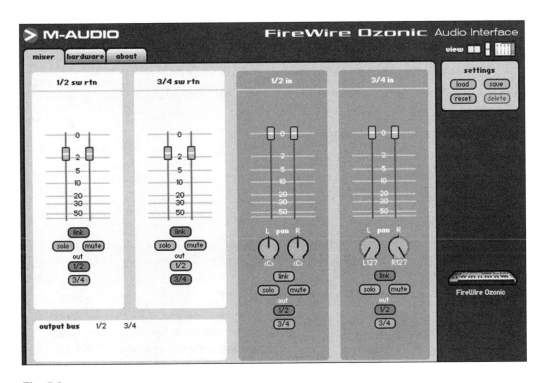

Fig. 5.9

Many audio interfaces come with control software that can be used to make settings independent of those made in the DAW.

this decrease the signal-to-noise ratio, it also prevents the recorder from working at its maximum headroom, thereby reducing sound quality.

The optimal level is as close to zero as possible, without going over into the clipping range. Use your recorder's input meter to judge the level of signal coming into the system. You'll want to average near the top—"in the yellow" section of the meter without hitting the red (which indicates clipping, sometimes referred to as an "over"). However, be aware that not all meters are reliable. For instance, some will read "over" before clipping actually occurs. Experiment by recording audio at various meter positions to see what works best.

■ INPUT MONITORING

Before you can record a track, you must be able to listen to, or monitor, the signal feeding it. Software recorders offer several different monitoring options.

MONITORING THROUGH THE SOFTWARE

As the heading implies, this option routes input signals through the audio software's audio engine and on to the audio interface's outputs. This way, you can audition your sound in context and add plug-in effects to the signal, if necessary.

With native systems, the process of passing signal through the audio system introduces some delay, or *latency*, into the monitor signal. (Refer to Chapter 2 for an explanation of latency.) While latency doesn't affect how the signal is recorded, the monitoring delay can cause some confusion as you play along with the track—a potential problem if you're recording a real-time performance in a multitrack environment. Latency is less of an issue if you're dealing with a prerecorded source in a 2-track environment. One of the biggest advantages of using a DSP-based audio system such as Pro Tools HD over a native system is that latency isn't an issue.

Low latency—under 15 ms—is acceptable for most users, and some folks can get by with latency as high as 30 ms. Anything higher introduces an audible delay and can affect your performance.

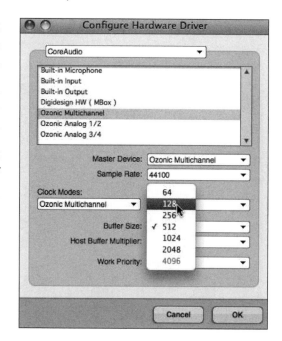

Fig. 5.10

Setting audio buffer size to reduce latency: The smaller the buffer, the less the delay between the audio input and its sound at the outputs—and the greater strain on your computer's resources.

You can lower latency by reducing the size of your audio system's input **buffers**, shown in **Fig. 5.10**. But there's a trade-off. Using a smaller buffer puts more strain on your computer's processor and can reduce your software's track count, as well as its ability to handle real-time plug-ins. One trick to get around this limitation is to set lower buffers when you record, then increase the buffer size for playback and mixing.

INPUT-ONLY MONITORING

This option lets you hear the input signal routed to a given channel, both during playback and when playback is stopped. When input-only monitoring is enabled, the mixer ignores any material already recorded to a track and lets you play along, even when the machine is not recording. This is useful if you want to play along with a track a few times before actually recording anything. You'll hear the track as it will sound on playback through the mixer, so if you add audio effects, the input signal will be processed through them.

TIP

Input-only monitoring is also useful if you need to integrate audio from an external source into a mix. For example, the output of a MIDI sound module can be included in your mix by routing it to a channel set to input monitoring.

RECORD-ENABLED MONITORING

With this option, you hear the input source only when the track is record-enabled. When the track is not record-enabled, you hear either silence or whatever material was previously recorded to the track. Signal at the input is muted.

PUNCH-IN, OR TAPE-STYLE MONITORING

This option toggles between monitoring prerecorded material and the input signal on a record-enabled track. When the project is in playback mode, you hear the prerecorded material. When it enters record mode, or when playback is stopped, you hear the source at the input. This is the preferred setting for punch-in recording (see "Punch-in Recording" later in this chapter).

"PRINTING" EFFECTS

In the early days of multitrack recording, recorders had fewer tracks and mixers had fewer channels than they do now. As a result, recording engineers commonly recorded tracks with audio effects in place. This practice became known as "printing" effects to tape. (Later it became more common to record tracks dry and only add some types of effects—especially EQ and spatial effects like reverb and delay—on mixdown.)

In a software environment, effects plug-ins are usually only used on playback and are not actually printed with the recording. This lets you make changes to the effects at any time during mixdown. However, you *can* print effects as you record a part, and while this may not offer the flexibility of the "playback only" option, it does free up computer resources for other things during mixing.

There are two ways to print effects. The first is simply to do what they did in the old days: set the sound up exactly as you want it with outboard gear, and use a microphone or direct input to capture it. We give an example later in this chapter in the section "Direct Monitoring."

Another option is to route the input signal through your software's plug-ins *before* it reaches the record-enabled track. To do so, you may need to create a separate auxiliary (aux) input along with the track on which you plan to record (some programs, including Ableton Live, let you route signal directly from one channel to another without creating an additional aux input). Then:

1. Enable input monitoring on the aux input.

2. Set the aux input to accept signal from the appropriate channel on your hardware interface. If your guitar is plugged into hardware channel 1, set your aux to accept hardware channel 1.

3. Insert whatever plug-ins you want to hear on the aux channel.

4. Set the aux channel's output to feed an unused internal path, or *bus*, in the software. For example, set the output of the aux channel to "bus 10." Doing so will initially cause the channel to become inaudible.

5. Set the recording track's input to match the aux channel's output. In our example, we'd set the track input to "bus 10."

6. Enable input monitoring on the track and check that there's signal going to it. The meters should fire, and the audio should sound as it did through the aux channel. You're ready to record!

MONITORING ON HIGH-LATENCY SYSTEMS

Even with today's fast computers, the low input buffer settings necessary for low-latency monitoring can cause processor overloads, which can cause playback or recording to stop in the middle of a take, or introduce audio anomalies, such as pops, clicks, or even white noise, into a take.

To solve the problem, you can bypass your software's mixer and monitor directly, using either the audio interface's internal routing or an outboard mixer to combine the input signal with that of your software.

To use a mixer: Route the input signal to the mixer first, and use the mixer's output to feed your audio interface. Route the audio interface's outputs back to the mixer, and monitor the mixer's output through your speakers or headphones, as shown in **Fig. 5.11**.

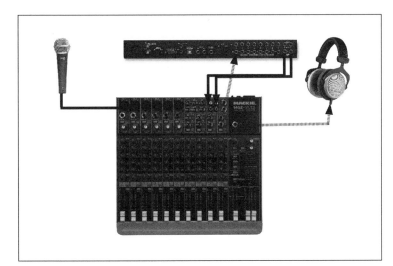

Fig. 5.11

Using a hardware mixer with an audio interface lets you monitor your input signal as you record while avoiding latency.

Be sure to disable the software's input monitor when you do this. Otherwise, you'll hear the source track twice—once through the mixer's input, and again as it's played back (and delayed) through the audio engine.

DIRECT MONITORING

Many of the better audio interfaces on the market offer ***direct monitoring***. Here, the audio interface routes the input signal to two places at once: to the software for recording, and to its own hardware output for monitoring.

This monitor signal bypasses the software audio engine, sending the signal from the input directly to the monitor speakers or headphones without passing through the audio software's mixer. To be clear: The signal *still gets recorded into the software* along with the existing tracks, and these tracks *are* routed to the audio interface, so you can play along with them. Most interfaces that offer direct monitoring let you determine the mix between the input signal and playback from the software. **Fig. 5.12** illustrates the difference between software and direct monitoring.

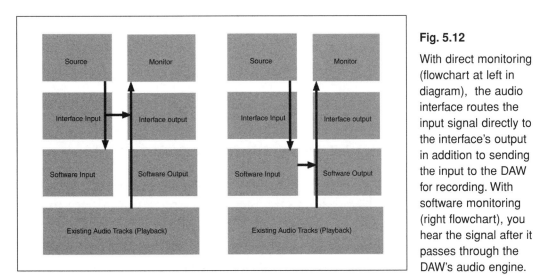

Fig. 5.12

With direct monitoring (flowchart at left in diagram), the audio interface routes the input signal directly to the interface's output in addition to sending the input to the DAW for recording. With software monitoring (right flowchart), you hear the signal after it passes through the DAW's audio engine.

While it can solve many problems, direct monitoring is not as effective if you need to hear the audio effects resident in the software as you record a part. If, for example, you're recording a guitar solo using the Guitar Rig plug-in to simulate the sound of a wah pedal and delay feeding into an overdriven tube amplifier, you won't be able to hear the "amp" or any of the associated effects if you bypass the software and monitor directly from the interface's input. As a result, the guitar will sound bland, and this will probably affect your performance. On the other hand, if you're miking up a real amp to create a similar sound, there's no need to monitor through the software.

TIP

If you prefer the flexibility offered by Guitar Rig and therefore don't want to commit to the sound of the amp, there's another option, though it's a little complicated. Send the guitar to a direct box (DI) and split the signal so that the guitar feeds both the amplifier and an input on the audio interface. Mic the amp, and route its signal to one channel of the audio interface. Route the DI output from the direct box to another channel of the interface. Next, create two tracks, sending the mic signal to one, the DI signal to the other. Record both, monitoring the amp only using the interface's direct monitoring feature. Once you're done recording, you can open the DI track, add Guitar Rig or whatever amp simulator you prefer, and use it in your final mix. Or you may find that the amp track works as-is. This "two-for-one" method also works on bass, keyboard, and other electronic instrument parts.

Some of the newer interfaces come with built-in effects that allow you to monitor reverb, for example, while in input-only mode. These effects are not "printed" to disk, and can therefore be replaced by your software plug-ins during mixdown.

■ 2-TRACK RECORDING

2-track, or stereo, recording is audio recording in its most basic form. The best example of a 2-track recording is a stereo mix—the kind of audio you'll find on a CD or other playback medium.

In addition to the number of audio channels that you can record and play back, there are some important differences between 2-track and multitrack recording, and each has a role to play in your production. Before we get into the mechanics of 2-track and multitrack recording, we need to establish the differences between the two.

2-TRACK VS. MULTITRACK RECORDING

A multitrack recorder is used to build an arrangement out of many discrete parts. You can record (or *track*—in studio jargon it's used as a verb as well as a noun) each part of a multitrack arrangement separately. The parts are then mixed down into a master recording. The most typical format for a master is stereo, or 2-track. Multitrack recorders are most commonly used for composing, arranging, and producing music.

Yet 2-track recorders have many uses in the desktop studio. They're great for recording mixes, for importing audio into your computer from a CD player or external sound source, and as an archiving tool for transferring old recordings (such as cassette tapes or record albums) into digital format. A 2-track recorder is often an ideal sketchpad for capturing ideas as they're forming. But it can also be used later, as a premastering and editing tool for preparing existing mixes for final distribution. Some software-based "2-tracks" like Bias's Peak and Steinberg's WaveLab, are very powerful tools for waveform editing and premastering.

A 2-track recorder is also handy for recording and editing *samples*, short recordings that can be played back by a keyboard sampler to recreate the sound of an acoustic instrument.

2-tracks can be used to record and edit short performances and turn them into loops, which can be triggered by samplers or imported into multitrack arrangements. All of these applications can take advantage of the 2-track's waveform-editing capabilities, which we discuss in *Chapter 6: Audio Editing and Assembling.*

Obviously, a multitrack recorder is capable of recording two tracks, and you can use multitrack recording software to perform many of the same duties as a 2-track. But because 2-track software is designed to handle and prepare master recordings, it offers a number of specialized tools that make it a better choice for many 2-track-only tasks.

2-track recorders are extremely nimble at handling multiple audio files from a single source (called batch processing). For example, you can use a program like Peak or WaveLab to record, organize, edit, master, and assemble a number of performances and then convert them into MP3s.

RECORDING FROM AN EXTERNAL SOURCE

An "external source" is any audio that you feed into your computer through the audio interface. The signal can be digital or analog in nature. Examples include:

- A stereo turntable, playing all those great LPs you found for a dollar at your neighbor's garage sale.

- The output of a cassette recorder, playing back the house mix of your latest gig.

- The analog or digital output of a DAT machine, playing back a mix you recorded before DATs became an endangered species.

- The analog or digital outputs of your hardware mixer, to mix down a multitrack recording from your other computer or multitrack tape machine.

- The signal from a microphone or instrument preamp.

Set and check levels, as detailed above. *Remember to watch those meters at all times.* You may choose to monitor your recording through your software, but if you're using the same hardware mixer for both the source signal and the monitoring, make sure that the software's output is not feeding back—through the mixer—into the software's input.

Start the recorder and start playback of the source. Don't worry about having silence at the start of an audio recording. You can edit this out later.

"RECORDING" FROM AN INTERNAL SOURCE

2-track recording software is also useful for dealing with audio that already exists in digital form. The most common sources include pre-existing audio files on your disk (which you open for editing), sample data from a commercial sample library, and audio CD tracks.

For pre-existing files or sample data, you'll simply open the file with the 2-track software. If you plan to make any destructive edits, be sure to save a copy of the file before you do anything else.

Copying audio from an audio CD, or *ripping*, is slightly more involved, but still fairly straightforward. Because this is a data operation, you don't need to use an external CD player. Simply load the CD into your computer's CD/DVD drive, and use your 2-track recorder's import features to convert the data from the CD to a form that your hard disk can handle.

TIP

Modern computer audio systems also allow for internal routing between applications. The most common example is ReWire, which we'll discuss in depth in Chapter 10. A program called Jack (jackaudio.org) lets you patch audio programs together much as you would hardware devices. You could use Jack to, for example, route the output of a stand-alone software instrument to the input of a 2-track recorder.

■ MULTITRACK RECORDING

Multitrack audio recording has become the primary activity in the desktop recording environment. A multitrack lets you build a complex arrangement consisting of any number of tracks playing in tandem. While a typical 2-track project consists of one audio file, a multitrack project can include many audio files and regions.

UNDERSTANDING THE MULTITRACK SYSTEM

Because it's designed to work with many audio files, multitrack software looks at audio a little differently than 2-track software does. The core hard disk audio components of audio file, region, and playlist remain, but the way these elements interact is different.

The primary difference lies in how files and regions are assembled in a playlist. In a typical 2-track project, audio files and regions are assembled sequentially. Each region plays until the end, then a new region takes over.

A multitrack system plays regions in sequence *and* in parallel, meaning that two or more audio files can play back simultaneously, and in any order. For example, you can have separate tracks for drums, guitar, and bass. These tracks may be routed to different outputs on an audio interface or combined together in the software's internal mixer.

We'll cover mixing in detail in *Chapter 10: Desktop Mixing*, but I mention it here because it is at the heart of the difference between 2-track and multitrack recording. 2-track: no mixing. Multitrack: mixing.

WORKING WITH TRACKS

The multitrack environment introduces a new element to go along with files, regions, and playlists: the *track*. Each track acts as an avenue for your files and regions, and just as any number of cars can travel independently via lanes on an interstate, your multitrack software allows you to record and play back independent audio files and regions.

FILES, REGIONS, AND PLAYLISTS IN A MULTITRACK SYSTEM

As we explained in Chapter 4, in a linear, tape-based system, a track and the audio it contains are inseparable. But in a hard disk system, the track is a separate entity that can contain audio files, regions, and playlists. In a hard disk environment, the distinctions between recording, editing, mixing, and arranging are pretty blurry.

Each time you record onto a track, you create a new audio file. This is true even if the file contains nothing but silence. A single file can take up the entire length of a track, or you can build a track made up of several different audio files.

Conversely, once it has been recorded, a single audio file can be assigned to more than one track, or you can simply move the audio from one track to another.

Tracks are recorded *nondestructively*. When we record a new take onto an existing track, we create a new audio file and a new region. *The old audio file remains untouched*, but the behavior of the region associated with that old file may change when you play the song back. What happens to this region depends on how your software is set up. There are three common scenarios:

1. The new region replaces the old. The old region is stored in the software equivalent of a bin or file cabinet, and can be dragged back into place or used elsewhere as needed.

2. The new region lays over the old on the same track. This was the default MO of sequencers like Logic and Cubase until recently. The topmost — or, if the start time of the regions varied, the latest — region would play back. Advantage: you can see all the regions associated with a given track in their original place. Disadvantage: you sometimes need to be clairvoyant to figure out which region is playing back.

3. Regions are collected in *lanes* or *takes,* and stored within a folder or *comp track*. This feature offers the flexibility of scenario 2 above, without the clutter or confusion. When you record, the software automatically organizes every audio file on that track

into a folder. In the Arrange window, you see what looks like one region per track. But you can open that folder to see all the takes within it (see **Fig. 5.13**). Each take represents a separate audio file. You can then choose among the takes to create a composite, or *comp*, something we'll discuss in more detail in Chapter 6.

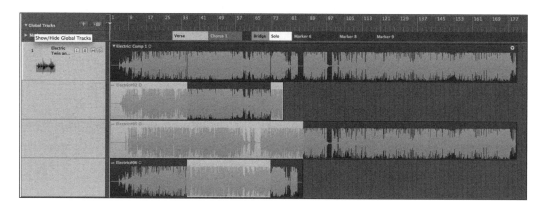

Fig. 5.13

In this comp track in Logic the top line shows the composite track. Below are the three individual takes, each in its own "lane," that provide source material for the comp. The dark areas represent the sections included in the comp; only one lane can be active at a time.

TIP

Note that in all three cases outlined above, a hard disk system gives you the option of creating a new playlist, or virtual track, for a given track before you record a take. When the track is empty, you'll just record to that track's default playlist. But let's say you want to try a lot of different takes, while keeping the first one easily accessible. By creating an alternative playlist, you can record new material and then switch back between the new and old versions easily.

PREPARING TO RECORD MULTITRACK AUDIO

Before you can begin a multitrack project, you must prepare your software. Start with the steps outlined above in "Setting and Checking Input Levels." Because you may be dealing with tens (and even hundreds) of audio files in a single project, the organizational elements of naming audio files and setting up and organizing folders to contain them is imperative.

CREATING A TRACK

Most software-based multitracks aren't restricted to a fixed number of physical tracks. They are open-ended systems that allow you to create as many tracks as you need for the project at hand. Step one in any recording project is to create a new track (see **Fig. 5.14**).

When you create a new track, you specify whether it will be a mono track (for sources like lead vocal, bass, and tuba) or stereo (for sources like drum overheads, keyboards, or dual-miked acoustic guitar). If your multitrack includes sequencing features (and these days, just about all do), you must specify whether your newly created track will contain audio or MIDI.

Fig. 5.14
Creating a new track in Logic.

With some programs, you'll also need to indicate what kind of timing reference will be used by the track. Audio tracks that are referenced to bars and beats (or recorded with embedded tempo information) can change speed if the song's tempo changes.

Set and check input levels and choose a monitoring option. Remember that if you're overdubbing (which we'll cover shortly), you'll need to hear both the input signal and the previously recorded tracks.

NAMING THE TRACK

I find that the additional step of giving the audio track a descriptive name (such as "Kick Drum" or "Room Mic Left") *before* I record is a big help. The software will generally include this name in all audio files and regions generated from the tracks.

TIP

You can save time by making template files that have a basic set of tracks and routing assignments already in place. You build a template by creating and assigning all the tracks you're likely to use in a typical project. Name and save the file before you record to any of the tracks. It's a good idea to use a descriptive name for the template, like "16 Audio Tracks" or "Full MIDI Rig."

Every time you use the template, be sure to *rename* the file before you record—this will keep the original template intact.

ASSIGNING A TRACK TO AN APPROPRIATE OUTPUT

In order to monitor your track, you'll need to hear it through your audio interface. You would typically assign it to your software's master mix bus feeding the main outputs, but you may also find it useful to assign the track to an individual output on your audio interface, to a subgroup within your software mixer, or elsewhere. We'll look at output routing in more depth in Chapter 10.

TIP

If you're using direct monitoring on the input signal as described earlier in this chapter, you may want to mute the output of the track to which you're recording until after you've finished tracking.

SETTING THE TEMPO AND CLICK TRACK

Tempo is important in all music, but it's especially crucial in computer-based multitracking. Whenever possible, it's a good idea to set the tempo of a song before you record any audio data. (MIDI offers more flexibility in this regard, which we'll talk about in Chapter 8.) Even if your software lets you change an audio file's tempo after recording, this operation can diminish sound quality—sometimes quite noticeably. The closer you are to the "right" tempo, the better. Once you establish a tempo, your software creates a grid based on it that serves as a guide for you when editing and setting markers (see Chapter 4).

A *click track* is an audible tempo reference built into music software that lets you follow the song and play in time, even when nothing else is recorded. Usually, the click sounds a little like a wood block, but some programs have clicks that sound like computer beeps from the 1980s.

TIP

Digital Performer has a great feature that lets you choose different patterns and sounds for your click, but you can also create a "custom" click by importing a drum loop, or setting up a MIDI drum pattern to play along with. These can be discarded later as your arrangement takes shape.

SETTING UP PRE-ROLL/COUNT-IN

In order to start the recording at the beginning of the song, it's useful to have a one- or two-measure count-in—sometimes called "pre-roll." This also reminds you of the tempo. Be sure the click is enabled for pre-roll, even if you're using a drum loop or other timing reference once the song starts.

RECORDING YOUR FIRST TRACK

After you create and name your track, you're ready to arm it for recording, check input levels (be sure to stay in the "yellow"), and start tracking.

Locate to the beginning of the song and hit Play + Record (this is usually accomplished with a quick key or virtual button push on the transport). Listen to the count-in, and when the first measure starts, begin playing.

TIP

If your part anticipates the beat, start recording at measure 1, but wait until measure 2 or 3 to begin playing. This way, you won't cut off the initial attack of your part. You can always move the audio file back to measure 1 later.

After you have finished recording the track, the software stores the audio file and creates a region, which it places on the track. The screen shows the region's position in the timeline (see **Fig. 5.15**).

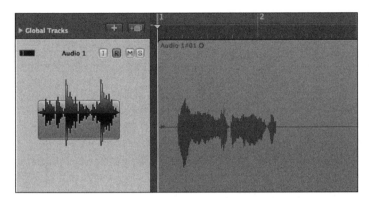

Fig. 5.15

A newly recorded region.

I always like to check the first take for sound quality before I record anything else. Once you're satisfied that levels are correct and the tone is what you're looking for, you have two options: recording a new take over the same track (don't worry, as we mentioned earlier, this won't erase the old material), or recording a new part on a new track alongside the first one. This is known as ***overdubbing***.

RECORDING A NEW TAKE ON AN EXISTING TRACK

You can record as many takes on a track as your disk space (and patience) allows. As mentioned above, recording a new take will not erase the old (unless you specifically tell the software to do so). A new file and region will be created in place of the original, while the old take will be stored for later recall.

There are a couple of different tactics for recording new takes. The first is to simply arm the track and start recording. New data will replace the old in the Arrange window, creating a new region for playback. This is the way to go if you're pretty sure you don't like the original take. You can keep it around for later reference, or you can delete it from the disk.

Another option is to create a copy of the track or the playlist. Various software packages handle this differently. In Pro Tools and Digital Performer, you can create a number of alternate playlists for each track. When you record or edit on a new playlist, the original is unaffected. Only one playlist can play back at a time, but you can hear alternative versions of the track by switching among the various playlists. A new playlist can start as a copy of the original, or can be blank, ready for a completely new performance. This approach conserves screen space.

In Logic, Cubase, and other programs, you can create a copy of a track and assign the copy to the same audio channel as the original. All the copies will be visible onscreen. By muting the original track, you can hear just the playback of the copy. Although this feature uses up more screen space, it also affords a quick visual picture of each take. That makes it easy to edit together a composite of the various tracks into a final take. You can also take advantage of the comp track feature we discussed earlier in this chapter. In fact, you can combine these two approaches, as shown in **Fig. 5.16**, where we see two copies of the guitar track, each with its own comp track. Later, these can be combined into one master composite.

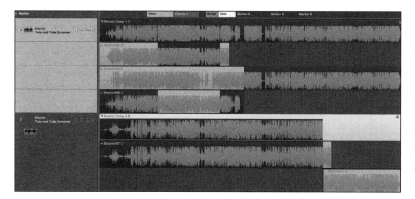

Fig. 5.16

Two versions of a guitar track, each with its own composite. These composites can be further edited to form one master composite.

OVERDUBBING

Once you've got your first track down, you're ready to build your arrangement by overdubbing. This involves a couple of additional steps:

SETTING UP EXISTING TRACKS FOR PLAYBACK

When you overdub, you need to hear the other tracks in the arrangement. If you've muted a track while monitoring the source directly from the hardware, unmute it now. And don't forget to take the first track out of record-enable before you record the new one!

CREATING AND ARMING A NEW TRACK

Make sure that the new track is assigned to its own audio channel within your software. (If it's assigned to the same audio channel as the first track, the first track won't be audible on playback.)

SETTING THE APPROPRIATE INPUT-MONITORING OPTION

You'll need to hear the previously recorded material and the input source. Set a monitoring level that feels most comfortable for performing. Remember, you can change the relative levels of the tracks at the mixing stage.

Follow the same steps you used to record your first track: Move the playhead to the spot where you want recording to begin, hit Play + Record, and start playing.

RECORDING MULTIPLE TRACKS SIMULTANEOUSLY

The number of tracks you can record at any one time is determined by both your hardware and software. Obviously, the number of physical inputs on your interface will be a factor.

Assuming that your gear will allow it, you can record eight or more tracks at once, allowing you to track an entire band "live." To do so, you must route the signal for each source to its own input, create a track for each input, and arm each track. **Fig. 5.17** shows the process for recording a basic rhythm section consisting of drum kit, bass, and guitar.

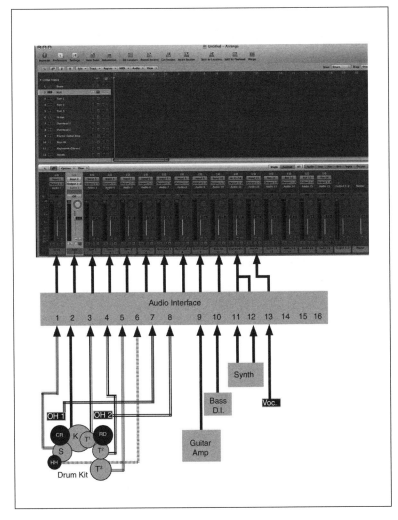

Fig. 5.17

Example audio assignments for multitrack-recording a full band.

TIP

Note that on many multitrack interfaces, the total number of inputs will include both analog and digital connections. So an interface offering "18 ins and outs" may actually have only eight analog inputs; the remaining 10 are digital. To use those additional inputs, you'll need an outboard A/D converter or a digital mixer capable of converting an analog signal to digital format.

PUNCH-IN RECORDING

Punch-in, or drop-in, recording is recording over a small section of audio without disturbing the adjacent audio regions. It's most commonly used for fixing mistakes—if you have a perfect guitar solo, except for one ugly clam in the middle, you can punch in over the offending note and replace it with something better (see **Fig. 5.18** and **Fig. 5.19**).

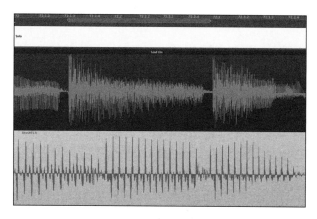

Fig. 5.18

Automatic punch in/out recording starts by defining the region to be replaced. The shaded bar below the timeline (starting around measure 72.1.3 and ending just before 72.3) shows the boundaries of the punch.

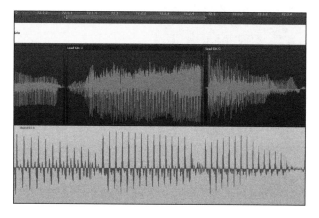

Fig. 5.19

The track shown in **Fig. 5.18** after automatic punch-in recording. A new audio region (shown with the shaded top) replaces the original in the playlist.

Punching in with software is much less risky than it is on a traditional tape recorder. If you miss a punch on a tape (by activating Record too soon, or leaving the machine in record for too long), you can ruin the original take. With software, the punch-in is nondestructive (unless you specify otherwise). You're creating a new region in place of the old, but the old data remains available. Not only does this provide a safety net in case you miss a punch, it also allows you more flexibility when combining the original take with the new section. You can use your software's editing tools to make a seamless transition between the original take and the punch, or combine elements of each take to create something completely new. And if you don't like it, there's always the old "undo" command.

PUNCH-IN MODES

There are several ways to punch-record. ***Manual punch*** is when you physically activate and deactivate recording as the track plays back. You can do this with your software's transport controls or (if your hardware supports it) via footswitch if your software and hardware support it.

TIP

By using key commands (addressed in Chapter 4), you can set up a MIDI controller—for example, a keyboard's sustain pedal—to manually activate punch recording.

In ***Auto-punch*** mode, you instruct your software to start and stop recording at prespecified locations, known as **punch points**, as illustrated in **Fig. 5.18**. In addition to letting you set up the exact punch you want (more precise than hitting a pedal on the fly), it also affords hands-free (or foot-free!) operation.

TIP

When you set up auto-punch, be sure to set the pre-roll so that you can hear audio before the punch point.

LOOP, OR CYCLE, RECORDING

While punch-in recording allows you to make one pass at a specific section, ***loop*** or ***cycle recording*** lets you take a number of shots at the same section.

Start by defining the loop's boundaries the same way you would set up punch points. Audition the loop and adjust the boundaries accordingly. You may want the loop to extend beyond the beginning and end of the part you want to play, to give yourself time to reset before each pass.

Begin recording: each time the loop plays back, the software creates a new region (see **Fig. 5.20**). You can take as many passes as disk space (and your ears) will allow.

To keep things moving quickly, some programs record loop takes differently than they do linear takes. Instead of writing a new audio file for each pass, they create a single audio file that contains all the passes. Each pass is stored as a separate region within the file. If you listen to the raw audio file, you'll hear each take play back in the order in which it was recorded.

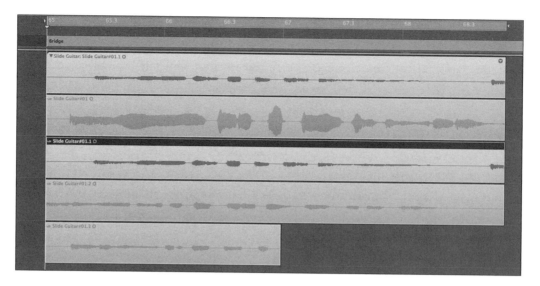

Fig. 5.20

Recording with the loop/cycle function engaged: each time playback loops, the software creates a new audio region. Note that the darker region is the one currently audible on playback.

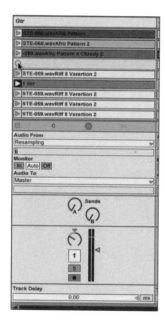

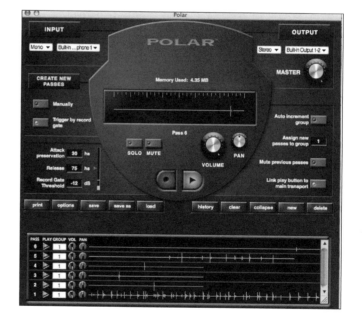

Fig. 5.21

Triggering a clip in Ableton Live.

Fig. 5.22

Digital Performer's Polar module lets you capture ideas quickly.

BREAKING THE LINEAR MODEL

As we've mentioned several times over the course of this book, most of the multitrack software we now use is modeled to some degree on hardware tape machines. But there are some notable exceptions.

Over the years, Ableton Live—now in version 8—has added features that are more in keeping with traditional DAWs, but the heart of the program remains its clips. *Clips* are short segments of audio or MIDI that are either prerecorded or created by the user. Instead of adhering to a traditional track grid, these clips can be assembled and triggered individually or in groups to create a performance or a complete arrangement. We'll explore all of this in more depth in the next two chapters, but while we're on the subject of recording and overdubbing, I want to contrast recording a Live clip with recording a track on a DAW.

In Live (see **Fig. 5.21**), you first arm a track, and then set a count-in as you would with a regular DAW. But instead of starting playback and playing along as a complete song unfolds, you can trigger a clip and play along to a small part of an arrangement.

As soon as you finish recording, the clip can be edited to create a loop, and the groove of that loop can be altered. To do this well requires a slightly different approach than that used to create a more linear recording. For example, if you stop recording too early, the boundaries of the clip may make it harder to use as a loop. At the same time, the clip you've created may not go with the rest of the arrangement, but *can* be used elsewhere. So you may find yourself just recording clip after clip, storing and editing all of them, and then using that material in many different ways.

Digital Performer, which is a more traditional DAW, includes a feature called Polar (see **Fig. 5.22**) that uses RAM instead of the hard drive, allowing you to quickly capture ideas and loop them, then "print" your work to the hard disk, where it will then be stored as tracks within the DAW project.

In both these examples, nontraditional approaches can be used instead of—or alongside—more conventional linear multitracking.

MOVING ON

Multitrack recording is exciting and powerful in and of itself, and there are plenty of situations where you can lay down a few linear tracks and move straight on to mixing. But the fun of the desktop studio really begins after the tracks go down. We cover audio editing and assembling in Chapter 6.

CHAPTER 6: AUDIO EDITING AND ASSEMBLING

IN THIS CHAPTER
- **BASIC EDITING AND ASSEMBLING AUDIO**
- **EDITING A MULTITRACK ARRANGEMENT**
- **WAVEFORM EDITING**
- **PREPARING FILES FOR WEB DISTRIBUTION**

In Chapter 5 we discussed the essentials of audio recording. But with a desktop studio, getting audio onto tracks is only the beginning of the production process. The ability to edit and assemble audio elements is what makes the software such a powerful and creative tool.

If you have not done so already, take a moment to look through Chapters 4 and 5, and pay close attention to the sections that explain how audio files, regions, and playlists relate to one another. You'll need to know this before you can fully understand how to edit digital audio.

BASIC EDITING AND ASSEMBLING AUDIO

Your music software's ability to work with audio files—and the regions within them—as independent entities offers you incredible flexibility when editing and arranging your project. This process can involve music you record yourself, previously recorded loops and clips, or a combination of the two. You can approach your audio editing in several ways:

- **The multitrack arrangement.** Here, you move audio regions in time and among tracks to create a multitrack arrangement. This kind of editing is as much art as it is science, and is often part of the composing and mixing process. Most of this work is *nondestructive*, meaning that the original file is unchanged. But just because it's nondestructive doesn't mean it's not precise: Even in a multitrack arrangement, you may find yourself editing regions on the sample level.

- **The waveform level.** Waveform editing is where you roll up your sleeves and get under your audio's hood (or maybe into its internal organs). Though waveform editing is more technical and utilitarian than arrangement-level editing, it has its creative uses as well. Since waveform editing directly affects the file, it is often described as *destructive*.

- **The 2-track playlist.** Like multitrack arrangement editing, 2-track playlist editing involves the creation and sequencing of regions. But where multitrack editing is used to build a single project that will be mixed down into master form, a 2-track playlist is most commonly used to assemble several complete mixes, or masters.

READING THE WAVEFORM

Before we go further, let's take a very quick detour into some important but basic physics. Sound travels through air in waves. The frequency of a wave—the number of times it oscillates through one cycle in one second—determines its pitch: The higher the frequency, the higher the pitch. This is easy to see if you're working with a simple sine wave (see **Fig. 6.1**). But most music consists of complex waves with many overtones mixed in with a fundamental frequency.

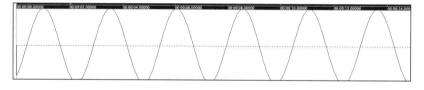

Fig. 6.1

A sine wave

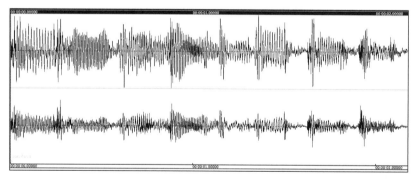

Fig. 6.2

A waveform is a visual representation of an audio wave.

A *waveform* is a visual display of the sound waves that make up an audio file or region (see **Fig. 6.2**). As you can see, a typical audio file's waveform is way more complex than a simple sine wave. But even with all that complexity, the display gives you two key pieces of information about your audio:

- **Duration** (along the x-axis) is measured in real time, SMPTE, bars and beats, and samples.

- **Loudness**, or *amplitude* (along the y-axis), is measured in **decibels** (dB). A flat horizontal line represents silence, or 0 dB. The higher the wave appears relative to that flat line—on most displays, the wave goes both above and below the 0 dB line—the louder the signal. The loudest signals are known as *peaks*.

These display conventions apply to any audio file display, whether you're working nondestructively or destructively, and are employed by virtually all audio software programs.

The amplitude and shape of a waveform can give you some clues about the audio it represents. For example, with a region containing drum hits, such as the one in **Fig. 6.3**, we can look for the peaks as a way of finding the beats. On a guitar track (see **Fig. 6.4**), the display shows where the guitarist plays and where he's silent. On a synthesizer track (see **Fig. 6.5**), we can see where a sustaining note builds up and where it fades out.

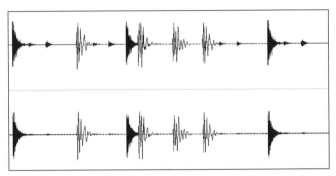

Fig. 6.3

The waveform display of a drum track shows distinct peaks, representing each drum hit.

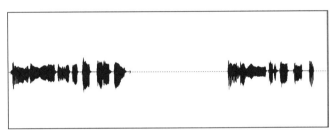

Fig. 6.4

The waveform display of a guitar track; note the low amplitude areas, which represent where the guitar part rests.

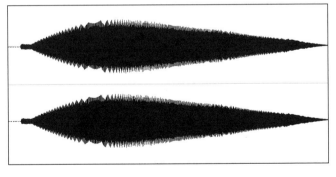

Fig. 6.5

The waveform display of a synthesizer part; as the note sustains, it builds in level, represented by the higher amplitude in the waveform.

GETTING A CLOSER LOOK

We discussed zooming in and out in Chapter 4. Zoom is an especially important tool for audio editing, where precision counts. **Fig. 6.6** shows the same audio region at two zoom levels. With the region zoomed out, the region boundary appears to begin at the start of the waveform. But when we zoom in, we see that the audio actually starts later than the region. At this view, we can make necessary adjustments so that the audio and the region line up.

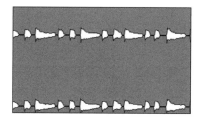
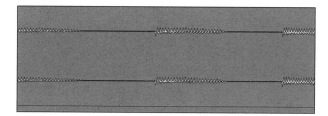

Fig. 6.6

The same audio material is shown at a wide (left) and tight zoom (right).

Because audio files contain so many samples, it can be hard to home in on an exact edit point. If you chop off a sound in the middle of a wave, you may hear pops, clicks, or other artifacts. You can choose precise edit points by looking for *zero crossings*—places in the waveform where the amplitude is at zero. You can do this manually by zooming very tightly (see **Fig. 6.7**). Many editors can automatically search for zero crossing points, even when you're zoomed out further.

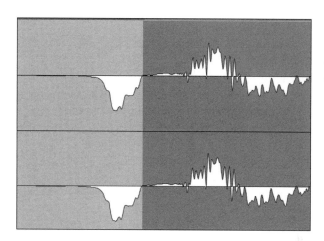

Fig. 6.7

Zooming in tight can help you find zero crossing points.

■ EDITING A MULTITRACK ARRANGEMENT

In Chapter 4, we examined the concept of the grid, and how it allows you to produce complex and dynamic multitrack arrangements. There are a number of techniques for editing audio regions relative to their grid position, which we'll examine below. But first, let's look at what happens to the audio you've recorded.

WORKING FROM A POOL

The regions that you create when you record and edit audio are catalogued in a master list that appears in its own window, separate from the main Edit/Arrange window. This list shows all the audio files associated with a project and every region contained within them. Think of

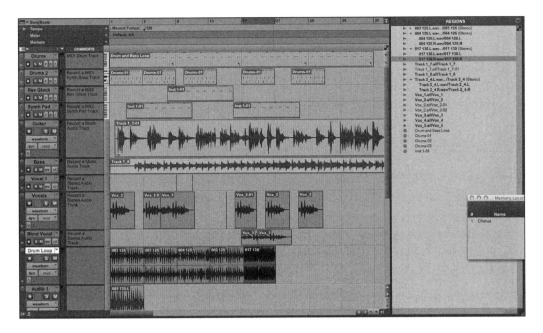

Fig. 6.8

Pro Tools' Audio window helps users organize all the files and regions in a project. Most DAWs offer similar project-management features.

it as a big file cabinet for your project. Various programs call this window by different names: In Cubase it's the Pool; in Logic it's the Bin; in Digital Performer it's the Soundbites window. In Pro Tools (see **Fig. 6.8**) it's simply called the Audio window.

But by any name, this audio "file cabinet" is one of the most powerful features in multitrack audio software. You can drag regions from this window into your arrangement, audition regions from the list, remove unwanted regions and audio files from your project (and from the disk), and import audio files from other projects or sources, such as audio CDs and loop library CDs, and add them to your project.

Because this list will contain all the audio files recorded with the project, you can also use it to replace a region you may have removed from your edit/arrangement—useful if you make a mistake or purposely delete something and later change your mind.

The Audio window also lets you perform important housekeeping operations, such as renaming regions and files, moving audio files to new locations, converting audio files to a format that matches the others in your project, and more. If your program crashes after you've done some recording but before you've saved your work, you may be able to locate the audio files you recorded and add them back into the project from this window. On many programs, you can launch an editor for the file from this window without importing the file into your arrangement.

TIP

Audio File Browsers

As mentioned above, most of today's music software provides a central window to help you organize the audio files in a project, and will automatically add new files to it. Modern music production techniques often combine project-specific tracks with pre-existing audio files like drum loops, etc. To make it easier to find and organize these items, most programs offer some sort of database function. This tool can be as simple as a "browser" that lets you look through the contents of your hard drive, audition files, and import them into your project. Other versions let you create a searchable library that can help you find files by criteria such as instrument, genre, tempo, etc. In either case, these files can be dragged into a project, where they'll be available alongside any other audio you've recorded. Spend some time learning these features and configuring your software to take full advantage of them.

DESTRUCTIVE AND NONDESTRUCTIVE EDITING

Before we look at specific editing techniques, let's jump back to some topics we introduced in Chapters 4 and 5 and go over how destructive and nondestructive editing affect your work with audio files and regions. Destructive editing operates on the *file* level. It changes the actual data written to disk. This will affect both the audio file and the regions it contains. We discuss destructive audio editing techniques in depth later in this chapter. Nondestructive editing works on regions but leaves the original file untouched. If you're unsure what type of editing you're doing, make a copy of the original file before you begin. Better to be safe and have extra copies of a recording that to risk ruining a great take because you've edited the audio file itself, and not the region.

TIP

One audio file may be used in many different regions within a project. Before you edit the file, be sure that the changes you make won't affect the other regions that use the file. For example, if you trim a noisy section at the beginning of an audio file and thereby shorten that file's duration, it may cause regions using that file to play back out of sync with the rest of the project. You will then have to move and/or adjust those regions to compensate.

BASIC NONDESTRUCTIVE EDITING TECHNIQUES

Most of your editing will take place in the Edit/Arrange (or Tracks) window, and most of the important tasks can be done with a mouse or trackball.

You can select single regions or groups of regions using the standard selection conventions that apply to your computer platform, though as we saw in Chapter 4, the behavior of the cursor may change depending on the active tool it represents.

Generally, clicking the mouse cursor on the middle of a region selects it (see **Fig. 6.9**). Shift- and Control/Command-clicking lets you add additional regions to the selection. Dragging the mouse around a group of regions selects all of them (see **Fig. 6.10**).

The cursor can also be used to select or define part of a region. **Fig. 6.11** shows how this is done in Pro Tools.

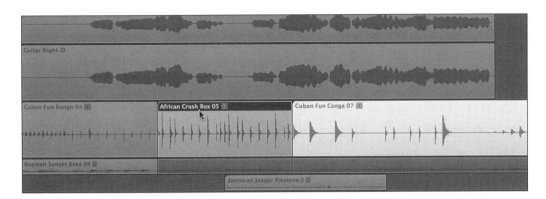

Fig. 6.9

Selecting a single region by clicking on it.

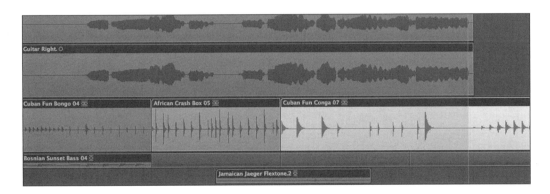

Fig. 6.10

Selecting multiple regions by dragging over them.

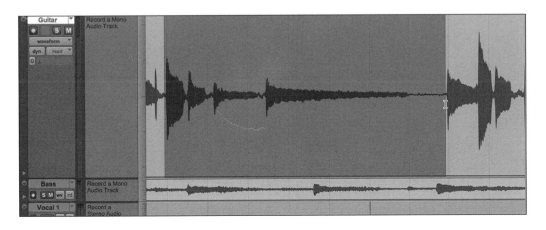

Fig. 6.11

Selecting a section within a region.

TIP

In addition to the mouse moves described below, you can use the clipboard for Cut/Copy/Paste editing in much the same way you'd work with a word processor or spreadsheet.

The following basic editing techniques apply to both audio and MIDI in virtually every desktop production program. While specific methods and terms may vary, the end result is the same.

- **Move.** Changes the location of a region. You can move a region to a new location on the same track, or onto another track. The region plays in its entirety from the new location.

- **Copy.** Duplicates a region. You can place the duplicate at a new location on the same track or assign it to a new track. You can also use duplicates to repeat a region, creating a loop-like effect on playback. These copies can be designated as independent regions, so editing one won't affect the content of the others.

- **Repeat.** Duplicates a region and places a specified number of copies in a series (see **Fig. 6.12**). You can achieve a similar result by **looping** the region. If you loop the region, the playback of the copies is affected any time you edit the original.

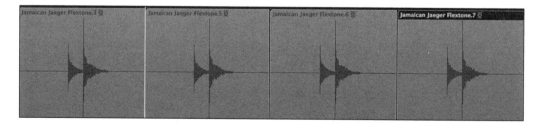

Fig. 6.12

The Repeat command offers a quick way to copy a region any number of times.

- **Split.** Divides one region into two new regions. Each of these new regions can be independently moved, copied, split again, etc. (see **Fig. 6.13**). The original region remains available for later recall.

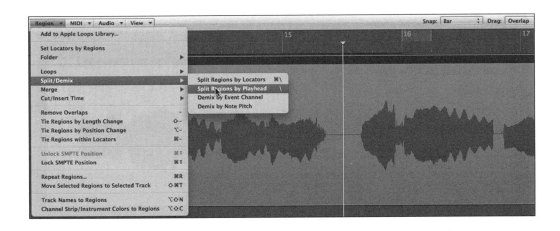

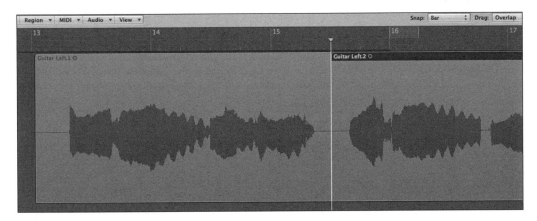

Fig. 6.13

Splitting a region into two new regions.

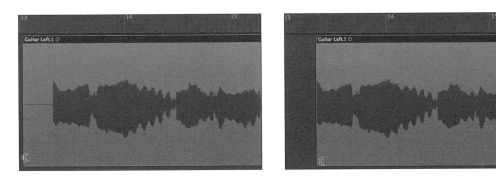

Fig. 6.14

Trimming the boundaries of a region without moving the contents within it.

- **Trim.** Changes the boundaries of a region by moving the start and end points. Conventional trimming alters where a region begins and ends playback, but doesn't change the location of the material contained within it (see **Fig. 6.14**). However, a second kind of trimming is available on many programs. Instead of altering the start and end points of the region to fit a certain length, it actually changes the speed of the audio to conform to that length (see **Fig. 6.15**). This is known as *time compression and expansion*.

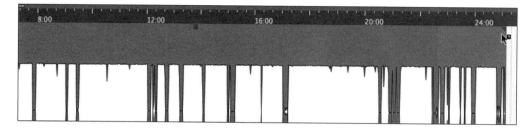

Fig. 6.15

Stretching a region with a time compression/expansion tool changes the duration of the material within the region.

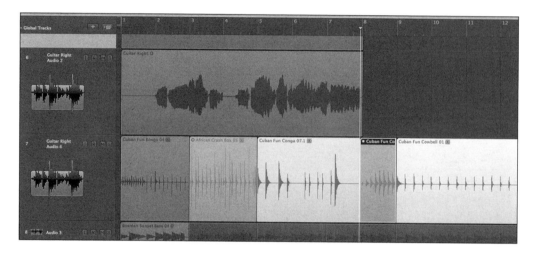

Fig. 6.16

Muting individual regions within an arrangement.

- **Mute.** You can disable the playback of individual regions by muting them in an arrangement (see **Fig. 6.16**). Unlike the Mixer's Mute button, muting an individual region has no effect on other regions in the track. This is a very useful tool for testing out arrangement ideas.

WORKING WITH THE GRID

In audio production, as in real estate, location is everything. When you copy and move regions in your arrangement, you want to be sure each element lines up correctly. Otherwise, your production will have about as much clarity as a man-on-the-street interview during Mardi Gras.

FREE-FORM OR SLIP EDITING

Free-form editing lets you drag a region to any location in the arrangement. How this works depends on whether or not you have your software set to conform, or *snap*, to a grid position.

With snap-to-grid turned off, the region will end up exactly where you leave it and not conform to any pre-established grid or marker position. Because your edits won't be restricted by the grid, you can preserve a subtle nuance, such as a slightly anticipated first beat, that might otherwise be cut off by a strict grid edit. This type of editing comes in handy for lining up regions that you recorded without a click, and for making small, corrective edits, as shown in **Fig. 6.17**.

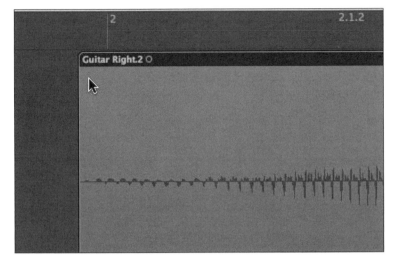

Fig. 6.17

Turing off Snap-to-Grid lets you make very precise edits.

When snap-to-grid is active, the software will automatically move the region to the closest grid position. In this case, the grid resolution will affect where the region ends up. **Fig. 6.18** shows what happens when I drag a region to the first beat in a measure. With the snap value set to a whole note, the region automatically lines up with the beginning of the measure. But when the snap value is set to one beat, the region snaps to the *second* beat in the measure—even though I dragged it to the same position on the timeline both times.

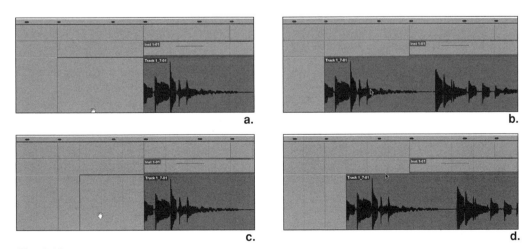

a. **b.**

c. **d.**

Fig. 6.18

Different snap values affect how regions will line up on the grid. With the grid set to a whole note, the material on measure 2 (a.) moves to measure 1, beat 1 (b.). Change the grid to one beat, and the material (c.) can now be moved to measure 1, beat 2 (d.).

Grid resolution can be defined in musical time (bars/beats/clicks), in SMPTE time (hours/minutes/seconds/frames), or in real time (minutes/seconds/milliseconds). Each of these settings can be useful depending on the type of work you're doing. The more precise the editing you're doing, the smaller the snap value should be.

TIP

Once you move a region to its new location, it stays there until you move it again. Changing the snap value from, say, a quarter note to a whole note will not cause previous edits to move; it will only affect any edits you make after that change.

SPOTTING

Spotting places a region at the exact location you specify by typing in the desired position, which can be either a bar/beat value or a real-time location. In addition to providing a precise way of placing regions in your arrangement, spotting tools allow you to return a region to its original recording position—a potential life saver if you've lost track of your edits. Spot editing (see **Fig. 6.19**) is especially useful when you're working with video, because it lets you line up your regions with video cues.

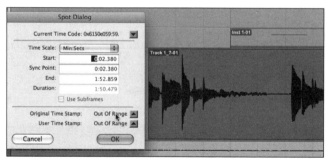

Fig. 6.19

Spot editing lets you type in an exact location for a region.

NUDGING

Sometimes you want to move a region by a specified amount, such as a measure or beat. As an alternative to using the cursor to drag the region by hand, you can *nudge* it to the left or right (earlier or later in the timeline). The amount of this move is called the "nudge value," which can be set separately from the grid value—for example, you might set the grid to a whole note, but the nudge value to an eighth note. You can use your computer keyboard (usually, the plus and minus or arrow keys) to move the region forward and back in your arrangement. You can still move it by a whole note—simply hit the nudge key eight times.

SETTING ANCHORS, OR SYNC POINTS

Working with a grid helps you keep your regions tied to a musical value. But sometimes a region's boundaries simply don't line up with the bar lines. Perhaps you're editing a region containing a guitar part that starts right on the beat, but trimming the region's boundary to that beat makes the guitar sound like it's cut off. To sound natural, you need the region to start a little *before* the first note is played. But when you snap to the grid, the start of the region—and not the first note of the guitar part—lines up with the beat.

An *anchor*, or **sync point,** is a marker within a region that you can use in place of a region's boundaries to conform the region to a grid position. For example, you could set the sync point to a guitar part's first note, as shown in **Fig. 6.20**. Now when you snap the region to the grid, the guitar will start right on the beat as intended.

SHUFFLE EDITING

Shuffle editing lets you change the order of adjacent regions. Rather than snapping to a grid value, each region snaps to the region that abuts it; it's as though the regions are magnets attracting one another (see **Fig. 6.21**).

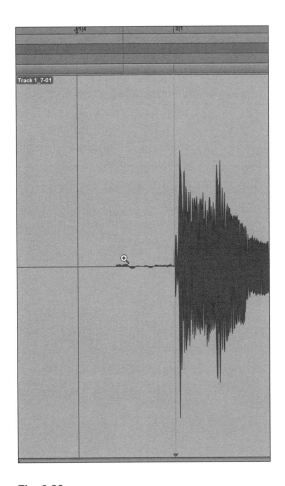

Fig. 6.20

Placing a sync point, or anchor, within a region lets you snap any note or beat to the grid without changing the boundaries of the region.

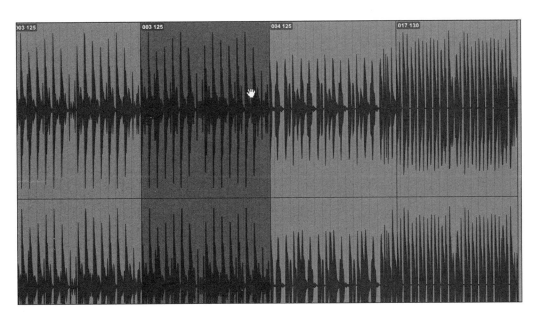

Fig. 6.21

With Shuffle editing, a region snaps to those adjacent to it.

Shuffle editing is great when you want to change the order of several regions of the same length (such as drum loops). If you delete a region in Shuffle mode, the following region in the track will move to occupy the deleted region's position. Similarly, if you trim the duration of a region in Shuffle mode, the regions around it will move to adjust to its new size.

Shuffle editing can also be useful when you want to perform more complex tasks, such as changing the phrasing of a vocal line or instrumental solo. Let's say you have two notes, and you want to shorten the first note, while having the second one begin sooner. First, divide the region so that each note is now in its own region. Next, in Shuffle mode, use the Trim tool to shorten the first region. The second one will move automatically to start where the previous one ends.

SCRUBBING

Though not specifically an edit technique, the *Scrubber*, often depicted by a speaker icon, is great for finding precise edit points. Scrubbing doesn't involve cleaning up your audio; it refers to a practice from the days of reel-to-reel tape when an engineer would manually move the tape over the tape heads (scrub) to hear a specific edit point. With software, the cursor takes the place of the tape head. You can scrub both forward and backward.

WAVEFORM EDITING

Think of your waveform editor as your audio medical kit. Here's where you fix problems, eliminate unwanted portions of a file (thereby freeing up disk space), prepare a file for mastering, and convert file formats. You can also apply effects and perform a few tricks that alter the audio's very nature.

LOOKING AT AUDIO IN A WAVEFORM EDITOR

Like a multitrack's Arrange window, a waveform editor displays audio along x and y axes. But the context of the waveform display is different. Where a multitrack editor shows each region in relation to other regions in an arrangement, a waveform editor focuses on one audio file at a time. The display's main components are the overview, which always shows the entire wave, and the work area, which shows the current edit position (see **Fig. 6.22**).

MAKING SELECTIONS

Because waveform editors treat audio at a fundamental level, most of the action takes place with the cursor (as opposed to the "exterior" tools available in the Arrange window editor, such as the Scissors tool, Trimmer tool, and the like). One analogy is that while an Arrangement editor shows a neighborhood, a waveform editor shows the inside of a house.

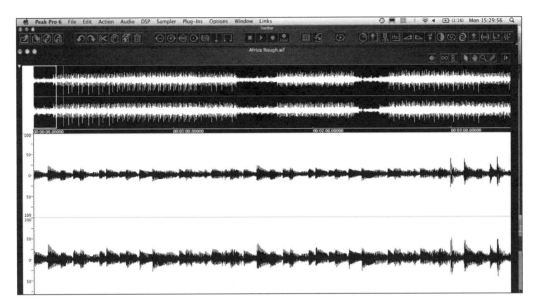

Fig. 6.22

Waveform editor Bias Peak shows one audio file at a time. The top pane shows the overview of the file; the pane below it shows the same file in more detail.

OPENING AN AUDIO FILE

Programs that function as waveform editors, such as Bias's Peak, Sony's Sound Forge, and Steinberg's WaveLab, *can* record audio directly—in which case they're functioning as 2-track recorders (see Chapter 3). But a waveform editor can also open existing audio files, and for those of you recording to multitrack software, that's how you'll use them most of the time. There are a number of ways to launch a waveform editor.

If your audio software includes a separate waveform editing feature (as do programs like Logic, Cubase, Nuendo, Digital Performer, and others), you can usually launch the editor directly from the Arrange window by double-clicking the region you want to edit, as shown in **Fig. 6.23**.

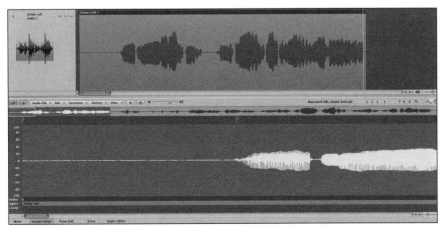

Fig. 6.23

Double-clicking an audio region in Logic launches that DAW's internal waveform editor.

Some digital audio multitracks (including Logic, Cubase, Performer, and Acid), also allow you to launch a third-party waveform editor from within the multitrack. When launched from your multitrack, the file you edit in the waveform editor will automatically link to the multitrack project; when you save your work in the waveform editor, it will be updated in your multitrack with the edits in place. (Use caution: Once saved, you can't undo changes made by the external waveform editor from within the multitrack.)

If you're not working with a multitrack, you can open an audio file directly in the audio editor either by opening it from your software's File menu or by double-clicking on the file on the desktop.

Many programs allow you to drag and drop audio directly from the desktop into the editor. This is the preferred method when you're working on self-contained material, such as a finished mix.

One thing to be aware of when double-clicking on a file on the desktop—it may launch the wrong application. Operating systems typically assign file formats to specific programs, and any time you click a file, that program opens up. For example, Windows might assign MP3 or WAV formats to Windows Media Player. In this case, you can either reassign the file to your waveform editor, or simply launch the waveform editor first and open the file from within it.

WAVEFORM EDITING TECHNIQUES

Like your multitrack software, a waveform editor allows you to create and work with regions within a single audio file. As a companion to multitrack software, the waveform editor is especially useful for fine-tuning a file's boundaries and performing signal processing.

In stand-alone applications, the waveform editor handles regions more directly, using them more for assembly than arranging. For example, you can define regions and then export them as new audio files. This is a good way to turn a 16-bar drum passage into a collection of one- and two-bar drum loops. You can also create regions for assembly in a sequential playlist (useful for preparing audio for CD), or select regions for format conversion (for example, converting WAV files to MP3 files).

CUT, COPY, PASTE, AND TRIM

Cut, copy, and paste are a waveform editor's most basic functions. The most common applications are:

- **Cutting** to remove a section of an audio file or region from your file. Cutting places the data on your computer's Clipboard, which allows you to paste it elsewhere in relation to the rest of the file (or even into a separate file). You can also use Cut to completely erase an audio file or region (by not pasting it back into any file). You can also erase material using your Delete key, but deleting bypasses the Clipboard—so once deleted, the material cannot be pasted anywhere. If you don't "undo," it's gone.

- **Copying** a selection and **pasting** it into a new file. This is a good way to extract and organize small pieces of audio taken from a longer recording.

- **Trimming** to remove excess audio at the beginning and end of a file. This is a little different than trimming in a multitrack arrangement environment. Here, trimming (also known as **cropping**) destructively edits a file so that *only the selected area* remains (see **Fig. 6.24**). This is one of the most useful features of a waveform editor.

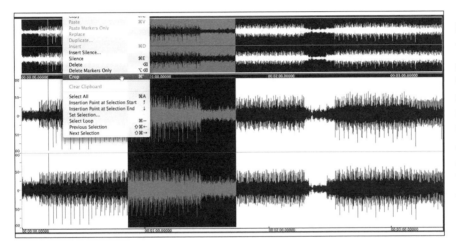

Fig. 6.24

Trimming a file in a waveform editor removes unwanted audio before and after the selected area.

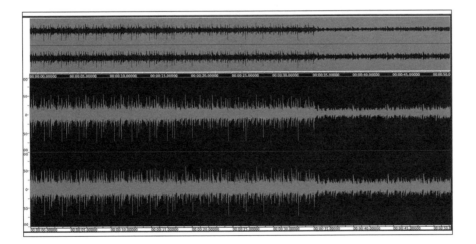

SPLICING

To *splice* is to join two sections of audio together. These can be two or more regions within the same audio file, or audio taken from different files. A splice can be destructive (when it's written to the original file) or nondestructive (either when you're splicing two regions in a playlist, or when you're taking material you've copied from one or more files and pasting it in another file). In a way, nondestructive splicing is not all that different from the type of region editing we discussed in the multitrack section of this chapter.

To splice two or more sections of audio together, you'll need to hear how the pieces fit together. You can audition the edit in context by using **pre-roll** and **post-roll** to play the sections before and after the edit point. If you hear noises or other audio glitches with pre-

and post-roll engaged, the problem most likely lies in the position of the edit points. Adjusting the selection area can generally solve the problem.

The most natural splices occur when musical factors match: for example, the pitch and volume of both sides of the splice should be the same. Look for obvious cut points, like the beginnings of notes — the start of a measure is ideal — or look for gaps between phrases where there's silence. Try to define both sides of the splice so that the cut happens when the waveform is at 0 — a.k.a., the zero-crossing point. Your software may be set to automatically conform to these points.

When making a splice, listen *very* carefully. Engineer, author, and Pro Tools expert Rich Tozzoli advises using headphones and monitoring with a limiter that will exaggerate any pops and clicks your edit may create; even if you don't plan on using these in the final mix, they can alert you to problems.

USING CROSSFADES

A crossfade overlaps the edit points of two regions by a small amount, mixing in elements of both sections. If adjusting the selection boundaries doesn't allow two regions to blend smoothly, you may need to perform a crossfade over the splice point. **Fig. 6.25** shows how this works.

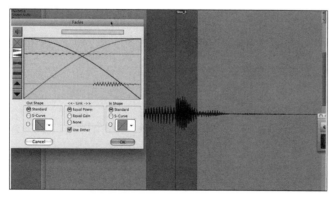

Fig. 6.25

A crossfade can help make an edit between two regions sound smoother.

FILE-BASED SIGNAL PROCESSING

When it comes to signal processing, your computer is like a world-class athlete: powerful, flexible, and capable of pulling off feats that amaze spectators. Signal processors are the tools you use to shape your sound, and we cover them in-depth in Chapter 11. But it's worth noting here that your software can tackle signal processing in two ways: in real time (so that the processing occurs as the signal plays back), and as a file-based operation, where the processor rewrites the audio data on disk. The latter is the most common way of working with a waveform editor.

Real-time signal processing takes place as the audio plays back. It is nondestructive and can be adjusted throughout the production process. The most common real-time processing is the use of plug-ins, which we discuss in Chapters 11 and 12.

File-based signal processing is destructive, and performs operations **offline**, which means that it works on the file while the music is stopped. Your work does not become permanent until you save the file. Often, plug-ins give you the option of working in both real-time or offline modes. Remember, if you're not sure you want to keep the changes you make, use "Save As..." to create a new version of your file!

File-based processing is also used for a range of specialized digital signal processing, or DSP, that's not possible in real time. This includes operations such as normalizing, adjusting the gain of part or all of an audio file, creating fades, correcting DC offset, and file-based (i.e., destructive) time compression/expansion and pitch shifting. Let's look at each of these.

NORMALIZING

Normalizing helps you set the optimal signal level of your file by adjusting the highest peaks to a maximum amount (usually 0 dB or just under 0 dB). Normalization is different from compression and limiting in that it does not change the relative dynamics of the material. Everything is boosted by the amount it takes for the largest peak to reach the maximum. This works especially well on audio of a consistent level because all of the audio will be boosted near maximum without going **over**.

For material with a wide dynamic range, it might be better to normalize the audio file in sections, excluding the hottest peaks.

GAIN ADJUSTING

Gain adjusting boosts or **attenuates** audio by a fixed amount. Unlike normalization, gain adjusting doesn't stop at a preset peak—if you're not careful, you can cause the file to distort.

FADES

A **fade** changes the level of a section of audio over time. The most common fade is the fade-out (see **Fig. 6.26**). Longer fades can sound similar to those created with a traditional mixing console. But the advantage of creating a fade in a DSP environment is that you can more precisely define the length and response curve of the fade.

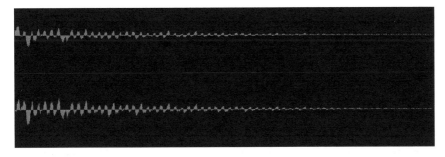

Fig. 6.26

A fadeout

Shorter fades are useful for smoothing out edits. For example, if your edit cuts off the beginning of a note's attack, the result will sound harsh. Creating a very short fade (a few milliseconds) at the beginning of the attack will make the edit less obtrusive.

DC OFFSET ADJUST

You might not be able to hear the results of **DC offset**, an audio problem that occurs when there's too much DC current present in a signal. This can push the waveform off the zero-axis and affect processing and editing, and can also adversely affect the performance of your audio system.

Your waveform editor can search an audio file and adjust DC offset so that the wave is centered at the zero axis. It's a good idea to check DC offset for every audio file you open.

TIME COMPRESSION/EXPANSION AND PITCH SHIFTING

Time compression/expansion changes the duration of an audio file without affecting the pitch, while pitch shifting changes the pitch without affecting the duration. While many programs can now perform this function in real time nondestructively (we'll discuss this in depth in Chapter 7), there are occasions when writing these changes to disk is beneficial.

When working with standard audio files, these operations work best in small increments. Time changes of over 10 percent can cause audible artifacts that diminish sound quality, though some algorithms can offer good results at much higher levels of expansion and compression. This is one area where you should experiment, listen carefully, and always work with a copy of the original file.

REVERSE

Reverse plays a selection backwards. You can use it to create psychedelic sounds—for example, recreating the "backwards solo" sound Jimi Hendrix popularized on *Axis, Bold as Love*—and other, more subtle effects. Try reversing a crash cymbal hit to create a swell.

SILENCE

Silence is pretty self-explanatory: it turns any selected region into absolute silence. You can use it, for example, to eliminate background noise between the verses of a vocal track.

FORMAT CONVERSION

One of the most important DSP functions, format conversion changes an audio file from one type, or format, to another. For example, you can change a WAV file into an SD2 file, or convert an AIFF file into an MP3.

Two related functions include sample-rate conversion and bit-depth conversion. In a typical audio project, you'll be working with one sample rate, and all audio files must conform to it. That's no problem if you're only using files that were originally recorded as part of that project. But if you import external files that have a different sample rate, you'll have to convert them to match your project. A common example would be importing CD audio (16-bit, 44.1 kHz) into a 24-bit, 48 kHz project.

Sample-rate and bit-depth conversion are also common at the mastering stage. You may, for example, record your mix as a 24-bit file to take advantage of that resolution's higher headroom and better fidelity. But a CD master must be in 16-bit, 44.1 kHz format, so you can use your waveform editor to convert the file to the appropriate format.

DITHERING

Dithering can help improve audio quality when converting a file from 24 bits to 16 bits. The conversion process sometimes introduces small amounts of digital distortion that can be audible on quiet passages (like fadeouts). Dithering adds a small amount of noise to mask this distortion. You would use dithering only when converting a file to a lower bit depth.

BATCH PROCESSING

Batch processing enables you to do file-intensive work on a number of audio files at the same time. This is a very useful tool for format conversion, adjusting the gain of a number of files from the same session, and other bulk-processing operations.

OTHER OPERATIONS

Some of the other operations you can do with a waveform editor include repairing audible clicks and pops; automatically finding and removing, or *stripping*, silent areas from a file; inverting the phase of an audio file; and more. These are pretty specialized tools, but worth exploring.

▇ PREPARING FILES FOR WEB DISTRIBUTION

Uncompressed audio files sound great, but they're much too big for most Web uses. Compressed formats, such as MP3, offer acceptable sound quality in files that are up to 10 times smaller than their uncompressed counterparts.

You can create MP3s from a variety of original files. Many programs allow batch conversions, so you can convert an entire CD's worth of audio in one operation. When making MP3s, you'll be given a choice between better sound quality (larger files) and faster upload/download (smaller files).

WORKING WITH SAMPLERS

Waveform editors are very useful for preparing *samples*—short recordings that are used as source material by hardware and software digital samplers. You can use a waveform editor to edit the boundaries of a sample, to adjust a sample's gain so that individual samples will sound cohesive when played together as one sampler instrument, and to adjust other sonic attributes of the audio. This is especially convenient if you're working with sampling software on your computer (see Chapter 12).

If your sampler supports it, you can also use a waveform editor to define a sample's loop points. When discussing samplers, the term *loop* (sometimes referred to as *sustain loop*) is a section of an audio sample that, when repeated, allows the sample to sustain beyond its original duration. This, for example, lets you create a long note out of a relatively short flute or violin sample.

There are several types of sustain loop, but the most common are 1) a single loop, where the looped section plays back one time; and 2) an infinite loop, where the sample continues to play for as long as you hold down a key (or for the entire duration of a MIDI note). Other types of loops include reverse (where the loop plays the audio backward), and bidirectional (where the sample plays both forward and backward). Some samples, such as individual drum hits, are usually left unlooped. These are called *one-shot samples*, because the wave plays once from beginning to end, no matter how long you hold down the key.

With a sustain loop, you usually want the boundaries of the loop to be as seamless as possible; the goal is to create a natural-sounding sustain. In most cases, simply repeating the entire sample won't work. The initial section of the sample, or attack, generally has a different character than the body of the sample, or sustain. Your waveform editor can help you select a section of the sample's sustain and assign it to a loop. To help ensure smooth playback, you should set loop boundaries at *zero-crossing points*, sections of audio where the waveform has an amplitude of zero. This can prevent pops, clicks, and other artifacts from being heard as the audio loops. A full-featured waveform editor can search for zero-crossing points automatically.

Once you've finished editing the sample, you can load it into your sampler software (or export it to your hardware sampler) and use the sampler's onboard editing tools to shape the note's overall tone and other performance characteristics.

CONNECTING A SAMPLER TO YOUR COMPUTER

Hardware samplers have become an endangered species, but there are many still on the market—at least, the used market—and some pros swear by them. You can probably pick one up at a bargain and may find it has a unique sound that you won't get from a software sampler. But you can still use your computer to transfer samples between your waveform editor and MIDI sampler. This can happen in two ways: via MIDI (which can take a long time), or over a SCSI cable using SMIDI (SCSI MIDI), if your computer has a SCSI card. Most waveform editors support hardware samplers from Roland, Akai, and E-mu/Ensoniq, which means that the software can import and export audio to these instruments in their respective formats. Support for software-based samplers, such as GigaStudio, Kontakt,

HALion, and others (covered in Chapter 12) is also common. Since these instruments reside on the computer's hard disk, there's no long transfer process.

ADVANCED WAVEFORM EDITOR FEATURES

As you get comfortable with the basic operations of your waveform editor, you should explore its advanced features. A waveform editor can work with audio on the sample level (see **Fig. 6.27**), where you can actually redraw waveforms to eliminate problems. This takes some practice, but it can save the day when pops and clips are ruining an otherwise perfect audio file.

Frequency analysis is another useful tool that's available in high-end waveform editors. You can use a frequency analyzer to study the frequency balance of your mixes. Comparing your own work against your favorite professional recordings can be an incredible learning experience, especially if you're new to audio mixing.

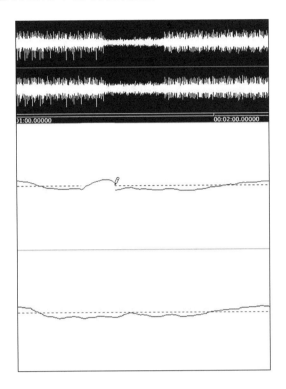

Fig. 6.27

By zooming in to the sample level, you can "redraw" the waveform to solve problems.

■ MOVING ON

The techniques we've explored in Chapters 5 and 6 have revolutionized audio production by allowing us to alter an audio recording after the fact. The final step in the progression from linear audio recording to true random-access production is the ability to manipulate existing audio files into components of an arrangement, regardless of their original pitch and tempo. We cover this technique, known as loop construction, in Chapter 7.

CHAPTER 7:   ELASTIC AUDIO: LOOPING AND PITCH SHIFTING

IN THIS CHAPTER   ▓ UNDERSTANDING LOOP CONSTRUCTION
         ▓ REAL-TIME BEAT-MATCHING TOOLS
         ▓ MAKING LOOPS WORK TOGETHER

Perhaps the most important technical development in computer-based audio over the last few years has been the ability to manipulate the timing and pitch of audio. Remember, in the early days of digital recording, as was the case with tape, there was a direct relationship between the pitch and the tempo of a recording. If you played the tape faster, the pitch got higher; if you played back a digital audio sample in a higher key, the tempo increased too.

Today, however, it's possible to alter the tempo of audio while leaving its pitch intact (time compression and expansion, or *compansion*), and to change its pitch without altering its tempo (pitch shifting). While today these techniques are widely used in many forms of music production, they first emerged as part of a style of music-making called loop construction.

Audio loop construction is one of the hottest trends in music production. While it first became popular in dance genres, almost all styles of pop music production use loops; in fact, while the core of loop production leans toward cutting-edge sounds and beats designed for dance clubs, there are libraries of loops that cater specifically to musicians who produce traditional styles of music.

Loop production allows you to assemble performances and sounds from a diverse array of sources and incorporate them into your own work. A loop in this context is usually a short phrase of music that can be repeated to form a longer part (as opposed to a loop used with a sampler, discussed in "Working with Samplers" in Chapter 6).

The most common examples are one-, two-, and four-bar drum patterns, bass lines, and other rhythmic figures, but just about any self-contained section of music can be turned into a loop.

Audio loop production features can now be found in every major DAW program, including Pro Tools, Sonar, Logic, GarageBand, Cubase, and Digital Performer. Some more specialized applications, such as Ableton Live, Propellerhead Reason and ReCycle, and Sony Acid, put slightly more emphasis on loop manipulation. There are even programs, like Submersible DrumCore, that help you organize and audition loops and then export them to the production software of your choice.

■ UNDERSTANDING LOOP CONSTRUCTION

Today's techniques for loop construction have their roots in three technologies, and though we don't need to deal with their old-school limitations these days, it's good to know what they were, in the same way that it is useful to understand how analog recorders and mixers worked in relation to their modern digital equivalents.

The first types of loops were on tape, which was physically connected to form a loop. This allowed the section of tape to play continuously, repeating the music on it until someone stopped it (or the tape broke). These loops weren't used much for mainstream music production (though an instrument called the Chamberlin, an early type of what we now call a sampler, actually did play back tape loops at the press of a key).

Early electronic instruments also had the ability to repeat parts that were programmed into memory. These "sequences" consisted of electronic pulses that could trigger sounds in a pattern. Unlike tape loops, sequences could change speed without changing the pitch of the notes they were triggering.

The first drum machines and sequencers had limited memory and weren't able to store very many notes in any one pattern. But by combining various patterns into a string, a programmer could create an arrangement suitable for a song. The tempo of the patterns could change to match the arrangement. This still holds true in MIDI sequencers and modern drum machines, though the patterns themselves can now contain enough data for a complete song. The problem was that while these patterns could trigger electronic sounds, they could not capture an audio recording of a live musician, the way tape could.

When digital sampling became affordable in the 1980s, it allowed electronic musicians to make digital recordings that were similar to the analog recordings of the first tape loops. This was the birth of modern loop construction.

Early loop construction artists would record sections of music into a sampler, and trigger the samples from a keyboard—another technique that's still in use today. With careful editing and a few slick performance moves, sampler users can make diverse snippets of music fit together.

The problem with looping audio in a standard sampler came when you tried to match audio that was originally recorded at a different speed, or tempo. Unlike a drum machine pattern or MIDI sequence, a standard audio recording has a fixed tempo and pitch. So while you *could* change its speed, in doing so, you'd also change its pitch (decrease the tempo, lower the pitch; increase the tempo, raise the pitch). An alternative was to use the sampler's DSP processing to time-compress or -expand the audio, but with the early instruments the results were inexact and compromised the audio character of the original file.

An effective—though tedious—solution for matching audio tempo involved slicing the loop into smaller components and triggering each slice individually via the keyboard or—more practically—via a sequencer. With this technique, an audio loop would be split and trimmed so that each beat was its own sample. Doing this by hand is no fun, but it works. You can then use a sequencer to trigger the individual samples in order, or to alter the order, and therefore the rhythm, of the loop.

But today's audio looping software takes the tedium out of this manual process. You no longer need surgical skill to create smooth loops and make it easy to change pitch and tempo.

LOOPS À LA CARTE

In a way, modern loop production is a collaboration between you, the producer, and the person who performed the loop—a remote character you might think of as a very reclusive session musician. Commercial loop libraries give you access to thousands of different performances, recorded at some of the finest studios in the world. You'll find pristine sounds, grungy noises, and everything in between. As the producer/arranger, your first job is to choose the parts you want. And while you can create quite a bit of music by simply dragging these prerecorded loops around, you can develop a better understanding for the creative potential—and limitations—of loop production by creating some loops out of your own recordings. So, let's start right there.

BASIC LOOPING TECHNIQUES

Before we proceed, you may want to review the basic audio editing techniques we discussed in chapter 6, especially cutting large sections into smaller regions, snapping, searching for clean edit points, copying, and pasting.

With that knowledge in hand, you can create a new arrangement out of audio you've recorded yourself. You can do this with any standard multitrack audio program because it requires no time- or pitch-shifting—at least, not yet!

SELECTING AUDIO FOR LOOPING
The key to creating a smooth loop lies in the selection process. Ideally, you want to choose a piece of audio that can repeat without glitches. The easiest way to do this is by activating your

multitrack's snap-to feature, and setting the snap value for a musically relevant duration—such as a whole or half note (one bar or half a bar in 4/4 time). Select one or two bars of audio and separate it into a new region, as shown in **Fig. 7.1**.

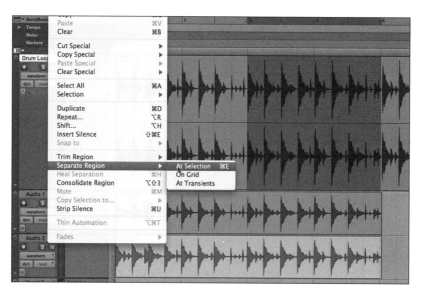

Fig. 7.1

Separating regions in Pro Tools

You may need to make fine adjustments to the region's boundaries in order to make it loop smoothly. For example, if a drum loop anticipates the beat (meaning it starts just before the new measure), you may have to move the start point slightly ahead (to the left) of the grid. However, be sure to adjust the end point by the same amount (again, to the left) so that the region's duration remains at a musically relevant value.

After fine-tuning your selection, you're ready to start looping—that is, repeating the selected material. This can be done by copying and pasting the region, as shown in **Fig. 7.2**, or designating the region for looping with a software command, as shown in **Fig. 7.3**. The

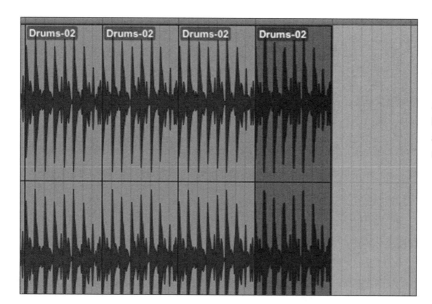

Fig. 7.2

Creating a loop-style arrangement by cutting and pasting regions.

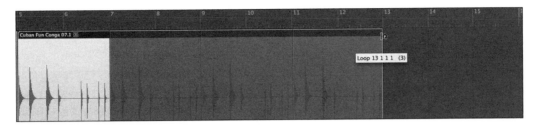

Fig. 7.3

Looping by dragging on a region with a loop tool (upper right corner)

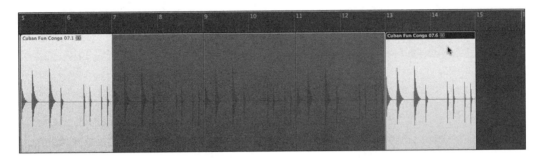

Fig. 7.4

Combining cut-and-paste editing and the use of the loop tool lets you quickly build complex arrangements.

advantage of the first approach is that you can easily remove, substitute, or alter any one of the copies you've pasted. The latter approach offers instant gratification—you can adjust the number of repeats and activate/deactivate the loops with one or two commands—but because the same region is literally triggered over and over, you can't add much in the way of variation as it repeats. But of course you can combine the two methods, as shown in **Fig. 7.4**.

MATCHING AUDIO TEMPO AND ARRANGEMENT TEMPO

The above techniques work well when the audio matches the project's tempo, but unfortunately, the audio you have at your disposal doesn't always cooperate.

When this is the case, you have two options:

1. Match the loop to the project's tempo.

2. Match the project's tempo to that of the loop.

Since the second option is more straightforward to explain, let's start with that. First, if you already know the tempo of the audio recording, it's pretty easy: simply enter that tempo into the project.

But what if you don't know the exact tempo of the audio recording? Fortunately, you don't need a stopwatch and calculator to figure it out: your DAW can help you. Select a portion of the audio—say, one or two bars—and define its duration in musical time. In essence, you're saying to your software, "This selection equals x number of bars." With that information, your software can calculate the tempo, as shown in **Fig. 7.5** and **Fig. 7.6**.

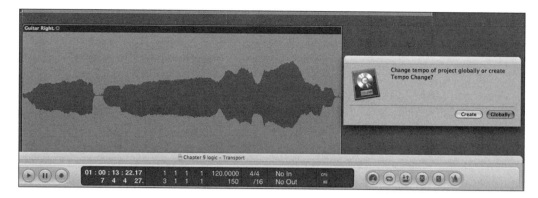

Fig. 7.5

By selecting a region and a duration on the timeline, you can calculate the region's tempo.

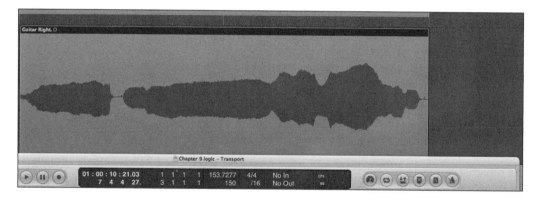

Fig. 7.6

With the project's tempo changed, the region now has a duration of two bars.

This method is most accurate when you're working with short sections of audio, simply because almost every musician's tempo will fluctuate over the course of a performance, even if his or her overall timing is solid (those who don't actually sound mechanical). If you are dealing with a longer performance, divide it into a number of one- or two-bar regions. You can then recalculate the tempo for each one. (To do this, you'll need to activate your DAW's *tempo map*, a feature that allows a project to change tempo over time.)

Once you have your tempo map in place, you can play along with your recording, add overdubs, MIDI parts, and even additional loops. Note, however, that this only works if one part defines the tempo. You can't, for example, use a rhythm guitar track to create the tempo map, and then grab a bass track and use *it* to create the tempo map for the same song. Once the tempo is established, any other audio you import will need to match it.

TEMPO-MATCHING MULTIPLE AUDIO FILES

Tempo-matching becomes more of a challenge when you're working with a group of audio files that were originally recorded at different tempos, as in a collection of rhythm loops taken from a variety of CD loop collections.

You *could* globally set your sequencer to match the tempo of one of the files as outlined above—but the others would quickly go out of sync. No matter which tempo you use as the base for your project, the rest of the audio must be brought into line, or you'll have a mess.

TIME COMPRESSION AND EXPANSION

Time compression and time expansion (called "time compansion," for short) let you alter the duration of an audio file. You can do this with or without changing the pitch of the audio.

When changing tempo and pitch, you have two options. The first works just like the sampler example we talked about earlier in this chapter: when the tempo increases, so does the pitch (and vice versa). While this method is a good way to alter time without degrading audio quality, there will be plenty of instances when you won't want to alter pitch along with time: for example, a bassline is in the right key, but is too fast to fit the drum loop. You can't slow down the bassline's tempo without lowering its pitch.

The time compansion algorithms (see **Fig. 7.7**) allow you to alter time *without* affecting pitch. Some work as offline processes (as opposed to the real-time solutions discussed below). These work well on short snippets of audio, as long as the time or pitch change is not too far from the original. More than a 10 percent variation can produce an audible effect on the sound. As with all offline processes, this will affect the actual audio file—so make a backup of the original before proceeding.

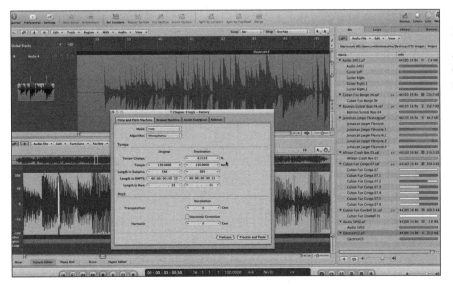

Fig. 7.7

A time compansion algorithm.

While various offline time compansion tools will have different specific features, all basically require that you enter the same data: the original tempo or length of the audio to be processed, and the desired tempo. As you can see in **Fig. 7.7**, the software indicates the percentage of change. Other common parameters include whether to change the pitch along with the speed or keep the audio at its original pitch, and the quality of the algorithm (higher-quality processing can take awhile, so you may want to audition a low-grade version before taking the time for the high-quality rendering). Some algorithms also let you define the nature of the audio—for example, bass, rhythmic, mono- or polyphonic, etc. This can help the software to produce clean and accurate results. Note that most of these offline operations are destructive—they're written to the file itself. Always work with a copy so that you can go back to the original if you don't like the results.

Many DAWs allow you to "draw" the time compansion right in the Edit/Arrange window. Unlike the offline processes mentioned above, this works on the region in a nondestructive way. **Fig. 7.8** shows how this works in Pro Tools 8.

Fig. 7.8

Pro Tools 8 lets users change a region's tempo by redrawing its boundaries in the Edit window.

REAL-TIME BEAT-MATCHING TOOLS

Offline editing can solve many time-correction issues, but if you're working with a diverse array of loops and audio **clips**, it can be a tedious process—not to mention that the results may not always be what you're looking for.

Fortunately, there are some cool software tools to help you integrate audio clips of different tempos into any arrangement. Propellerhead's ReCycle, Sony's Acid, and Abletons Live were among the first applications to specialize in time manipulation; these programs remain popular, and have influenced developers of more "traditional" DAWs.

PITCH SHIFTING

The converse of time compansion is pitch shifting—the ability to transpose or change the pitch of audio without affecting its tempo. As with time compansion, early pitch-shifting tools were offline processes that required you to write a new audio file with the new pitch.

These days, you can still use offline processing, which at its best can deliver incredibly good results. That's probably your best bet if you're changing the pitch (or duration) of a critical mix.

But for multitrack arranging, it's more fun and creative to use real-time transposition; the software changes the pitch of a section of audio on playback without rewriting the original file. This technology can be used as a type of signal processing for pitch correction and for generating harmonies (both of which we'll discuss in Chapter 11). But in the context of this chapter, we'll examine how it can be used to automatically match audio material to a desired base pitch—even when that material was originally recorded at a different one—and also change the pitch of audio regions as they play back in an arrangement.

Before we go further, let's clarify a few terms as they apply here:

Loop: A single audio file or region with a clearly defined start and end. The file/region is edited in such a way that it can play back continuously. But it does not need to. A file intended for looping can be played once, and then stop, or transition seamlessly into another loop.

One-Shot: A file/region in a loop library that's intended to be played once and decay naturally, instead of repeating. For instance, if you're looking for a cymbal hit to end a song, a "one-shot" sample is a better choice.

LOOP CONSTRUCTION SOFTWARE AT A GLANCE

"Loop construction software" is becoming an obsolete distinction, much the same way the boundaries between sequencing and multitrack audio software became blurred a few years ago. As we've mentioned a few times already, most DAWs now include some loop construction features.

That said, these features generally echo those developed by the pioneers of loop construction. Their work, too, has evolved, so programs like ReCycle, Acid, and Live remain cutting-edge creative tools that can be used either on their own or in tandem with more traditional DAW software.

RECYCLE AND REX FILES
ReCycle is a stand-alone music application that resembles a 2-track recorder/waveform editor in that it works on one audio file at a time. ReCycle analyzes the audio file and inserts markers at the peaks in the waveform.

These markers are used to define special regions called *slices*, which can be exported as individual samples. Initially, ReCycle was designed to work with short phrases (ideally one- to four-bar loops) and to send the slices to a hardware sampler via MIDI. The slices would then be assigned to consecutive keys on the keyboard. Triggering them all in order would produce the original audio file.

ReCycle can also save the component slices into a special audio file format called **REX** or RX2, which can be opened within DAWs such as Cubase, Logic, Pro Tools, and others, be imported into software samplers, or be opened in Propellerhead's software instrument suite Reason, which includes a special REX player instrument (see **Fig. 7.9**). This is the way "ReCycled" loops are most often used these days.

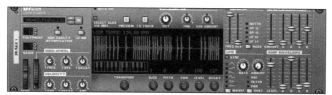

Fig. 7.9

Dr. Rex is a module in Propellerhead's Reason that can play REX files.

DEFINING SLICES

Once you load an audio file into ReCycle, you can adjust the number and position of the slices and fine-tune the start and end points of the loop without altering the original audio. **Fig. 7.10** shows a drum loop with a slice point for each beat. Once you set the start and stop boundaries of the loop, you can define its length in musical terms. From there, ReCycle calculates a tempo.

When ReCycle analyzes an audio file, it can generate an accompanying MIDI file that follows the groove of the original audio, assigning one MIDI note for every slice point (see **Fig. 7.11**). This MIDI file allows a sampler to trigger each slice just as it occurred in the original performance, its relative position intact. Because the slices are short, you can control the speed of the loop without changing the pitch or degrading the audio quality by adjusting the tempo

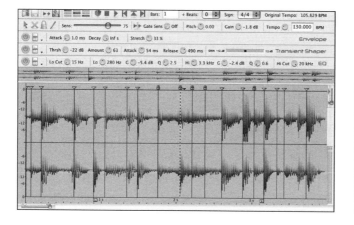

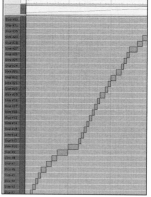

Fig. 7.10

ReCycle "slices" a drum part to create an individual region for each attack.

Fig. 7.11

A MIDI file generated by ReCycle follows the groove of the original audio file. Each MIDI note triggers a slice.

of your sequence. Reason's REX player can automatically export this MIDI data to a track in Reason's sequencer.

ReCycle offers a lot of flexibility. In addition to playing the groove back faithfully, it allows you to edit the MIDI file to change its timing (say, from a straight-eighth groove to a shuffle). You can also change the order of the slices by altering the pitches of the MIDI notes. This MIDI data can also be copied and assigned to trigger a different set of sounds. (See chapters 8 and 9 for more on MIDI techniques.)

TIP

One cool trick is to generate MIDI from a drum pattern and copy it to a MIDI track assigned to a bass sound: You'll need to change the pitches of the bass notes, and maybe remove a couple to make the part less cluttered, but you can create some very interesting grooves this way.

REX files can be imported directly into many DAWs. Each slice will appear as a separate region, as shown in **Fig. 7.12**.

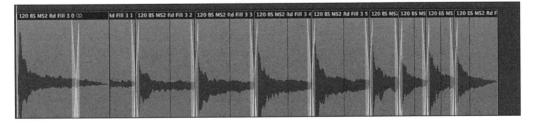

Fig. 7.12
A REX file after it's been imported into Logic.

ACID AND ITS FOLLOWERS
Sony's Acid (see **Fig. 7.13**) may be one of the most influential pieces of software to emerge in the last 10 years. Like ReCycle, it analyzes an audio file and builds groove information from the peaks in the waveforms. But unlike ReCycle, Acid is a full-featured audio multitrack program, capable of working with many audio files at once.

Acidized **audio** files are encoded with extra information called *metadata*, which tells the software the audio recording's original tempo and pitch. Using this data as a reference point, Acid can nondestructively stretch and contract the audio to conform to the tempo of an arrangement.

TRANSPOSING LOOPS

The pitch information included in these encoded files also allows for real-time pitch shifting. This lets you use content, such as basslines, orchestral loops, guitar rhythms, and other

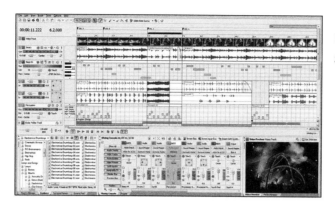

Fig. 7.13

Sony Acid

melodic material, much more freely than you can with more traditional loop production. Like the tempo map mentioned earlier in this chapter, Acid lets you define a project's base pitch, and then insert key changes as the song progresses. Pitch changes can be applied to all the tracks in an arrangement, or to individual parts.

This same method has been incorporated into other programs as well, such as the Apple Loops format used by Apple's Logic, GarageBand, and Soundtrack. As with Acidized files, Apple Loops are encoded files that will automatically conform to a song's defined tempo and pitch. In Logic, for example, you can import Apple Loops for drum parts or basslines, and they will match the song's tempo and key. Non-encoded files will play at their original tempos and pitches.

TIP

Apple Loops actually come in both audio and MIDI forms; the latter type lets you change the sound and even the performance within a loop.

ARRANGING LOOPS

Building an arrangement in the Acid style gives new meaning to mix-and-match. You can draw from a pool of loops, which may or may not be related to one another, and freely place them in your project. No matter that the walking bassline loop was originally recorded at 110 bpm in the key of C, the rhythm guitar at 120 bpm in E, and the drums at 90 bpm: If your project tempo is 115 bpm and the song's key is D, the software will have an easy time making the loops go together.

Regions made from encoded audio files are stretchable—you can drag the region's boundaries to the length of a loop within your arrangement. This technique is much faster and more intuitive than cut, copy, and paste editing. You can, however, also copy/paste the loops and edit them to alter the loops somewhat. This is where the editing skills we discussed in chapter 6 come in handy.

The feature that makes Acid-style editing so powerful is its ability to change the audio's pitch and tempo *during playback* without losing sync.

But that doesn't mean that all loops actually *sound* good together. Aside from the obvious creative choices (does that bassline really fit the drum groove? Is the guitar part too funky for the song?), you should also be realistic about the technology. In the example above, the original components were all similar; both the tempos and keys were close. But what if the original drum loop was recorded at, say, 180 bpm instead of 90? The software will still make it play back at 115 bpm, and its groove will remain intact. But it may sound a little strange; think of it as the audio equivalent of how you feel when you wake up early in the morning after three hours of sleep. Now, sonically, that's not necessarily bad: in fact, the slowed drum groove can have a lot of flavor. But it won't sound as natural as drums recorded within 20 percent of the song's tempo.

Similarly, in addition to the pitch-base of a loop, pay attention to its actual key. A rhythm guitar loop recorded in A minor, for example, might not sound good with a bassline recorded in A major. Their bass pitch is the same, but each uses a different scale.

ABLETON LIVE

Live, a program from the German developer Ableton, offers yet another approach to pitch/time compansion and loop-based production. In some ways, it's like a cross between a MIDI sampler and a multitrack DAW. While it does allow you to record audio and MIDI parts in a linear arrangement that's similar to what you'd find in Acid or GarageBand, it also feaures a unique work area called the Clips view. Here, you can organize, trigger, record, and mix individual sections of sound called Clips (see **Fig. 7.14**).

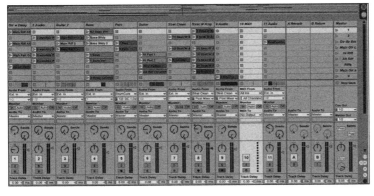

Fig. 7.14

Ableton Live lets users trigger individual audio and MIDI segments called clips.

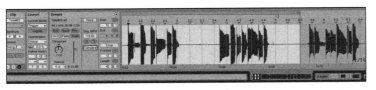

Fig. 7.15

Live's clip editing pane lets you define how the software will manipulate an audio file's tempo, groove, pitch, sound, and more.

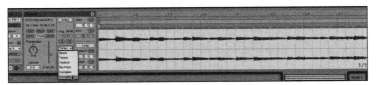

Fig. 7.16

Live applies different processing to various types of source material.

141

Live can analyze any file it opens and turn it into a potential loop, which can be independently transposed and time companded (Ableton calls this "warping").

Live's clip editing tools are very extensive (see **Fig. 7.15**). You can change a clip's length and select what part of it will loop, transpose the clip, alter its gain, and even program what happens after the clip is finished playing, using it to automatically trigger another clip on the same channel. But that's just the beginning of the story.

The program offers several different algorithms to help it more accurately analyze audio content (see **Fig. 7.16**). You can tell it that a source file contains rhythmic material (Beats), monophonic melodic material (Tones), polyphonic material (Texture), or full songs (Complex). All of these modes let you speed up and slow down the audio without affecting its pitch, but Live also has a Pitch mode, which changes the audio's pitch along with its tempo — making it higher as you increase the clip's tempo, lower as you decrease it — the way that old samplers and tape machines did back in the day.

With Live, you can actually change the groove of an audio clip by telling the software where you want the beats to fall. You can do this with prerecorded loop library material, or with audio you've recorded yourself. **Fig. 7.17** shows a short guitar part as it was originally played. You'll notice a couple of things: there's silence before the first note, which starts around measure 2; and some of the high-amplitude waveforms don't fall directly at any of the beat divisions. It's not that the part is wrong — it actually has a nice groove — but it's not quantized to the grid.

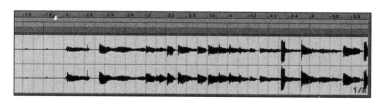

Fig. 7.17

Altering the groove of an audio file with Live.

We can, however, change the rhythmic feel of that guitar part by moving the beat markers in relation to the waveform. You can do this globally — changing the position of the clip in relation to the downbeat but preserving the relationships between the beats in the clip — which is useful when you want to create a neatly edited clip of, say, a bassline that has the feel you want but just started a little before the downbeat.

However, things get really interesting when you start morphing a groove by selecting and moving individual tempo markers. Check out **Fig. 7.18**, which shows the guitar part from **Fig. 7.17** after this kind of editing. You'll notice that the first note of the figure is now defined as 1 — we've told the clip to start the measure there. The third note, which previously *anticipated* a beat, now falls directly on beat 3; the next three notes, which had a dotted eighth-note feel, now trigger on quarter notes.

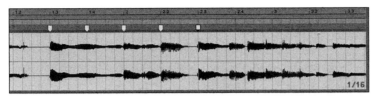

Fig. 7.18

The guitar part shown in **Fig. 7.17** after its groove has been redrawn in Live.

You can do this kind of editing as the clip loops, so you can hear your changes as you go. Even better, you can listen to the loop in Solo or you can hear it in context. This lets you match the groove of one part to another by ear.

Clips in Live can be "played" the way you'd play individual notes and chords on a piano. You can assign MIDI or QWERTY keys to trigger one clip or a group of clips, which allows you to perform a "mix" on the fly.

More than one clip can be assigned to a mixer channel. The clips sit in "slots," and each channel can play one slot at a time. This lets you stack a group of similar drum loops on a channel and switch between them quickly and seamlessly. You can also, however, build complex mixes with multiple channels. One of my favorite techniques is to copy the same group of clips to two different channels. If you were to do so with the set of drum loops I referred to above, you could alternate individual loops with layers consisting of two loops.

Making all of this even more powerful is the way Live relates any edits you make to the clip's source file. Live sees each clip made from an audio file as an independent element. So going back to the guitar example in **Fig. 7.17** and **Fig. 7.18**, if you were to Option-drag the original clip to make a copy, you could then change the copy's groove without affecting any other clips based on that audio file. All the parameters, including the start time, loop boundaries, transposition, etc., can be altered on the copy. But when you go back and trigger the original clip, it'll play exactly as you left it. As you can see, this lets you get a lot of variation out of one audio file.

While clips automatically retain all these edits within an arrangement, you also have the option of saving the clips as independent files, which allows you to import them into other projects and retain the edits you've made.

Note: Live can also trigger sounds through software instruments and external devices via MIDI. It comes with MIDI loops that can be edited using a similar interface to that used for audio editing, but basically uses a grid-style editor similar to what you'd find in a sequencer. We'll be discussing MIDI in more detail in chapters 8, 9, and 12.

COMBINING RANDOM AND LINEAR EDITING

Live's most unique feature is its Clips window, but the program also includes a more traditional Arrange/Edit-style window (see **Fig. 7.19**). Here, you can record audio and MIDI in a more traditional linear fashion, and also capture and automate the way material is triggered from the Clips window. Audio you record here can be edited and made into clips if you like, or it can be left as-is, to play back as it would in a conventional DAW.

Fig. 7.19

Live's Arrange window is similar to that of a conventional DAW.

SOUND MANIPULATION

Like most music software, Live lets you add effects to its mixer channels as you see fit. Many of the effects it comes with seem to encourage unusual sounds, and the program's graphical interface makes it easy to change effects parameters as the music plays. The way clips play back can be automated, as well as all effects and mix moves (something we'll discuss in more detail in chapters 10 and 11), which can be saved for easy playback. One of my favorite features is the ease with which you can route the output of one channel to another channel for recording. So, for example, you can run a clip through some crazy echo and filter effects, and then record it as a new audio file, with the effects added. That kind of interactive sound design is not only fun, but can be a useful way to build a library of your own unique sounds that you can then import into other projects.

Live is one of the few multitrack programs to really break with the old tape-based model while still offering the ability to record traditional as well as experimental music. Its uniqueness is something you need to experience to appreciate, but fortunately Ableton has always offered free demo versions of its software on its website (ableton.com). I highly recommend downloading it.

RE-GROOVING A LOOP

As discussed above in the section on Ableton Live, it is possible to alter the groove of a prerecorded loop by changing the position markers in relation to the waveform. Another way to do this is to move the slices in a REX file (when it's imported into a DAW's Arrange/Edit window), or to change the position of the MIDI notes triggering those slices when the file is assigned to a sampler or Reason's REX file player.

TREATING AUDIO LIKE MIDI DATA

When MIDI first appeared, the most exciting thing about it was the way musicians could edit individual notes in a track after they were recorded. Want to change that C into a C♯? No problem. Want to move the snare drum an eighth note later? Just grab it and move it.

The whole loop construction revolution began as a way to offer this kind of control to people who wanted to work with real audio. In the last few years, developers have taken this idea even further by allowing MIDI-like note-by-note editing of audio data.

Celemony's Melodyne (see **Fig. 7.20**) analyzes audio for pitch and time, and generates a display not unlike the MIDI piano roll editor we'll be looking at in the next two chapters. (It can also generate traditional music notation.) Individual notes can then be edited freely: you can change a vocal melody based on a major scale to one based on a minor scale, change the phrasing, change the duration of individual notes, and correct the pitch. You can then save the edited audio as a new file and export a MIDI file based on your edits. Melodyne, which can function as a multitrack recorder and mixer complete with effects, works as both a stand-alone program or as a plug-in within a DAW.

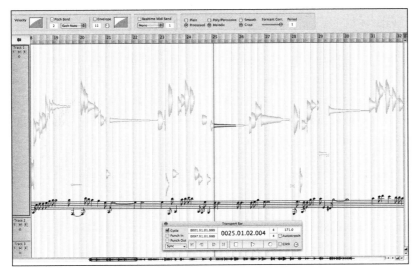

Fig. 7.20

Melodyne allows MIDI-like editing of audio.

Note: Cubase 5's new VariAudio feature, introduced in 2009, offers similar functionality "native" to that DAW. I'm guessing that by the time you read this, MIDI-style editing will have spread to more programs as well.

As we go to press, Celemony is about to release a version that can recognize individual notes within a chord, with impressive results.

CHANGING TEMPO AS A SONG PLAYS

When an audio region is tagged for loop construction, it's not only capable of following the song's base tempo, but it can also follow any changes programmed into the song's tempo map. So, if you start a song at 120 beats per minute and assign a drum loop to lock to that tempo, you can then program the song to change tempo to, say, 125 bpm on the 64th bar, and the drum loop should follow suit. If the audio region is *not* tagged, it will fall out of sync. These transitions work best when the change is not too radical, and it can be tricky to create natural reitards, but it works pretty well for most applications.

■ MAKING LOOPS WORK TOGETHER

When you record music using traditional methods, your ability to play and sing, as well as your imagination as a producer and your skill as an engineer, all play a role in the quality of your finished project. If you're composing with prerecorded loops, you don't have to deal with the performance and engineering factors (at least, not unless you plan to combine live recording with your loops). Therefore, your judgment as a producer and your ability as a mixer become even more important.

Loop collections can include a range of audio recording styles. Often, material originally recorded on a multitrack—for example, a drum kit, horn section, or bass and drum combination—will be mixed down into one stereo file. This mix may or may not feature audio effects like reverb, delay, and chorus, but it's a good bet that it will have been mixed with compression and EQ. The advantage here is that you don't have to mix the audio—a pro has done it for you.

The disadvantage is that the pro, like the player on the loop, is a remote collaborator. He has no idea what else will be playing along with the loop. Heck, you're the producer, and even you may not know what's going to be on your track at this point! That big fat bass with the funky '70s auto-wah might sound good on its own, but when you drag it into your arrangement, it's stepping on the acoustic guitar.

An alternative is to look for loops that are "dry"—recorded with minimal or no effects. You'll need to do more actual mixing, but will have more control over the final product.

Some loop collections even include *stems*: the individual tracks from a multitrack mix. For example, a deluxe drum collection might include a stereo mix of a two-bar drum groove, but may also offer individual two-bar loops of the kick drum, snare, toms, cymbals, hi-hat, and so on. This gives you the best of both worlds; you can build your arrangement using the mixed loop, but if you want to, say, add reverb only to the snare part, or give the kick some special EQ, you have the option.

BUILDING AND MANAGING LOOP LIBRARIES

If you haven't upgraded your music software in a while, you may notice that the requirements have changed for many DAWs. Some now require 4 GB—and more!—for a full install. That's because these programs now come with content libraries full of loops. (Those of you reading this in 2012 may be saying, "Only 4 GB? That's nothing!" Such is the nature of computer-based audio.) Specialized loop production programs like Acid, Live, GarageBand, and Reason also come with lots of content. Then there are third-party libraries that can run to multiple gigabytes. I have one collection that came with 8 GB of data—more space than I had left on my laptop's internal hard disk at the time.

So there are two things to keep in mind: No matter how many songs you produce, you'll never use all the loops stored on your hard disk; and no matter how many loops you have in your collection, you'll want to add more from time to time.

ORGANIZING YOUR STORAGE

While you could keep your loops on the CD/DVD-ROMs they come on, it makes more sense to copy them all onto one hard drive—preferably not your system disk. (This may not be so easy if the loops are installed as part of your DAW software, as is the case with Logic, which puts its content in the operating system's Library file.) You can then organize the content as you wish. You may want to keep each collection separate, or you may want to combine all the drum loops into one master folder, organize loops by tempo or genre, and so on.

But even after you've set up your disk and copied and organized all your loops, with all those gigabytes divided into relatively small, short audio files, how do you *ever* find what you need?

The term "data management" may sound like the most boring thing a musician can face, but it's an important part of every form of computer-based music making. It's even more vital when working with collections of loops. You wouldn't dream of writing a song on piano if you couldn't find the keys; you can't produce with loops if you can't find the parts you're looking for.

Fortunately, the folks who make the music software—who seem to be into this whole data thing anyway—have made it relatively easy to keep track of your stuff—if you take the time to learn and use the tools they've provided.

TAGGING

Among the many brilliant ideas the developers of Acid had, the least "musical" may have been the most important (okay, the second most important, next to that whole time and pitch compansion thing): the ability to search for audio files from within the program.

This feature lets users search through their loop libraries by using *tags*—a special form of metadata that provides information about the audio in the file, such as instrumentation, mood, key, musical style, sound quality, and more. As of this writing, Apple's GarageBand, Soundtrack, and Logic, as well as Steinberg's Cubase, all allow users to tag audio files and use these tags in searches.

Using tags, you can search your library for drums, Latin instruments, distorted instruments, acoustic instruments, etc. Loop collections usually come pre-tagged, but you can also add your own tags. **Fig. 7.21** shows how this is done using the Apple Loop Utility. This not only allows you to edit the tag on a loop someone else produced, but also lets you tag loops you've made from audio you recorded yourself.

Fig. 7.21

Tagging an audio file.

READING FILE NAMES

Since not everyone uses software that includes a database capable of searching through tagged files, library developers have come up with a simple and clever naming convention. They'll often add the original tempo as a number in the file name. So if you see 90_FunkDrum.wav, you can bet that you're looking at a funky drum loop originally recorded at 90 bpm. 120_Am_Skank.wav might be a reggae-flavored guitar part recorded at 120 bpm in A minor.

TIP

Even if your software doesn't let you search for such things directly, you can use your computer's operating system to look for these indicators. For example, point your Explore/Finder at the folder containing the loops and search for "120_": you should get all the loops recorded at 120 bpm.

PRO TIPS

Jack Freudenheim is the drummer/co-producer for the band 46bliss, whose music is in the Top 10 All-Time charts on the Podsafe Music Network, and who have been heard on CSI-NY *and* Veronica Mars. *He is also the creator of the generative music software Sounder (sounder.com), and has written tutorials for* Computer Music *magazine on Reason 4. His drumming website is realdrummer.net.*

Not all loops sound good together. Feel is everything, and any two loops can have very different feels from each other. Using Reason 4 and REX files, loops can now easily slide into the same feel, thanks to the Groove Mixer.

If you're using Reason and have drum loops in REX format, each drum hit is a sequenced hit that you can move around. In Dr. Rex, press the To Track button to dump the hits into the sequencer. Then grab those hits in the sequencer and quantize them. Even cooler, grab the hits to a drum loop you love, right-click, and choose "Get groove from clip." Open the Groove Mixer, and that groove you just chose is now called User 1 in the Groove Mixer. Select another drum (or bass, or any other type) loop in another Dr. Rex, and set its track to use the same channel in the Groove Mixer. Slide the groove fader up or down and hear how the two loops now lock into the same groove.

With Ableton Live, anything can be a loop. Drag an MP3 into an audio track, and Live slurps it up and detects its tempo. Drag the start and end arrows to the bar or bars you want to loop, and press the Loop button in the Sample window. The Seq. bpm box tells you what tempo is detected; if your song tempo is different from that, it will already be playing the loop at your song's tempo. It's really important to play with the Warp Mode possibilities: if the loop is made up of a full music track, choose Complex—it uses up more CPU than Beats, but the sound will be so much better if you push the tempo up or down by a larger amount. Set it to Repitch if you want the pitch of the loop to go up or down proportionately to the tempo change, just as if you sped up or slowed down a tape machine or turntable the old-fashioned way.

In Ableton Live, if you have a beat that doesn't groove quite the way you want, you can move any point within the loop to fit your feel. Zoom into your loop and find a note or hit that doesn't feel good. See how it's too far before or after the beat (or subdivision of a beat)? Double-click on the triangle at the top of the closest grid subdivision (for instance, 1.2 for the second beat in the first measure). A yellow rectangle will appear around the 1.2. Now drag that yellow rectangle to the left or right to match up with the hit you were unhappy with. Now play back the loop, and you'll hear the hit happen dead on that second beat. Of course, you can use the same technique to push notes ahead of or behind the beat as well.

▪ MOVING ON

Because it's fast, convenient, and opens musical doors to people who don't have musical training, loop-based production will continue to gain in popularity. For songwriters and producers who play traditional instruments, loop construction can speed up the composing process by helping to flesh out ideas or build realistic drum tracks. For those interested in using loops as an "instrument," the possibilities are extensive and expanding as developers come up with more ways for users to customize prerecorded material. Far from being a lazy way to make music, the best loop construction requires a combination of imagination, judgment, and sonic creativity.

For more about working with tempo and loops in the MIDI realm, see chapters 8 and 9; for more on samplers, see chapter 12.

PART III   WORKING WITH MIDI

CHAPTER 8: MIDI BASICS

IN THIS CHAPTER
- ▓ HOW MIDI DIFFERS FROM AUDIO
- ▓ MIDI SIGNAL ROUTING
- ▓ PREPARING TO RECORD MIDI
- ▓ MIDI RECORDING TECHNIQUES
- ▓ MIDI AND TIMING
- ▓ MIDI LOOPING
- ▓ CREATING MIDI FROM AUDIO

Computer recording has its roots in the realm of MIDI. Most of the top digital audio workstation programs—including Digital Performer, Cakewalk (now Sonar), Logic, and Cubase—began life as MIDI sequencers.

▓ How MIDI Differs from Audio

MIDI (Musical Instrument Digital Interface) is designed to transmit control information, called *messages* or *events*, between devices. Unlike an audio recorder, which captures actual sound waves, a MIDI recorder captures MIDI messages, and these in turn trigger the sound in an external device, such as a synthesizer (see **Fig. 8.1**). The playback device is called a "slave," while the triggering device is called a "controller," or "master." Chapter 2 describes the hardware elements of a MIDI system and outlines some setup procedures.

Today, you're as likely to use MIDI sound generators resident on the computer, called software instruments, as you are to trigger external devices. But the principles remain basically the same.

MIDI messages include notes, controller data, timing information, and **System Exclusive**, or SysEx, which is used to control a device's internal parameters. Once you record a MIDI performance, you can tweak it in fine detail: if you like, you can alter the pitch, duration, velocity, volume, and more of individual notes.

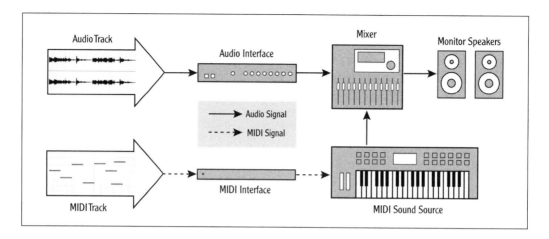

Fig. 8.1

Unlike audio recorders (top of diagram) MIDI recorders capture commands that trigger sounds on external devices.

MIDI RESOLUTION

One of the most important things to understand about MIDI is the way a sequencer assigns each event to a location in time. MIDI divides each quarter note into parts called *pulses*, and the number of pulses per quarter note is known as the **MIDI resolution**, or **PPQ** (pulses per quarter note). Early sequencers had low resolution—as few as 4 PPQ. This would limit the playback of the MIDI recording to 16th notes, even if the original performance included notes of smaller values, like 32nd notes. This restriction can make a performance sound robotic.

Software sequencers typically offer much higher PPQ resolution, ranging into the thousands. A high-resolution setting will capture the subtleties of a performance. Because there's no actual MIDI cable between the notes generated by the sequencer and the instrument, software instruments can take advantage of this higher resolution in ways that external instruments can't.

■ MIDI SIGNAL ROUTING

Like audio, MIDI signal travels from a source (your controller) to a destination (a track in your sequencer). The sequencer in turn routes the signal to a destination that can produce sound, like an external sound module or an internal software instrument.

A MIDI assignment consists of two elements: the output port or MIDI cable, and the **MIDI channel**. Each port can transmit up to 16 MIDI channels.

When working with software instruments, the routing is internal—there are no MIDI ports. But the same concept applies: The data on a track can be assigned to *any* instrument.

In a single-port setup, you can assign each device to its own MIDI channel. However, you must daisy-chain the devices by routing the signal through each one's MIDI Thru port. You then activate the desired channels on each device, muting any MIDI channels that are assigned to other devices in your system. If you're using a **multitimbral** device (capable of playing back separate instruments on more than one MIDI channel), you may want to assign it to more than one MIDI channel, as shown in **Table 8.1**.

CHANNEL	DESTINATION	SOUND
1	Keyboard Synth (controller)	Piano
2	Multitimbral Rack Synth 1	Bass
3	Multitimbral Rack Synth 1	Strings
4	Analog Synth	Pad
10	Multitimbral Rack Synth 1	Drums

Table 8.1

One multitimbral device can generate independent sounds for up to 16 MIDI channels.

If you connect each MIDI device in your system to a separate port, each will be able to receive 16 independent channels. This is especially handy when you're working with multitimbral instruments. **Table 8.2** shows an example of signal routing in a system with multiple MIDI ports. Note that the channel and port assignments need not be sequential.

PORT	CHANNEL	DESTINATION	SOUND
1	1	Multitimbral Rack Synth 1	Synth Pad
1	2	Multitimbral Rack Synth 1	Upright Bass
1	3	Multitimbral Rack Synth 1	Organ
1	4	Multitimbral Rack Synth 1	Cello
1	5	Multitimbral Rack Synth 1	Trumpet
1	10	Multitimbral Rack Synth 1	Drums
2	1	Keyboard Synth (controller)	Piano
2	2	Keyboard Synth (controller)	Synth Bass
6	1	Rack Sampler	Strings
Internal	1	Software Synth	Analog Pulse

Table 8.2

A system with multiple MIDI ports allows for far greater flexibility.

INTERNAL MIDI ROUTING

MIDI can also be routed between different software applications on the same computer. The ReWire protocol allows the master program to send MIDI data to the slave program. So, for example, if you have Reason connected to Cubase via ReWire, you can assign a MIDI track in Cubase to play an instrument in Reason.

Another way to route MIDI internally is to use a utility such as the IAC driver found in the Mac OS's CoreMIDI. Windows users can use a utility like the free (and very funky) MIDIox (midiox.com).

■ PREPARING TO RECORD MIDI

Although MIDI recording differs from audio recording in the type of data that's recorded, the recording process is very similar. You start by creating a MIDI track and assigning it to a MIDI output. You must also assign a controller source, such as a keyboard, to the track.

When you record-enable, or arm, a track, your sequencer goes into **Thru** mode, which routes signal from the controller to whatever MIDI instrument is assigned to that track's MIDI output. This allows you to hear the MIDI instrument as you play the controller. Once you're satisfied with your sound, you can put the sequencer into Record and start playing. It's that simple. **Fig. 8.2** shows a typical MIDI track that's ready for recording.

Fig. 8.2

A MIDI track armed for recording.

THE ELEMENTS OF A MIDI MESSAGE

A typical MIDI event consists of the following parameters, all of which can be freely edited after the recording:

- The note's pitch

- The note's location in time (its note-on and note-off status)

- The *velocity* of the note—the speed, or force, with which a key is struck—usually controls the loud/soft dynamics of individual notes, but can also be assigned to affect other parameters, such as tone

- Controller data, such as **pitch bend**, **modulation**, and **aftertouch**

It's a good idea to separate the different types of MIDI data, such as note events and controller events. For example, velocity is a characteristic of every note event, whereas controller events, such as pitch bend, modulation, **MIDI volume**, and aftertouch, are independent of individual notes. Still, this controller data can be recorded at the same time (and into the same tracks) as note data. For example, you could apply aftertouch to create a vibrato effect as you play a violin sound, or use MIDI volume to create a fadeout on a brass part.

One of the areas where audio and MIDI differ most is the degree to which you can edit an individual event. With MIDI, you have control over every aspect of each event: the pitch, timing, duration, loudness, sound parameters, and more. Although, like audio, MIDI notes and other events are grouped into tracks and regions, the events themselves are independent entities.

Here's an example. Let's say you've just created a MIDI drum part consisting of kick drum, snare, and hi-hat. Because each part is triggered by separate MIDI note events, you could copy just the kick drum part and place the copy in a second track that's assigned to a bass guitar sound. In the bass track, you could then edit the pitches of the notes (leaving the timing alone) so that they play a melodic bass line. Finally, you could go back into the drum track, copy the notes assigned to the snare drum, paste them into a third track, and assign them to play a tambourine sound, trigger a guitar sample, or anything else that sparks your imagination.

SOUNDS AND EVENTS

As mentioned earlier, MIDI events are independent of the sound they actually produce. You can record a part with one sound, or *patch*—say, a sampled piano—and play it back using another sound, such as a sampled acoustic guitar.

You can audition sounds by changing programs on your MIDI module as you play your controller (prior to recording), or, after recording, you can try out alternative sounds as the sequence plays back. The thing to remember is that you *always* have the opportunity to reassign a MIDI track, either to a different patch within a device, or to a completely different device.

Like other cases where technology seems to give you unlimited choices, this flexibility can be a double-edged sword. On one hand, it's nice to be able to lay down a track without worrying too much about the sound. You can focus on your ideas and the successful execution of the performance, then get the sound together later. I keep a library of generic patches for this very purpose; as my ideas come together, I reassign my tracks to more interesting and appropriate sounds.

Unfortunately, a typical MIDI device is capable of holding at least 128 sounds, and many can literally store thousands. It's possible to forget which sound you like best. I wish I had a dollar for every time I've gone searching through the memory banks of my Proteus 2000 in search of that *perfect* bass patch I used the day before. The longer I hunt, the better that missing sound seems in my recollection.

There are a couple of ways to avoid this problem. One is to use your sequencer to transmit a program change message to your module that calls up the sound you want. This offers the best of both worlds: Your computer will remember the correct patch, even if you don't, but you can still choose a different sound by editing the program change value.

The second alternative (when working with an audio multitrack program) is to "print to disk" by recording an audio track of your MIDI module's output (see **Fig. 8.3**). Think of this as a final step; your MIDI tracks have been recorded and edited and need no further work in the MIDI domain. But printing the audio of your MIDI parts to disk allows you to mix them alongside your audio tracks.

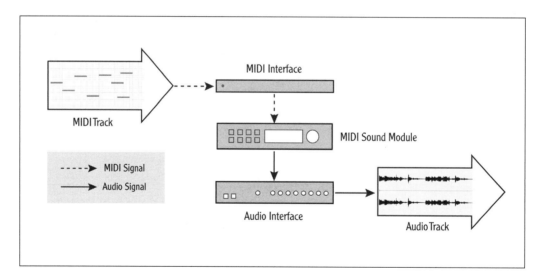

Fig. 8.3

Routing the audio output of an external MIDI device to an audio track.

MIDI RECORDING TECHNIQUES

As with audio, there are several ways to go about recording MIDI. You can work in a linear fashion, recording each track from beginning to end. Or you can record in sections, punching parts in and out as you go along, similar to the audio techniques described in the "Punch-in Recording" section in Chapter 5.

But MIDI recording also throws a few curveballs our way.

CYCLE RECORDING

We explored cycle, or loop, recording as it relates to audio in Chapter 5. Using cycle recording for MIDI offers one additional benefit: you can change tracks and record new material as the cycle plays back, without having to stop the sequencer. (With most audio software, you must stop playback before record-enabling a new track, as it involves a disk-based operation.) This allows you to build arrangements very quickly. Each track can be assigned to a separate output on the fly.

MERGING/LAYERING

Although you can set up your sequencer to overwrite (or erase) previously recorded material with each recording pass, as you would do with a linear audio track, MIDI technology lets you **merge**, or combine, newly recorded material with existing material in the same region, as shown in **Fig. 8.4**.

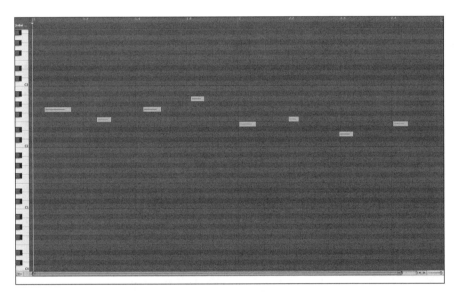

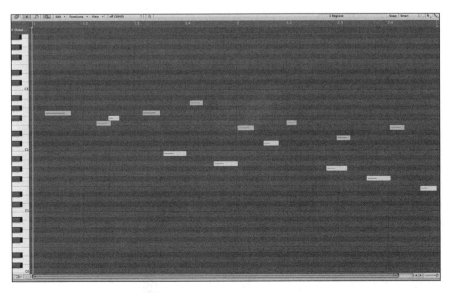

Fig. 8.4

Before (top) and after (bottom) merging new material with the existing data in a MIDI region.

You can merge incoming MIDI data into the same region as previously recorded material, or you can set your sequencer to create a new region for each recording pass by assigning both regions—each on its own track—to the same destination, as shown in **Fig. 8.5**. Unlike with audio, a second region assigned to play the same channel at the same time won't mute the first.

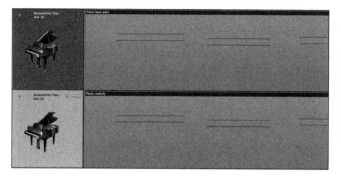

Fig. 8.5

By assigning two MIDI tracks to trigger the same sound generator, you can record and edit two sections of a part separately; as in this example showing the treble and bass notes in a piano part.

TRACKS

Splitting a MIDI signal across several tracks gives you a lot of flexibility, especially when you're composing a new piece of music. You can, for example, record the lower voice of an organ part on one track. Then, by opening a new track that is assigned to the same MIDI device, you can record the upper ranges. Each pass can be edited separately. You could quantize the lower voice (to tighten up the bassline) while leaving the upper registers untouched (so that the melody remains more expressive and less rigid).

After you've recorded and edited the parts, you can merge them into one master track (and unlike with audio, the MIDI events can be separated again later with your sequencer's editing tools).

STEP RECORDING

Step recording allows you to enter notes one at a time, with the sequencer stopped. In the early days of hardware sequencing, this was the *only* way to record a sequence—you had to manually program each note.

While real-time recording is a lot more fun—and results in a much more human performance—step recording can be more efficient for mundane tasks, like programming a sequence of notes with the same rhythmic value, or creating a basic drum loop. It can also save you when your playing technique isn't up to a particularly difficult or rapid passage.

Most sequencers provide a special module for step recording (see **Fig. 8.6**). You must tell the computer the duration of each step, but you can play the actual pitches on your controller. You can also step record by inserting notes in a MIDI editor, which we cover in Chapter 9.

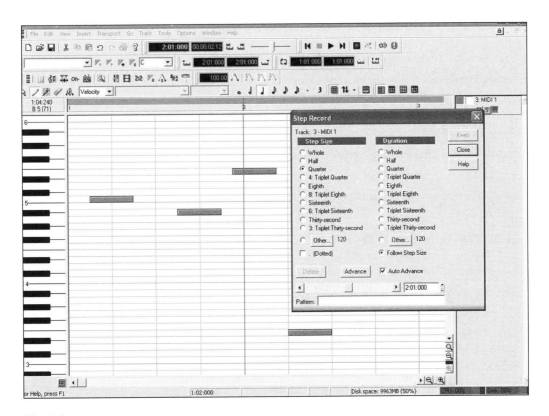

Fig. 8.6

Sonar's step entry module.

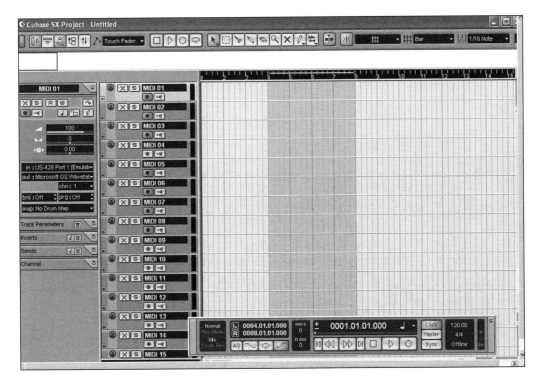

Fig. 8.7

Multichannel MIDI assignments

MULTICHANNEL RECORDING

The most common way to record MIDI is one channel at a time. But some situations call for multichannel recording; for example, when transferring data from an external sequencer into your software, or when recording the output of a multichannel controller, such as a guitar synthesizer.

In order to do multichannel recording, each input channel from the source device(s) must be assigned to a separate MIDI track, as shown in **Fig. 8.7**. Otherwise, all of the data will be merged into one track, regardless of its original source channel.

RECORDING AND FILTERING CONTROLLER DATA

Notes may be the most common type of MIDI event, but there are many other important MIDI messages, and your sequencer can record them all. Controller messages, including volume, modulation, aftertouch, piano sustain, and so on, are used to change the parameters of a MIDI device in real time.

When you record a passage on your keyboard, controller data is recorded along with the note events. Controller data such as modulation, sustain pedal, pitch bend, and aftertouch can add flavor to a MIDI track. Controller data can also be used to automate effects devices and mixer moves.

By recording in merge mode, you can add controller data retroactively. Try laying some modulation on top of a bassline, or adding pitch bend to a drum sample. If you're unsure whether you want the controller information to remain part of the performance, record it on its own track and assign it to the same MIDI output as the target instrument (see **Fig. 8.8**). By muting the track with the controller information, you can compare the results of your work—with controllers and without.

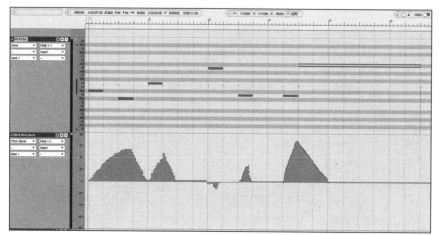

Fig. 8.8

This Digital Performer part has note controller data recorded to separate MIDI tracks.

Controller information can clog up the MIDI data stream, so if you're not going to apply a controller to a particular part, you can filter it as you record. For instance, filtering aftertouch information from a piano patch (which wouldn't ordinarily respond to this controller) can improve MIDI timing accuracy and performance.

ADVANCED MIDI INPUT PARAMETERS

Unlike an audio recorder, a full-featured MIDI sequencer can do more than just record your actual performance. Most sequencers can process and alter incoming information in real time, changing the very nature of the performance as it happens. This is sometimes referred to as **input-processing**, because the information is altered as it comes into the sequencer.

Common input processes include **transposing**, which converts your performance into another key; **input-quantizing**, which corrects the timing of the notes you play as you play them; and **velocity scaling**, which alters the speed, or strength, of your attacks to fit within a specified range.

MIDI AND TIMING

Another difference between MIDI and audio recording is the way each is connected to time. Once recorded, an audio track's speed and duration are fixed (unless it's a specially encoded track designed for loop construction). A five-second guitar passage will play back for five seconds, even if you change the arrangement's tempo.

MIDI messages, on the other hand, are always affected by tempo. If you record a quarter-note figure at 120 bpm, and play it back at 60 bpm, the quarter notes will trigger at half the speed, but will retain their position relative to the grid. The pitch of the notes won't be affected by this tempo change, nor will the audio quality of your MIDI module's output. The only change will be the tempo of the passage.

Conversely, you can record a part at half tempo (at 60 bpm) and then speed it up later (to 120 bpm); this is an effective way to record material that exceeds your playing ability.

MAP

A *tempo map* tells your sequencer when to speed up, when to slow down, and when to change time signatures. When you're working with MIDI, you can create a tempo map before you ever record a note, or after an entire arrangement is completed. The sequencer will follow along. You can program your sequencer to create a *ritard* or other time-based changes, as shown in **Fig. 8.9**.

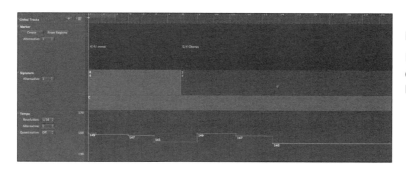

Fig. 8.9

Programming a series of tempo changes with Logic's tempo track.

WORKING WITH A CLICK TRACK

You *can* record MIDI without using a **click** track, but locking your music to a specified tempo allows you to later make edits based on the grid. As we discussed in Chapter 5, a click track can be a simple metronome or a programmed rhythm part. I like to use short drum loops with the appropriate feel instead of a simple click because they get me more in the mood to make music.

If your project will include audio as well as MIDI, remember that you need to establish your tempo map *before* you record your audio tracks.

CHANGING TEMPO INFORMATION AFTER RECORDING

If you feel that working with a click is too confining, you can record without one. To establish a grid, you can create a tempo map retroactively. Most sequencers allow you to enter a manual click, or guide track, by playing along with the previously recorded material. You can also define tempo by selecting a region and assigning it a duration, such as a whole note (four beats) or double whole note (eight beats). This is especially handy when you want your music to stay within the confines of a grid, but have it speed up and slow down.

■ MIDI LOOPING

The concept of looping—building tracks from repeating regions—was introduced in Chapter 7. MIDI offers enormous flexibility when building loop-based arrangements.

As with audio, you can create loops either by cutting and pasting a region to fill out a section, or by selecting a region and using the software's repeat/loop commands to streamline the process.

Loops that are based on a single repeating object have a couple of advantages in the MIDI realm. First, because you can turn the loop on and off with a single command, this is a very quick way to flesh out a basic arrangement. Second, any changes made to the original object are reflected in the loop.

You can, for example, create a basic drum pattern as the backbone of a song, and have it play for the entire arrangement. As other parts come together, you can fine-tune the loops, or replace them with parts that fit the changes in the arrangement.

USING LOOPS TO CREATE POLYRHYTHMS

The flexibility of sequencing software makes it easy to create arrangements that would be very difficult to achieve with conventional audio tools. One of my favorites is to turn ordinary percussion parts into a polyrhythmic figure. For example, take two percussion patterns: a two-bar drum part, and a two-bar conga part. Edit the conga part so that it is now five beats long. Loop both parts. As you can see in **Fig. 8.10**, the conga part's original downbeat will move a beat later in each measure.

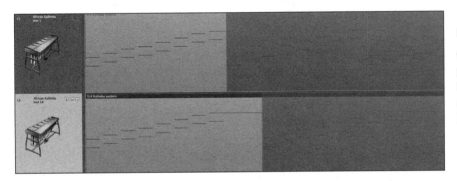

Fig. 8.10

Creating polyrhythms by copying and moving MIDI regions.

■ CREATING MIDI FROM AUDIO

In Chapter 7 we discussed ReCycle and Melodyne, programs that can build a MIDI file that follows the groove (and in Melodyne's case, the pitch) of an audio file. Some DAWs also offer features that analyze the pitch and timing of an audio region and create a MIDI track—complete with pitch information—based on it.

Audio-to-MIDI conversion can be useful in a number of ways. It allows you to use an audio track you've recorded with, for example, electric guitar or voice to trigger a MIDI sound such as sitar or strings. In a pinch, it can be used to create music notation for a part you may have improvised and want to relearn. But its most common application is for replacing unsatisfactory sounds in an audio recording with samples triggered via MIDI.

SOUND REPLACEMENT

Sound replacement is a technique where you substitute an audio recording with digital samples. This technique is most often used to replace poorly engineered multitrack drum recordings. This is done by generating MIDI notes that follow the exact timing and dynamics of the audio recording.

Sound replacement is most effective when it's applied to individual drums and isolated sounds—for example, replacing a snare recorded with a mic with a snare sample. **Fig. 8.11** shows an example: you see the original audio region with a MIDI track below.

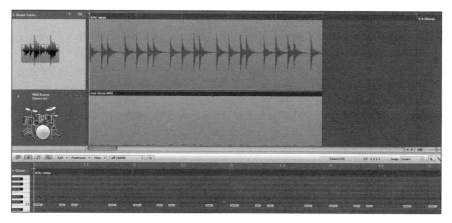

Fig. 8.11

A MIDI track assigned to trigger a sampler can be used to replace an audio part. This is especially effective for drum tracks.

There are several ways to accomplish this task. If you have a drum trigger controller, you can feed the audio generated by the recorded tracks to the triggers, which will generate MIDI data. This method is really challenging, however: first, you must be sure the source sound is totally isolated, and that the triggers are set to follow its dynamics perfectly with no dropped notes. Then you have to account for the latency inherent in routing audio out from the computer, and sending MIDI back to it. You must make sure that the MIDI track's quantize settings don't interfere with the drum groove. Finally, when the MIDI is on the computer, you may find yourself doing a *lot* of editing to get the parts to match.

Another option that's even more tedious is manually entering the MIDI notes that correspond to the beats of the drum part. I'll go out on a limb now and say that you'll go nuts if you try to do that with anything but the shortest and simplest parts.

Fortunately, software has come to the rescue yet again. ReCycle (see **Fig. 8.12**), which we looked at in Chapter 7, may be more commonly used on loops for any kind of audio. But in this application, you would open the isolated snare track in ReCycle and carefully edit the slices to match the snare's performance. Then, generate a MIDI file. As usual, ReCycle will

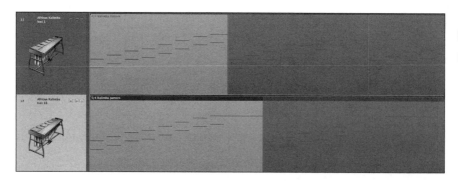

Fig. 8.12

ReCycle

generate a different note for each snare hit. Import this MIDI file to a track that's assigned to trigger the snare sample you want, then edit the MIDI on the track so that each note is the same pitch (usually, it's D3) as the snare sample. This is easier if your sequencer has some of the macro features we'll look at in the next chapter, because you can use one keystroke to make all notes D3.

TIP

If you're using ReCycle to replace sounds in a long audio track, you might want to divide the track into smaller regions and export each region as a separate audio file. It's a little more work on the "front end," but might make it easier to look at and manage your edits in ReCycle.

Digidesign's SoundReplacer (see **Fig. 8.13**) software caught on with Pro Tools users as a way of analyzing a waveform and triggering up to three samples based on its output. SoundReplacer works as an AudioSuite plug-in within Pro Tools.

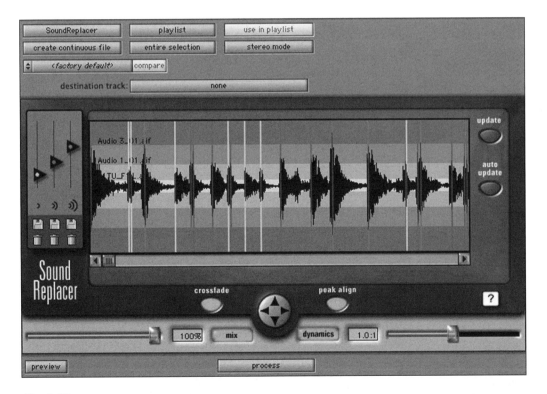

Fig. 8.13

SoundReplacer

Toontrack's Drumtracker (see **Fig. 8.14**) is a stand-alone program that can import multiple audio files and generate MIDI data for each one. It allows you to audition the MIDI sounds and make adjustments before generating the MIDI file.

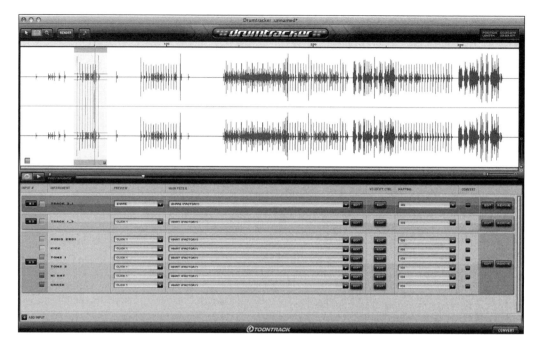

Fig. 8.14

Drumtracker

In all of these cases, the trick is to accurately identify the attacks in the audio file. You do this by setting the *threshold* control, similar to the way you would use a noise gate (see chapter 11), so that the software recognizes each note in the performance. This can get tricky if the original drum part has little subtleties, like ghosted notes and flams. **Fig. 8.15** shows Drumtracker focused on a snare track section. The lines above and below the center (red onscreen), show the threshold in relation to the peaks in the snare part's waveform.

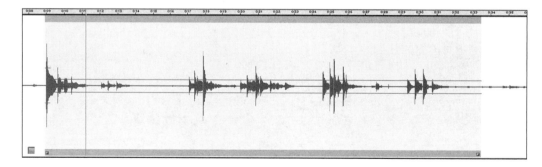

Fig. 8.15

Drumtracker analyzing a snare section; the horizontal lines intersecting the waveform represent the threshold; amplitudes at or above that line will generate MIDI notes.

Before generating the MIDI output file, you can fine-tune how the software outputs velocity data, whether it tracks to tempo, whether it generates one MIDI note or more than one for the track, and so on. **Fig. 8.16** shows the MIDI files generated by the snare track section we

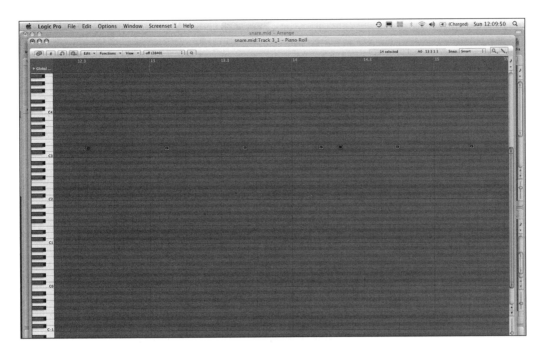

Fig. 8.16

The MIDI notes generated by the snare part shown in **Fig. 8.15**.

selected for editing in **Fig. 8.15**. The notes came in at a range of velocities, and include overlapping note events, hits slightly before the beat divisions on the grid, and so on—all of which follow the original feel of the drummer's performance.

TIP

If you want to replace sounds on a part that's been edited from several different audio files, you should create a new audio file that reflects those edits, and open this new file in your sound replacement program. Depending on your DAW's modus operandi, you can either render the new file by selecting all the regions in the track, or bounce a "mix" of the track with all its edits in place. If you're using the second method, be sure the track you want is soloed so that the new audio file has only that track's sound on it. Note that when rendering, start at measure 1 of the song, no matter where the part actually comes in. This way, the notes in the MIDI file you generate with the sound-replacement software will be positioned correctly when you import it into your DAW.

USING MELODYNE

Melodyne, which we also discussed in Chapter 7, analyzes audio and lets you edit its pitch and timing in a MIDI-like way. Because it can generate a MIDI file for each audio track, Melodyne can also be a very accurate sound-replacement tool, especially for drums. Because it works as both a stand-alone program and as a plug-in with many DAWs, you have two options:

1. Open the audio file for each drum track in Melodyne.

2. Send audio from your DAW to Melodyne via the plug-in's "Bridge" connection.

The advantage of the latter option is that you don't need to render an edited version of your track: Melodyne will be reading the audio as you've edited it in your Arrange/Edit window.

FINE-TUNING A DRUM REPLACEMENT

No matter how you've generated your MIDI data, the final part of the process is to fine-tune the MIDI to match the audio performance.

Be sure the MIDI track is assigned to an appropriate drum sound (it doesn't have to be the final choice, but it should be close enough that the part has the right basic feel when triggering it).

Solo the audio track you're replacing. Solo the MIDI track. Cycle/loop your DAW to play all or some of the section you're replacing. Listen carefully to the blend of the performances. The MIDI should trigger at exactly the same time as the original. Use the editing tools on the MIDI track (see Chapter 9) to bring the timing and dynamics of the MIDI notes into line.

BLENDING PARTS

One question that you'll face when replacing drum sounds is whether to replace every track or just a few in a multi-mic drum recording. The latter scenario requires very precise accuracy.

For example, let's say the close-miked snare track is tinny or distorted, but the snare is also present—and sounds good—in the overhead mics and in the room mics. When you replace the snare sound on the close mic, it needs to track *exactly* with the snare heard in the overheads and room mics. The sample you use should also be close to the sound of the original snare. So, as you adjust the MIDI audition, disable the Solo button from time to time and listen to the part in the context of the whole kit. Make sure the new part blends!

■ MOVING ON

MIDI recording may share many of the same attributes as audio recording, but it offers its own unique set of powerful editing and arranging tools, which we'll tackle in Chapter 9.

CHAPTER 9:   MIDI ARRANGING AND EDITING

MIDI has been around for more than a quarter century now, and yet it still seems revolutionary in the way it allows us to get inside a performance and edit it with such persnickety detail that the term "control freak" doesn't even scratch the surface.

When MIDI sequencers first emerged, they were both praised for offering this level of control and criticized for turning recording into more of a science than an art. MIDI was thought to rob a performance of its natural, creative feel and turn musicians into robots.

Both views, of course, have merit, yet the truth *does not* lie in the middle, as so many political pundits like to say, but actually at each extreme. MIDI *does* give you, the musician-producer, more control than ever before. And it *can* cause your music to sound robotic. But by understanding how to harness the first and avoid the second, you'll be able to create compelling recordings. (Of course, if you're into electronica genres that actually *should* sound robotic, only the first part applies.)

First, let's dispense with a few common misconceptions. MIDI performances can be recorded in a very linear fashion. If you're a traditionalist who happens to be working with a MIDI-equipped computer, you can play your parts into a DAW just as you would when recording audio. You may need to disable some of the sequencer's quantizing features to hear the performance play back naturally (input quantize should be off), but it can be done.

MIDI technology also allows you to edit your performance in fine detail. You can change one note in a performance, or all of them. You can speed up a passage, slow it down, cut it in half, or split the upper and lower pitches so that they make different sounds. You can correct your mistakes or create completely new ideas by rearranging old ones.

Music notation software, such as Finale (by MakeMusic), Notion (by Notion Music), and Sibelius 5 (by Sibelius) can record MIDI and display the performance as notes on a staff. Many DAWs also offer this kind of score display, which we'll touch on later in this chapter.

■ A NOTE ABOUT MIDI REGIONS

We've been discussing how DAWs allow you to freely arrange audio segments, called regions, on a grid. You can apply many of these arrangement-level editing techniques to MIDI as well. You can, for example, split a MIDI track spanning the length of a whole song into smaller parts and rearrange these regions on the grid. You can loop a MIDI region to flesh out a track, copy that region from one track to any number of others, and apply MIDI effects that alter the way the notes in the MIDI track play back. Regions can be split and rejoined, or merged into other regions to create new, denser parts.

One key difference between audio and MIDI is the way DAWs see the data inside regions. Audio regions point to an audio file, but when you edit a region, the file itself is untouched. You can chop up a guitar region and rearrange the order of the notes, then listen to the original audio file from which that region was created, and the guitar part will play in the *original* note order.

Usually, a DAW treats MIDI data a little differently. When you chop up a MIDI performance and move the material around, you're actually *changing the order of the notes in the original performance*. There's no separate file to use as a reference. (The exception is if you've imported a standard MIDI file into a track; in that case, the MIDI data from the original file is written into your DAW, but the original MIDI file itself is left alone.)

So, before doing any radical edits on a MIDI performance, you may want to make a copy of the track and work with the copy. **Fig. 9.1** shows this in Logic Pro: both tracks are assigned to the same sounds. The original track is muted so that it doesn't send note data. The second track contains the exact same data as the first, but has been chopped up into separate regions and is poised for editing.

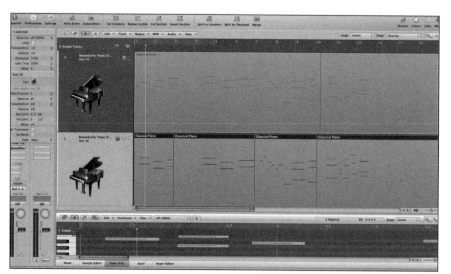

Fig. 9.1

By making a copy of a track (and muting the original), you can edit the MIDI data within it while preserving the original for later reference.

■ MIDI ARRANGING

You can manipulate MIDI on two levels: the overview (the arrange level) and the inside look (the editing level).

The arrangement level involves moving complete passages of music—using many of the same techniques we discussed in Chapter 5, such as subdividing a single track into regions that can be copied, rearranged, and assigned to other tracks; looping a section so that it repeats indefinitely; and so on (see **Fig. 9.2**).

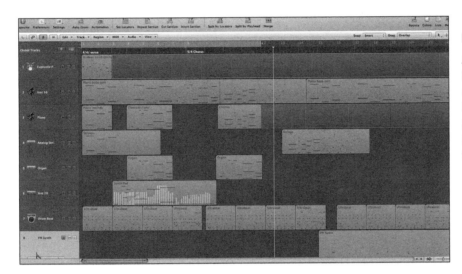

Fig. 9.2

A Logic Pro MIDI arrangement showing MIDI tracks and the regions within them.

On the arrange level, you can apply nondestructive (or playback) MIDI processing, such as basic quantizing, transposing, and velocity scaling, which will only affect the way the software plays back your MIDI messages, but not the original recorded data itself.

MIDI ARRANGING TIPS AND TRICKS

At the arrange level, MIDI editing is very similar to audio editing. But there are some things you can easily do with MIDI that are difficult or impossible to do with audio.

One is to create a layer of two or more sounds playing the same part. You do this by copying the data from one track to another, then assigning the second track to a different MIDI channel or instrument. For example, we can use a copy of the piano part seen in **Fig. 9.1** to trigger a mellow pad sound on an analog-type synthesizer (see **Fig. 9.3**).

There are many possibilities once the second layer is in place. You can simply blend the two parts together in the final mix. Or maybe have the pad only come in during the song's chorus. Perhaps as the arrangement unfolds, the piano itself isn't as effective as the pad, so you only keep the pad. Or perhaps you want the pad to play an octave lower, or to only include the top or bottom note of a chord. All of these options, and others, are possible.

Fig. 9.3

By making a copy of a piano part and assigning it to trigger a synthesizer sound, you can create a complex layered sound (note instrument assignments for the upper and lower tracks).

Another option is to offset two regions that contain the same material so that they generate a more complex rhythm. In this scenario, the piano part is copied to a new track, but all the regions in the copied track are moved so they start one beat later (see **Fig. 9.4**). The offset track can be assigned to the same MIDI output/channel as the original (in which case both tracks trigger the same sound) or to a different channel.

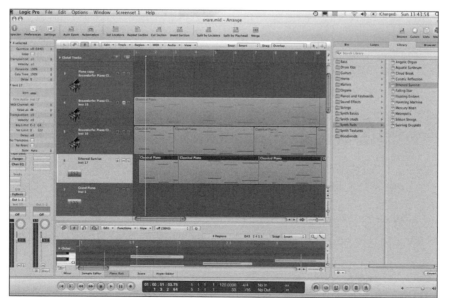

Fig. 9.4

Offsetting regions to generate complex rhythms.

The layered approach can also be used to create quick and easy harmony parts. You can tell your DAW to transpose the entire track by a set interval (for example, seven semitones higher, which would generate a part a perfect fifth above the original), or transpose individual regions (see **Fig. 9.5**).

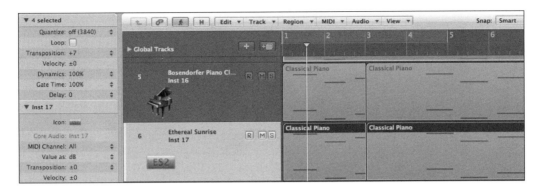

Fig. 9.5

Copying, layering, and transposing a part to create a harmony. The track assigned to Ethereal Sunshine is raised by seven half-steps (see upper left of window).

All of the above examples can be done quickly and nondestructively from the Arrange/Edit window in a typical DAW. But the real power of MIDI unfolds when you go inside the tracks and work with individual editors.

■ MIDI Editors

MIDI editors are work areas within a DAW that allow you to see your tracks and regions on an event-by-event level. A typical DAW or sequencer gives you a number of different ways to look at the same data, and each editor has an application in your work.

As with the Arrange/Edit window, MIDI data editors offer different sets of tools designed to give you hands-on control of your music. While these vary depending on both the software application and the editor you're using within it, typical tools include the following:

The *Pointer,* for selecting events, including individual notes or groups of notes, note velocity messages, and controller data. The pointer can be used to move events in pitch and time, change their duration, and select them for other types of processing.

The *Pencil,* for inputting new note and controller data. (In a drum editor, this may become a drumstick.)

The *Eraser,* for deleting events.

The *Scissors,* for splitting events such as notes into two or more pieces.

Glue, for joining two or more events—used mainly to convert a pattern of notes playing the same pitch into one long note.

The *Magnifying Glass,* for zooming the window's view in closer for more individual detail or farther away for a "big picture" overview.

Other tools might include *Mute*, which allows you to stop a note from triggering MIDI data without erasing it; *Quantize*, which allows you to apply timing correction to selected notes while leaving others as they were originally performed; and *Velocity*, which lets you use the mouse to quickly change the velocity of selected notes.

With some programs, right-clicking (Windows) or control-clicking (Mac) on a selection will call up a submenu offering even more commands that are relevant to the data in the window.

THE PIANO ROLL OR GRAPHIC EDITOR

A **graphical editor**, or **matrix editor**, like the one from Cubase 5 shown in **Fig. 9.6**, displays MIDI events on a grid. The vertical axis displays the pitch of each event, while the horizontal axis shows the event's location in time. Because the pitch reference along the left of the window looks like a piano keyboard, this editor is sometimes referred to as a *piano roll* display.

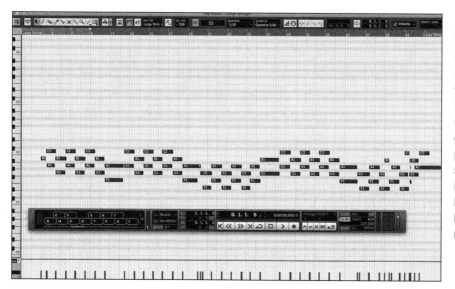

Fig. 9.6

Cubase's matrix (or "piano roll") is typical of the type. It displays individual notes on a grid with vertical position representing pitch, horizontal position location, and length of the bar note duration.

The graphic editor is great for click-and-drag MIDI editing. You can move events around while seeing how they fit together musically. You can set up your sequencer to trigger an event every time you select it—this lets you hear the edit as it's happening.

You can add events by drawing them in the graphic editor using the Pencil tool, select events for MIDI processing such as quantizing, or delete individual notes or groups of notes. You can change the length or velocity of individual or groups of notes, and you can draw and edit controller information, as shown in **Fig. 9.7**.

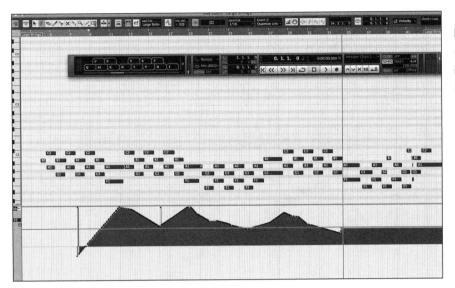

Fig. 9.7

Editing controller information in the Matrix editor.

THE DRUM EDITOR

The **drum editor** (see **Fig. 9.8**) is a variation on the graphical editor. But instead of focusing on only one MIDI channel or instrument, the drum editor lets you view all of the drum channels in one central window. Drum names replace the pitches seen in the piano roll editor, and you can assign—or *map*—each drum to any destination you wish. For example, the "snare" sound displayed in the drum editor might be routed to a digital sampler loaded with an acoustic drum set, while the kick is assigned to a MIDI module with an analog drum patch, and the hi-hats are assigned to a software drum machine.

Fig. 9.8

A drum editor can display multiple MIDI channels. Rather than keyboard pitches, each note is displayed by what drum sound it's assigned to trigger.

THE EVENT LIST

The **event list** lets you see each MIDI event in sequential order, represented numerically. The event list may not be as intuitive as the graphical display, but it's handy when you need to place an event in a specific time location (see **Fig. 9.9**).

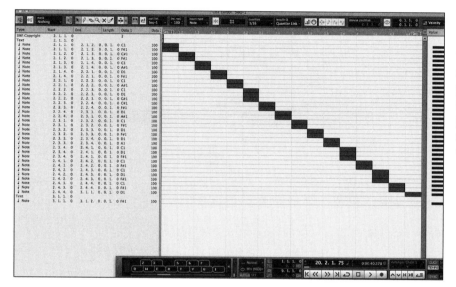

Fig. 9.9

The event list uses text to display MIDI events: type, location, pitch, duration, controller value, velocity, etc.

Because it doesn't display measures graphically, an event list is useful when searching for events positioned far apart in time. By activating a **display filter**, you can use the event list to find and edit specific events, while ignoring others. For example, you could set the event list to filter out notes and show only pitch-bend data, which you can then select, edit, and even erase without affecting the notes that were recorded along with it (see **Fig. 9.10**).

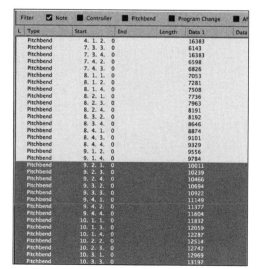

Fig. 9.10

Filtering an event list's display lets you edit only the type of MIDI events you want to change, while leaving others unchanged.

SCORE OR NOTATION EDITING

For many musicians, notation is still the preferred way to look at music. A MIDI score editor (see **Fig. 9.11**) lets you look at your performance on a traditional staff. You can move, insert, and delete notes on the staff much as you can with the graphical editor. Score editors can be found in all of the leading DAWs (Pro Tools added it in version 8), and are also available as stand-alone programs.

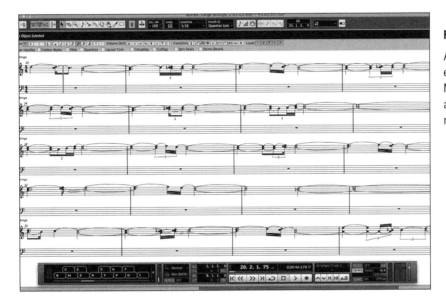

Fig. 9.11

A score editor displays MIDI events as traditional musical notation.

One drawback to using a score editor within a DAW is its inability to display unquantized MIDI in a form that's easily readable. If, for example, you rush a note in a performance that would normally be written as a downbeat, the score editor may be literal in how it's displayed, showing it as a tie from the previous measure. The display can become pretty confusing.

However, some score editors have a feature called *display quantization*. This lets the software make its best guess about where the note is supposed to fall in relation to the song's tempo, and display that onscreen without actually quantizing the actual performance of the note. If you play a note that starts a few clicks before the measure, the score editor will show it as falling on the first downbeat of the measure. **Fig. 9.12** shows the same material selected in Cubase's Key (matrix/piano roll) and Score editors. In the Key display, you can see that the first note anticipates the measure. But the score shows it exactly on the downbeat.

In addition to editing MIDI events, you can use a score editor to create charts and print them out. Some score editors allow you to create multiple staves, add guitar chord symbols, and more.

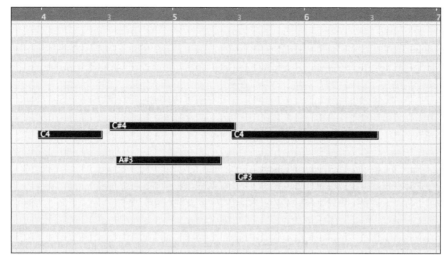

Fig. 9.12

The same MIDI events as shown in Cubase's matrix (top) and score editors (bottom).

STAND-ALONE SCORE EDITING SOFTWARE

Stand-alone score editing programs offer many features that go far beyond what you'd find in a typical DAW. Software like Finale and Sibelius (see **Fig. 9.13**) is designed not only for composers, but also for people who create printed music for a living, such as transcribers, music editors, and engravers.

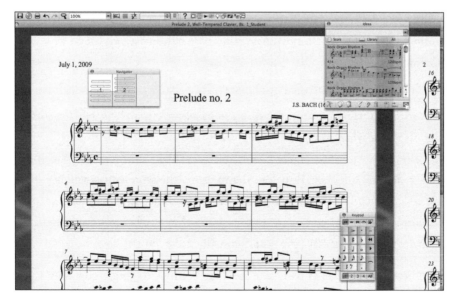

Fig. 9.13

Sibelius 5

Originally designed just for print, today's score editing software is like a cross between a sequencer (because it can record and edit MIDI data), a software instrument (because it can trigger the appropriate sounds as the score plays), and a graphic design program (because it allows for extensive editing of notes, text, symbols, and so on, and lets you prepare a manuscript for publication).

Score editors can record a performance played on a MIDI controller. Users can also manually input notes. You can develop a complete work in a score editor and generate an audio file of it by bouncing the score editor's output down to disk. You can also export Standard MIDI Files (SMFs) and open these in your DAW. Conversely, you can open an SMF in a score editor, and edit it using the score editor's notation features.

The one feature stand-alone score editors don't have—at least as I write this—is the ability to record and edit audio DAW-style. But for those who aim to compose complex scores with MIDI instruments, these programs may be preferable to a more general-purpose DAW.

CONTROLLER EDITING

Although you can display controller information in the event and graphical editors, there are times when it's useful to have a separate view of just the controller information in a track. A MIDI mix, for example, will consist of many controller events occurring at the same time. A controller editor like Logic's Hyper Editor (see **Fig. 9.14**) lets you look at multiple controller events side by side. As with the event list, you can filter out unwanted controller events and focus on the material you need at the moment.

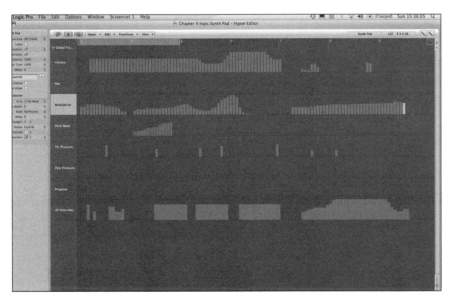

Fig. 9.14

Logic's Hyper Editor

MULTICHANNEL EDITING

Most MIDI editing is done one track at a time, but there are occasions when you'll want to get a detailed look at a number of tracks simultaneously. The drum editor mentioned above is a very specific application of this idea, but drum editing isn't the only activity that can benefit from the ability to scope out more than one channel/instrument at a time.

Multichannel editing is also handy for looking at related material, such as bass and drum tracks, or parts of a string quartet.

Many DAWs allow you to view the events contained in multiple MIDI tracks in a single window. To do so, you select all the tracks you want to edit, and activate the appropriate editor. This technique is especially effective when using a graphical key or drum editor because it allows you to see individual events in context. If your sequencer supports it, use color to identify the events by track.

GROUPING TRACKS INTO FOLDERS

One advanced sequencing feature is the ability to group multiple tracks (or sections within an arrangement) into containers (called *folders* or *chunks*, depending on the software). A folder can contain a complete multitrack arrangement, including both MIDI and audio data. The folder can then be treated as a single region or event within the larger arrangement. For example, you could group all the tracks that make up the chorus of a song into one folder, and group all the tracks that make up the verse into another. By copying and pasting the folders, you can restructure very easily. All the individual tracks that make up a section can be moved *en masse* — much easier than dealing with the tracks individually.

Similar to the way *comp* tracks work in audio editing (see Chapter 6), you can also use a folder to store a group of different tracks that make up one part. For example, if you have a MIDI drum part split over three tracks (one each for the kick, snare, and hi-hat), you can group these into a folder (as opposed to merging them into one MIDI track). Since the tracks remain individual entities, you can assign each to its own MIDI output and apply MIDI processing — such as quantizing — to each track separately. But you can use the folder to arrange the drums as a unit and, if you like, apply additional MIDI processing (such as velocity scaling) to all of the tracks in one move.

EDITING WHILE THE MUSIC PLAYS

The editors described above may seem data intensive — and they are. Retyping a note's start time or velocity in an event editor can seem about as musical as filling out your tax return. But you can eliminate a sequencer's "word-processor" vibe by editing while the music plays back.

One of my favorite techniques is to set up a cycle/loop for a region, and then edit, input, and delete notes on the fly. This gives me instant feedback on how the edits fit the track and the arrangement as a whole.

■ MIDI PROCESSORS

Despite the power afforded by individual editors, manually moving every event in a long MIDI track can become very tedious. MIDI processors help you control your MIDI tracks and regions without having to edit every event by hand.

A MIDI processor can work in two ways. In real time (or nondestructive) mode, the processor governs only how the sequencer *plays* the data. The original information is untouched.

In destructive mode, the sequencer actually rewrites the data to the track, changing the performance itself. Of course, you can undo unwanted edits, but it's advisable to apply these kinds of edits to a copy of the original performance, especially if you have any doubts at all about what you're about to do.

TIMING CONTROL: QUANTIZING

Quantizing is a method for adjusting MIDI timing information. When you quantize a region or track, you move the events within it closer to a grid value, defined as notes or parts of notes. For example, when you quantize a selection of notes to a quarter-note grid, all notes will play as quarter notes, regardless of their original timing. **Fig. 9.15** shows two regions derived from the same performance; one is quantized, one is not.

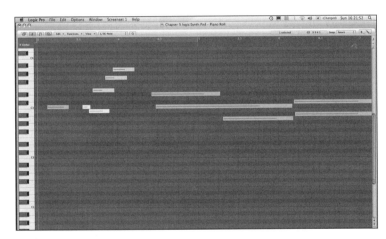

Fig. 9.15

Compare the unquantized region (top) with the same material after quantization has been applied (bottom).

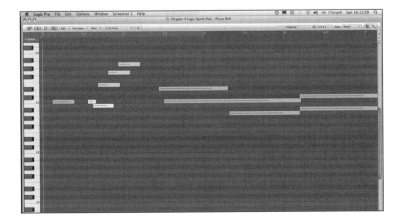

QUANTIZATION PARAMETERS

Because strict quantization can make a performance sound mechanical, there are several parameters that let you control the degree of quantization. Common quantization parameters include:

- **Note value:** Sets the position of the quantized notes on the grid.

- **Strength:** Sets the percentage by which the quantized notes will move toward the grid. A strength of 100 percent puts the notes right at the grid; 90 percent moves them 90 percent closer to the grid position, etc.

- **Range:** Selects which notes will be quantized. With range enabled, only notes a given distance from the grid will be affected. For example, if you have the quantize value set to a quarter note, with the range set to 10 percent, only notes close to the quarter-note position will be quantized; the others will be unchanged. This is an excellent way to tighten up a performance without robbing it of its feel (which often happens in between the quarter notes).

- **Offset:** Moves the quantize grid forward or backward in relation to the song's tempo. This is useful when you want to quantize a part that anticipates the beat—if you offset the grid a few ticks early, you can quantize without losing that anticipating feel.

- **Swing:** Swing is a way of changing the relationship between note values on the grid. Swing value is tied to a specific note value, so we'll use an eighth-note swing to show how it works. The default swing setting is 50 percent, which means that all eighth notes are evenly spaced. If you set the swing to divide the two notes into 66 percent and 33 percent of the beat (long-short), the second eighth note of each beat will be delayed to the value of the third triplet in an eighth-note triplet, giving the music a swing, or shuffle, feel.

GROOVE QUANTIZING

Quantizing to an exact grid doesn't always provide natural results. **Groove quantizing** conforms your MIDI data to a user-defined grid. Most sequencers come with a number of third-party grooves, or quantizing grids, that are derived from the performance of a live musician. You also create and save your own grooves by using a MIDI or audio track as a template.

Groove and standard quantizing are not mutually exclusive. You can quantize material in the standard way to a standard grid, and then spice it up by applying a groove template on top of it.

A groove template can affect velocity as well as timing—an effective way to add dynamic realism to an otherwise static part.

CHANGING DURATION

The Change Duration command alters the length of a MIDI note. You can use it to make a staccato passage sound more legato, or to shorten the length of notes in a drum track to make them easier to see and edit.

You can change a note's duration by a percentage, or you can assign it an absolute value. Some sequencers also let you automatically scale the duration of each note so that it reaches—and stops at—the following note, producing a legato feel (**Fig. 9.16**).

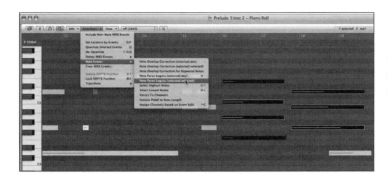

Fig. 9.16

Changing duration of a group of notes to create a legato feel.

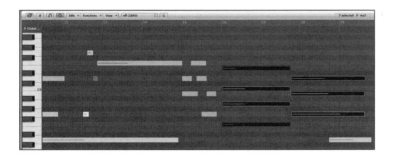

SHIFTING AND SPOT EDITING

Your sequencer's Shift and Spot Edit commands are similar to each other. They each let you change the location of events, but their applications are different.

The **Shift** command moves a MIDI event by a specified amount. You can shift MIDI events by musical values (measures, beats, and ticks), by **absolute time** (minutes, seconds, and milliseconds), or SMPTE values (hours, minutes, seconds, and frames).

Spotting is similar to shifting, but instead of moving events by a specific amount, you move them to a specific location. Spot editing is especially useful when you want to match a MIDI note to an audio performance that doesn't adhere closely to the grid. It's also handy for things like lining up sound effects to film cues and the like. See Chapter 5 for more on spotting.

PITCH CONTROL: TRANSPOSING AND HARMONIZING

Transposing, or changing a note's pitch, is another useful MIDI routine. You can change the key of an entire track (or range of tracks), or transpose a few notes within a track.

Harmonizing is similar to transposing, but instead of altering the original passage, you're adding new notes to play along with it. There are two types of harmonization:

- *Interval* transposition transposes all the notes by the same value, regardless of the key of the music. If you choose a major third as your interval, all the notes will be moved by four half steps, no matter where they are in the original scale. This will cause some of the transposed notes to fall outside the scale. For example, in C major (C, D, E, F, G, A, B), simply transposing the scale by four half steps will produce the notes E, F♯, G♯, A, B, C♯, and D♯—all of the sharps fall outside the key of C.

- **Intelligent**, or **harmonic, transposition** transposes notes by a scalar value (such as a third above or a fourth below), but conforms the harmonies to the appropriate key. Harmonic transposition of a third on the C scale would produce a mix of pitches that are three and four half steps above the note being harmonized, keeping the harmony within the key of C. The result would be E, F, G, A, B, C, D.

DYNAMICS CONTROL: CHANGING VELOCITY

Velocity measures the intensity of a MIDI note event. It's usually assigned to control the loudness of a note, but you can set up your MIDI gear to respond to velocity in a number of ways. One example would be assigning velocity-switching to trigger different samples assigned to the same key in a drum kit.

Velocity editing is most commonly used to correct the dynamics of a performance, but it can also help compensate for your equipment's inconsistencies. Not all MIDI devices respond to velocity in the same way. So, if you reassign a piano track to a different device (or even to a different patch in the same device), the velocity response might be very different from what you intended. If you're generating MIDI from audio, as discussed in Chapter 8, you may also need to edit the velocities of the MIDI notes the software has generated.

As with pitch and timing, you can edit individual note velocities by hand. However, it's often more efficient to use your sequencer's velocity editor, especially when you need to cover a range of events (see **Fig. 9.17**).

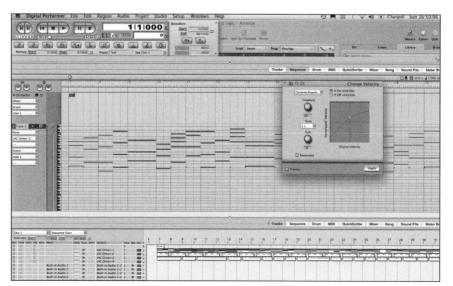

Fig. 9.17

A velocity editor can save a lot of time when you need to change the velocity of a group of notes.

Typical velocity edit parameters include:

- **Maximum and/or minimum velocity:** This lets you determine the absolute loudest and softest notes you'll hear. You can use this parameter in tandem with the others.

- **Increase/decrease velocity by a specific amount:** This adds or subtracts an absolute number for every velocity value.

- **Scale velocity by a percentage:** As with audio compression, the loudest and softest events are more affected than those with moderate velocity.

- **Set all velocity to the same specific value:** This is useful when you want to have a consistent level on a sound such as a kick drum.

LOGICAL SEQUENCER EDITORS

Logical editors are used to select data for editing based on specific criteria, leaving all other data untouched (see **Fig. 9.18**). This is useful in a number of instances. Let's say you want to remove only the lowest notes from a track, or change the velocity of every note assigned to the pitch C1: a logical editor can do this without altering the rest of your data. Here are a few examples:

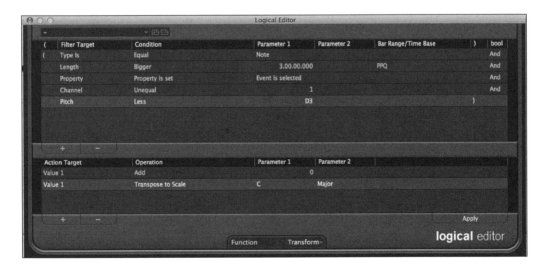

Fig. 9.18

A logical editor lets you select only data meeting your specific criteria for editing.

- **Split by note:** Separates notes in a track based on pitch. You can set a split point, or choose to remove the highest (or lowest) notes in a chord. You can also erase the split notes or assign them to another track.

- **Split by channel:** Separates MIDI events that are on different MIDI channels. This is useful for creating individual tracks out of a single-track, multichannel MIDI recording.

- **Split by event type:** This is a good way to extract controller data from a track for further editing.

- **Find doubles:** When you record in merge mode (or merge two tracks together), you may find that two of the same MIDI events are occupying the same space. Not only does this waste bandwidth, but it causes a double trigger from the MIDI device, which can produce a flanging sound. Tracking down these doubles can be a pain in the neck—a logical editor can find them for you.

- **Erase short or quiet notes:** Short and quiet (sometimes called "ghost" notes) are often the result of performance mistakes. You can set your sequencer to find and eliminate these ghosts.

You can also use a logical editor for more esoteric operations, such as selecting and processing every third note in a series, or processing only notes of a specific pitch. For example, you can use a logical editor to select all the "two" and "four" beats of a snare part in the chorus section of a drum track (the backbeats) and make them louder; then select snare beats two and four in the bridge region and make them quieter—while delaying them by a couple of clocks to create a more laid-back backbeat than the one used in the chorus. This is one area where a little digging through your sequencer's manual is definitely worthwhile.

OTHER MIDI EFFECTS AND REAL-TIME PROCESSORS

In addition to being a champ at nuts-and-bolts MIDI editing, a full-featured sequencer can produce some unusual effects in real time. Like logical editors, MIDI processors are sometimes neglected by the average user, but are a great boon to creativity.

An *arpeggiator* creates patterns based on chords (*arpeggio* is the musical term for "broken chord"). It is one of the most popular effects in electronic music. An arpeggiator that works within a sequencer is always in sync with your project.

Other interesting MIDI processors include *chord generators* (hold down one note and a chord plays back), *transformers* (input one type of event, and the sequencer generates another), *splitters* (these route each note to a different MIDI channel, port, or instrument), and *MIDI delays*, which cause MIDI events to repeat to create echo-like effects.

■ EDITOR/LIBRARIANS AND MIDI CONTROL SOFTWARE

An editor/librarian is any program that allows you to store, edit, and organize parameter data for your synthesizers, effects, and other MIDI-equipped devices. In the days when external MIDI modules were the norm, a good editor/librarian program was almost a requirement for serious sound design. Today, many desktop producers use software instruments, which in effect include their own editor/librarian interfaces.

At the same time, the current generation of hardware synthesizers and samplers often comes with dedicated control software. Many of these devices also offer large displays and computer-like interfaces, which makes it much easier to edit sounds using the hardware's own controls.

Yet editor/librarians can be incredibly useful, especially if your studio includes "vintage" hardware sound modules, many of which can be had for very little money these days. Editor/librarian software lets you access all of a synth's parameters at once; edit sounds, or *patches*; and organize them into collections called *libraries*.

A universal editor/librarian (see **Fig. 9.19**) such as SoundQuest's MIDI Quest (Windows) and MOTU's Unisyn, is designed to offer this kind of in-depth editing for a range of instruments from different manufacturers, all within one program. It makes it much easier to both manage the sounds you have and create sounds of your own.

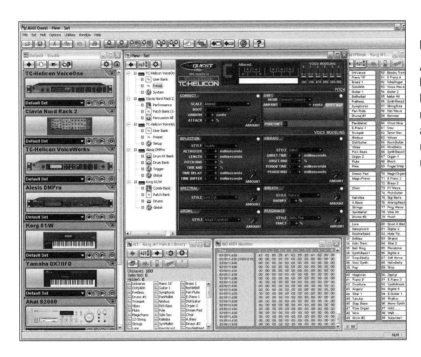

Fig. 9.19

A universal editor/librarian such as MIDI Quest can manage sounds and patches for multiple MIDI modules.

Note: When Emagic, the original developer of Logic, was bought by Apple, the company's cross-platform editor/librarian SoundDiver didn't come along for the ride. (But free beta versions of the program—which require Logic's old USB XSkey to work—can be found online for both Mac OS X and Windows. Using beta versions can be problematic in general, so proceed with caution!)

WORKING WITH SYSTEM EXCLUSIVE

Your software can control the internal parameters of your MIDI devices through special MIDI messages called *System Exclusive*, or **SysEx**. Unlike note and controller data, which are universal to all MIDI devices, SysEx messages are specific to each device (see **Fig. 9.20**). This allows your software to address the specific parameters of one device without affecting the others in your system.

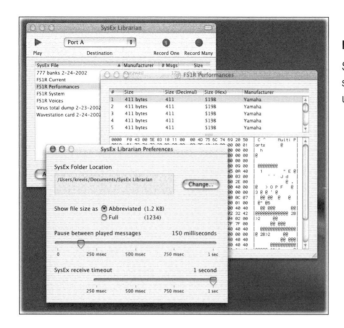

Fig. 9.20

System-exclusive messages shown in the free Mac OS X utility, Snoize SysEx Librarian.

MAKING CONNECTIONS

Editor/librarians communicate over the same MIDI connections used by DAW/sequencing software. However, the connection must be bidirectional, meaning that you must connect both the MIDI input and MIDI output of the target device to the computer—even if the external device is not acting as a controller in your system. A multiport MIDI interface is ideal for this application because it lets you dedicate one port to each module.

INSTALLING PROFILES

The next step in using an editor/librarian is to tell the software what to look for. Before you begin, check the program's documentation to see what special settings, if any, you need to adjust on each sound module to enable it to communicate with the software. You may need to change the MIDI channel, ID, and SysEx transmission settings on the module itself before it can communicate with the computer. These requirements may be different for each type of device in your system.

There are two ways for an editor/librarian to initiate communication with a device. The first option is to have the software scan your system for compatible devices. This is the easiest way to start communication, but it is by no means foolproof. My experience has been that these auto scans sometimes fail to detect compatible devices, even when all the connections and settings are correct.

The second option is to manually install each **profile**. You can use this method to troubleshoot the connection process. If the software fails to detect the device even after it's been manually installed, the problem most likely lies in the connection (always check your MIDI cables), or in the way the device is configured to transmit SysEx.

Universal editor/librarians are cosmopolitan by nature: they can communicate with a wide variety of units from a range of manufacturers, each with its own implementation of SysEx. Unfortunately, this can lead to some inconsistencies in support. Not all profiles are created equal.

UPLOADING PATCHES

Once your devices are connected and tested, you can start transferring sounds. When you're uploading, you have several options: uploading an individual patch, uploading a single **bank** of patches, or uploading the entire contents of each module's memory.

Uploading the entire memory can be time consuming, especially with modules that contain hundreds of patches. But once all the data is in the computer, you won't need to upload from the module very often; all of its patches will already be archived on the computer.

AUDITIONING PATCHES

One of the coolest things about working with an editor/librarian is having immediate access to your sounds. You need only click on a patch with your mouse, and it is transferred into your module, ready for playback. This is the ideal way to compare similar patches—for example, bass sounds—that might be scattered throughout your module's memory banks.

EDITING PATCHES

An individual editor gives you access to all the parameters in a specific patch, as shown in **Fig. 9.21**. In order to take advantage of the software, you'll need to do some homework on your MIDI device's capabilities: while some parameters are self-explanatory, others are more esoteric.

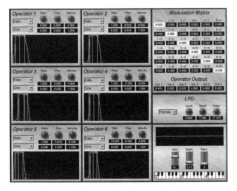

Fig. 9.21

Editor-librarian profiles let you adjust individual patches from the computer.

Because you can store your edits in the computer, you can create many variations of a sound without overwhelming the storage capabilities of your MIDI module. For example, you can create a basic orchestral patch, and use the editor/librarian to store versions with various effects assigned to them, or with slight variations in some of the filter settings.

IMPORTING THIRD-PARTY PATCHES

Even if you're not interested in editing your own sounds, you can use an editor/librarian to load third-party sounds. Many commercial and shareware sounds are available in formats compatible with popular editor/librarian applications.

SOUNDS

Computers were great data organizers long before they became valid musical tools. Editor/librarians exploit this facility for information-gathering in musical ways. You can reorganize the memory of your sound modules to put the sounds in the most convenient locations for your needs. You might organize banks to contain similar sounds, or set up a bank to hold all the sounds you use for a particular song.

You can use an editor/librarian to organize the sounds of one instrument, but you can also go further by organizing libraries that encompass all of the instruments in your studio. You can organize patches by category (such as strings, pianos, or synths), by project, or by any other criteria you like.

LINKING WITH SEQUENCERS

One of the most powerful features of an editor/librarian is its ability to link directly with a sequencer. The editor/librarian can create and organize your patches, and then export the proper settings into your sequences as part of the song. The correct patch is available each time you start a song.

Unfortunately, there's no standard for linking editor/librarians to third-party sequencers. However, MOTU's Unisyn can link to MOTU's popular Digital Performer sequencer.

EDITING SYSEX FROM YOUR SEQUENCER

If you don't relish the prospect of adding another complicated piece of software to your system, have no fear: most sequencers also let you record and edit SysEx data. You can upload, or *dump*, patch information into a sequence track, and when the track begins to play, it transmits the SysEx back into the sound module, ensuring that the correct patch plays back every time.

Many of the leading sequencers also let you build mini applications that can communicate directly with your sound module via SysEx. To do so, you need to know how the module uses controller and or SySex data.

These *consoles* (also known as *environments*) let you access many of the editing capabilities of an editor/librarian without leaving the friendly confines of your sequencer. Moves you make in a console or environment can be exported to a MIDI track for playback in real time. You can often find free console patches online in user groups, such as the Korg Trinity controller for Logic shown in **Fig. 9.22**.

Fig. 9.22

Add-on system-exclusive modules like this Korg Trinity controller for Logic can be used to alter the sounds of external MIDI devices from within a DAW.

Your software may even ship from the factory with a number of consoles preconfigured for instruments in your studio (look in the "extras" folder, or its equivalent).

MOVING ON

With MIDI and audio, you have all the tools you need to build complex and diverse multitrack arrangements. Next, it's time to turn those tracks into a finished product by mixing, adding effects, and mastering.

PART IV   THE FINISHING TOUCHES

CHAPTER 10:   DESKTOP MIXING

In a conventional recording studio, a mixer serves as the central hub for all audio routing. It blends the incoming signals from multitrack tape recorders, effects processors, microphones, and other sources, and sends them to an appropriate destination, such as a monitoring system, multitrack input, or mixdown deck. You can use a mixer to send a vocalist's microphone to one channel of your multitrack, and later use the same mixer to blend *all* the tracks of your multitrack into a stereo master mix.

A computer-based mixer works in essentially the same way. It allows you to route signals to and from your audio tracks, process those tracks as you see fit, and eventually, create a final master recording that can be played back somewhere outside your studio.

▓ MIXER LAYOUT AND SIGNAL FLOW

If you want to understand how your mixer works, you have to go with the flow—signal flow, that is. *Signal flow* refers to the path a source signal takes on its way to a destination. The most obvious example: sending your audio tracks to your audio interface's outputs. Along the way, the mixer lets you process the signal, combine it with other signals, adjust levels, and give it the polish needed to sound great to the outside world.

A mixer has three main areas: the channels (which handle your tracks and inputs), the auxiliary and effects sends/returns (where you add effects and send the signal to individual outputs), and the master, or output, section.

Software mixers have the advantage of being built right into the recording system—you don't have to patch things together with physical cables as you do in the hardware world. Still, most software mixers use a similar layout for the main mixing environment. **Figs. 10.1–10.4** show the mixer sections for several leading software packages. Note the similarities in their respective layouts.

Fig. 10.1

Pro Tools LE

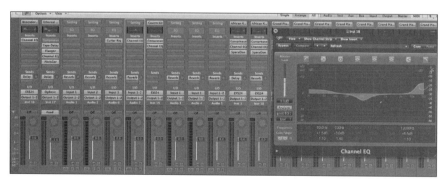

Fig. 10.2

Logic Pro

Fig. 10.3

Cubase

Fig. 10.4

Sonar

Fig. 10.5

An auxiliary mixer channel can be used to add external signals to the DAW's mix.

With a hardware mixer, you must manually connect each source to a channel, connect all effects to sends, and connect the master outputs to a mixdown deck. In a software environment, the mixer is usually preassigned to audio and MIDI tracks: when you create a new track, the software creates a corresponding mixer channel.

Software mixers are also more flexible in dealing with stereo tracks. In most cases, you can create both stereo and mono mixer channels as needed. In addition to routing the tracks in a multitrack project, many software mixers let you add inputs for interfacing outboard gear with your mix; auxiliary buses for adding effects to your mix; and channels for interfacing with other pieces of software or MIDI gear (see **Fig. 10.5**). In addition to mixing in stereo, many of today's DAWs can also mix in a range of surround-sound formats.

THE SOFTWARE SIGNAL CHAIN

Your mixer has two jobs: sending signals from the inputs to the tracks, and taking signals from the tracks to the outputs. **Fig. 10.6** is a block diagram showing the signal flow in a typical software mixer.

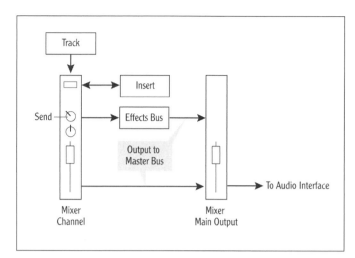

Fig. 10.6

Audio signal flow in a software mixer.

TRACKS VS. CHANNELS

The terms *track* and *channel* are sometimes used interchangeably, but we need to distinguish them here. A track contains either audio or MIDI data. A channel is the passage through which the data travels on its way to its final destination (an audio or MIDI output). Think of tracks as part of your recording/playback system, while channels are part of your mixing system.

SIGNAL ROUTING

We introduced audio signal routing in Chapter 5, and MIDI signal routing in Chapter 8. As the central conduit of all audio signals, your software mixer can handle all signal routing assignments, either inputs or outputs. MIDI signals are a little different: although some sequencers group audio and MIDI into one mixer window MIDI I/O assignments can be handled in other ways, so we'll set aside MIDI from the discussion for now.

A typical mixer channel includes mini-menus that let you set the input source and output destination, as shown in **Fig. 10.7**.

TYPES OF SIGNALS

The typical software mixer handles four types of signals:

• **Analog:** Common analog sources include microphones, preamps, electric guitars, keyboards, drum machines, and other electronic instruments with analog outputs.

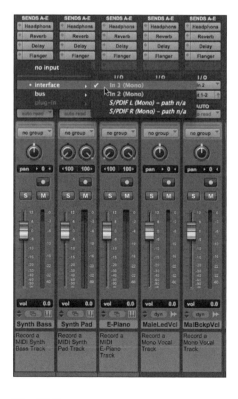

Fig. 10.7

Most DAW mixers feature pop-up mini menus that offer context-specific commands, such as this one showing input and output assignments for a channel in Pro Tools LE.

- **Digital:** Digital sources include digital mixers, outboard A/D converters, effects devices with digital outputs, and outboard digital recorders.

- **Internally Routed Signals:** Internal signals include effects and mix buses within the host software, outputs of software plug-in instruments, and outputs from audio programs that enter your main mix via ReWire.

- **Tracks:** Material being played back by the software, including audio recorded to disk and sounds generated by software instruments.

INPUT ROUTING

The input routing, or assignment, lets you set the source that will feed the mixer channel or track in your multitrack.

PHYSICAL INPUTS

A **physical input** is any hardware input that is routed to your computer via the audio interface. This includes both analog and digital inputs in any format.

The channel's input should be assigned to one of the physical inputs of your audio interface when recording from an analog or digital source, or when routing the output of an outboard effects processor into your mix. See Chapter 5 for more about preparing physical inputs, choosing input monitoring options, and arming tracks for recording.

INTERNAL INPUTS

A software mixer isn't limited to just accepting signal from the audio interface. One of the most powerful recent developments in desktop audio is the ability to interconnect two pieces of audio software, incorporating the output of one application into the mix of another. **ReWire**, developed by Steinberg and Propellerhead Software, has become the standard way to connect third-party applications to DAWs.

With ReWire, programs such as Propellerhead's Reason, Ableton's Live (see **Fig. 10.8**), Celemony's Melodyne, and Submersible Music's DrumCore can be incorporated into the mix of a host program such as Cubase, Logic Audio, Digital Performer, or Pro Tools. The connection includes both audio and sync information, so that both programs work in tandem as one big system.

As with physical inputs, your host software must activate the ReWire inputs in order to bring them into the mix. **Fig. 10.9** shows the ReWire setup for using DrumCore in Cubase.

Note: Live can be either a ReWire slave (routed to a DAW like Logic or Cubase) or a ReWire host (accepting signal from Reason, Melodyne, DrumCore, etc.).

Fig. 10.8

Ableton Live's mixer

One thing ReWire does *not* do is allow different DAWs to share signal routing with one another. You can, however, use a free utility like Jack for Linux or Mac OS X (jack.org) to do just that.

SETTING INPUT LEVELS

Unlike hardware mixers, software mixers typically lack the **trim** control that lets you set a channel's input level. Each channel's input level therefore depends on the output level of the device feeding the channel. Some audio interfaces include physical input level controls; others don't. If yours doesn't, you'll need to set the output level of the source to match the input level of your mixer channel.

We discussed levels in Chapter 5, but it bears repeating: proper levels are *crucial* to getting the optimal sound out of your gear.

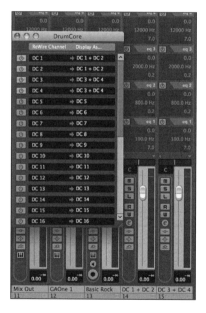

Fig. 10.9

Enabling ReWire inputs in Cubase 5.

■ OUTPUT ROUTING

One of the jobs of a mixer channel is to route signal to an output. Outputs include the physical outputs of your audio interface, auxiliary sends that feed other mixer channels, and effects buses.

A typical mixer channel can send signal to more than one destination at a time. For example, the channel's output may be assigned to your mixer's master bus, which in turn sends it to your audio interface's outputs and on to your speakers, while an **auxiliary send** may be assigned to an effects bus, as shown in **Fig. 10.10**.

PHYSICAL OUTPUTS

"Physical outputs" refers to any of the outputs on your audio interface. The most common physical outputs are the stereo, or main, outputs. If you have a multichannel audio interface, you can route signal to individual outputs as well as to the main outputs. This allows you to send individual tracks from your software mixer to individual inputs on a hardware mixer, or to send a signal from your software mixer's effects bus to the input of an outboard effects processor.

In mixer parlance, a *bus* is a common path that signals share to reach a single destination point. Examples include the **master bus**, or **main bus**, which sends signal to the audio interface's master outputs; **auxiliary buses**, which send signal to auxiliary mixer channels; and effects buses, which route signal to an effect within the mixer. Typically, the output of an auxiliary or effects bus feeds the mixer's master bus and is incorporated into the master output, but buses can also be used to route signal to individual outputs on your audio interface.

One of the most powerful features of a software mixer is the flexibility it affords for routing signal from tracks to buses (and from buses to tracks). The most common use for buses is as effects channels, which we'll discuss below. But you can also use buses to accomplish more esoteric goals. For example, you can use buses to **group** related tracks, process them as a group, and route the group to a new set of record channels. For example, let's say you have three drum tracks—a mono kick track, a mono snare track, and a stereo overheads track. Normally, you would route the output of each of these tracks to the master output bus. But let's say we want to process the drums and record the result of this processing to a new stereo track. We can do this by sending the drum tracks on a little detour.

First, we route the output of each drum track to an auxiliary bus (we'll call it "Aux 1"). Next, we create a stereo channel ("All Drums"), and

Fig. 10.10

This Cubase 5 mixer channel is simultaneously sending signal to the stereo bus (top) and to two different effects buses.

assign the input of All Drums to Aux 1. The channel should now be receiving signal from all three drum tracks exclusively. None of the other tracks in our hypothetical mix are feeding the All Drums channel.

From here, we have several options. We can use the fader for All Drums to control the overall level of the drum tracks. This way, we can set the balance of each individual drum relative to the drum kit with its respective fader, and set the balance of the drum kit as a whole relative to the mix using the channel fader for All Drums. Also, by using the inserts and effects sends on the All Drums channel, we can apply EQ, compression, and reverb to the entire drum part at once. The effects we apply on All Drums could be in addition to any effects we might apply to the individual drum channels. Finally, we can assign the output of All Drums to *another* bus (called "Aux 2"). Then we can create a new stereo track, set its input source as Aux 2, and use it to record the output of the All Drums channel, a technique known as *bouncing*. So now the drums are recorded as a unit on a stereo track. This kind of bus routing, or **submixing**, can be effective for handling any set of related sources (such as a horn section, a group of background singers, or a multi-mic setup for an acoustic instrument).

Another application for this type of internal routing is when you want to record an analog source like electric guitar or voice using effects processors built into your software mixer. You may, for example, want to record the sound of the software amp simulator you're using on the guitar. Typically, these processors affect the audio on playback only. But you can "print" their sound to disk by using the track-to-track routing outlined above.

Note: Some software allows direct connections between the output of one track and the input of another. Ableton Live is one example.

MIXER CONTROLS

A mixer can seem intimidating, with all its knobs, sliders, and buttons. Fortunately, appearances can be deceiving: there's a lot of duplication of function in a mixer, and the operation of one channel is similar to that of the others. The key to understanding a mixer is knowing your way around the *channel strip*. **Fig. 10.11** shows a typical channel strip you'd find on a physical mixer. A software mixer channel is similar. The main difference is that with a software mixer, you can customize some of the components to suit each project—no soldering required.

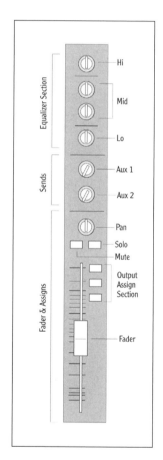

Fig. 10.11

A physical mixer's channel strip typically includes controls for EQ, effects buses, pan, level, mute, and solo. An input Gain control (not shown) is also usually present.

FADER

The **fader** is the control you use the most when mixing. It sets the output level of the channel on its way to its final destination (typically, the master bus). Higher fader settings produce a louder signal.

PANORAMA (PAN) OR BALANCE

The panoramic potentiometer, or pan pot, positions the track in the stereo field. Turning the pan pot left sends signal to the left side of the output bus. With a stereo channel, the pan pot is replaced by a **balance** control that governs the relative level of the left and right sides of the stereo source.

If you're mixing for surround sound, you need a special pan pot that can spread signal among multiple channels, like the one shown in **Fig. 10.12**.

MUTE

The **Mute** button turns off a track, so that its output cannot be heard in the mix. In a software environment, you may find several ways to mute material. In addition to the mixing console Mute button, your software may allow you to mute specific sections of a track from the Arrange window, or mute individual notes in a MIDI track.

Fig. 10.12

Logic Pro's panner for surround 5.1 mixing.

SOLO

The **Solo** button isolates the playback of one track—or a group of tracks you specify—by muting all the others in the mix. Soloing is useful for fine-tuning the sound of a single track or group of tracks. Isolating a track with the Solo function can also help you perfect your edits, especially if you're working on critical transitions, such as crossfades.

SEND

Auxiliary and effects **sends** allow you to route sound from the track to a destination of your choosing without interrupting the channel's main signal flow. A send is typically used to route signal to an effects bus or to a secondary output on your audio interface.

RETURN

On a physical mixer, a **return** is an input that accepts signal from an outside source (such as an outboard effect) and assigns it to the master output. With a virtual mixer, you can use an auxiliary input as a return by assigning it to a physical input on your audio interface.

METERS

The meters display the level of signal going through the channel. They show you the average level of the signal and the peaks—loudest points—in the signal.

■ ADDING EFFECTS

Effects processing is a key component in getting a polished sound out of your production. With a computer-based audio system, effects come in the form of **plug-ins**—helper software that adds to the capabilities of the main host program. We take an in-depth look at plug-ins in Chapter 11.

As with a hardware mixer, a software mixer gives you two basic ways to add effects, and each has a different application in your mix.

INLINE EFFECTS OR INSERTS

Inline effects, or *inserts*, interrupt the signal flow of a channel, and route 100 percent of the channel's signal through the effect, from which it flows through the rest of the channel's signal path. Because they're placed in series with the source material, insert effects are sometimes known as series, or serial, processors. **Fig. 10.13** shows the signal flow through an insert effect.

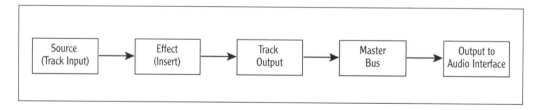

Fig. 10.13

When using an insert to add effects, 100 percent of the track's signal goes to the effects processor(s).

Common applications for inline effects include **dynamics processors**, such as compression, limiting, and gating; **equalization** and other filter effects; and any effect you need to limit to one channel at a time, such as **pitch correction**. Amplifier emulators are also typically used as inserts. In all these cases, 100 percent of the original signal passes through the effect.

Though they're more commonly used as send/return effects, you can also insert processors such as modulation, delay, and reverb into an individual channel. Unlike dynamics processors and EQs, these types of processors usually don't sound good with 100 percent of the signal passing through them. So if you use them as inserts, you'll probably want to use the effect's control panel to adjust the ratio between the original (or *dry*) signal and the affected (or *wet*) signal to get the appropriate sound.

SEND-AND-RETURN OR BUS EFFECTS

Unlike an insert effect, which works on one channel at a time, a bus effect can be applied to many channels at once. You use a send to route signal from a channel to an effects bus. Multiple channels can feed the bus simultaneously. This routing scheme is sometimes called *parallel* because both the channel and the send route the same signal to independent paths. **Fig. 10.14** shows how a parallel signal scheme works.

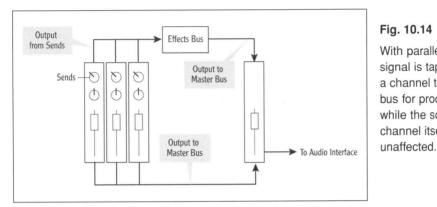

Fig. 10.14

With parallel routing, signal is tapped from a channel to an external bus for processing, while the sound in the channel itself remains unaffected.

A parallel bus is the most common way to add modulation and spatial effects like delay and reverb. You can also use a parallel bus to route signal for output to individual channels on your physical mixer, and more.

Fig. 10.15 shows how a channel can feed both series and parallel effects. As you can see from this illustration, the reverb is actually *inserted* into the effects bus. The amount of signal

Fig. 10.15

Feeding both serial (insert) and parallel (bus) effects.

feeding the reverb is controlled by the individual sends. In the example shown in **Fig. 10.15**, the guitar channel is sending more signal to the reverb than the vocal channel is.

ENABLING PLUG-INS

In most situations, the effects you assign to your mixes will be in the form of software plug-ins. Plug-ins can be added to individual channels (via channel inserts) or to buses (via the inserts on bus channels). In either case, you can insert more than one plug-in into a given channel, as shown in **Fig. 10.16**.

The mixers in Steinberg's Cubase and Nuendo programs have dedicated effects buses, as shown in **Fig. 10.17**. Here, you don't need to create a new auxiliary channel and assign it to a bus. You merely open the window and assign the effect.

Fig. 10.16

Adding multiple plug-ins to a Pro Tools channel.

Fig. 10.17

Creating an auxiliary channel for effects in Cubase 5.

INTERFACING WITH OUTBOARD GEAR

Another way to add effects is to use outboard hardware processors. If your audio system's latency is low enough, you can patch a hardware processor into your audio interface and incorporate it into your software mix.

There are several ways to do this. You can patch a piece of hardware directly into a channel or bus insert. You do this by routing the insert to one of your audio interface's outputs, as shown in **Fig. 10.18**.

Fig. 10.18

Adding an outboard hardware effects processor in Logic Pro.

You can also use a send to feed an outboard processor via your audio interface. You have two options for returning the outboard processor's output to your mix: 1) You can set up an input channel to receive the processor's output (see **Fig. 10.19**); or 2) If your studio includes a physical mixing board, you can simply patch the processor into an open channel on the physical board, and use the mixing board to blend the processor's signal with your sound card's output (see **Fig. 10.20**), then output it to a mixdown deck. The second option used to be standard, but since most users now bounce mixes internally—and have low enough latency to support the real-time routing of external processors — the first option has become more common. Once you're happy with the effects' settings, you can "print" the output of this effect processor to an audio channel assigned to a DAW track, thus eliminating the need to keep the outboard unit physically routed to your mix.

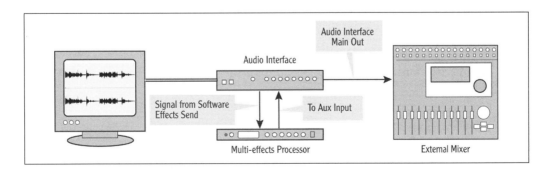

Fig. 10.19

You can use your interface's outputs (assigned to your DAW's sends) and inputs (used as returns) to add an outboard effect to your mix; this works best if the system has low latency.

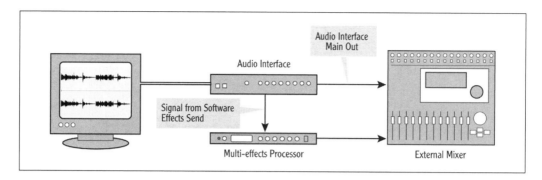

Fig. 10.20

An outboard mixer can be used to blend the sound of an effects processor with that of your audio interface.

▮ AUTOMATION

A finished multitrack mix will often involve making a lot of adjustments to individual channels as the song plays back. Perhaps the lead guitar needs to be louder on the solos and quieter on the fills, or the vocal needs more reverb at the end of the song. Maybe the acoustic guitars come in and out of the verse, and the bass and drums play a breakdown with all the other instruments muted. And what if the tone on the piano needs to be mellow during the intro and brighter later in the song? These are just some examples of the many small and large changes, or moves, that can be made over the course of a mix. And unless you're an octopus, you might have trouble executing all of them in real time. *Automation* allows you to record and edit mix moves so that they play back automatically. If you're mixing with a mouse, automation is a must.

REAL-TIME AUTOMATION

Real-time automation records your mixer moves as the track plays back. A typical software mixer lets you automate virtually all mix parameters, including a track's volume, pan position, EQ, the levels feeding sends, and the control settings of plug-ins.

Automation varies among applications, but the basic method goes like this:

- Set the mixer's controls at what you consider to be a good starting point. This should include the fader and pan positions for each channel, the effects settings, mute status, and so on. Don't worry if you're not sure whether these will be your final settings; you can change your mind later and adjust the mix.

- Enable the automation's **write** (or record) **mode** for each track you wish to automate and run through the mix. As soon as playback starts, the mixer will note the position of every control. If desired, adjust the channels as the song plays back.

- When you play the song back a second time, the mixer will return to the positions you set for the beginning of the song, and follow any moves you made with the controls during playback.

Once you make a pass, you can fine-tune your automated mix in several ways. During playback, you can select any and all channels and enable one of three "update" methods:

1. *Touch* mode changes the value of a control only while you hold it—when you release the control, it returns to its previous position.

2. *Latch* mode changes a control from the time you touch it until playback stops, even if you release the control during playback. Both touch and latch modes will only affect the parameters you select during the update pass. For example, if you touch-edit a send level, the fader, pan, and other settings will remain as they were when you first ran the mix.

3. *Overwrite* mode—which you do by putting the channel back into write mode—replaces *all* of the automation on the channel with new data.

EDITING AUTOMATION DATA

After you automate a mix parameter, you can edit the automation data by using your sequencer's controller edit tools, or by drawing automation settings, called *envelopes*, in the Arrange/Edit window. We'll look at this in more depth later in this chapter.

▉ MIXING MIDI TRACKS

So far we've focused mostly on audio mixing. However, MIDI instruments such as synthesizers and samplers can be mixed much the same way as audio tracks. These devices respond to control signals—MIDI controller #7 for volume, MIDI controller #10 for pan, and others—that can affect their sound in real time. **Fig. 10.21** shows a MIDI mixing module.

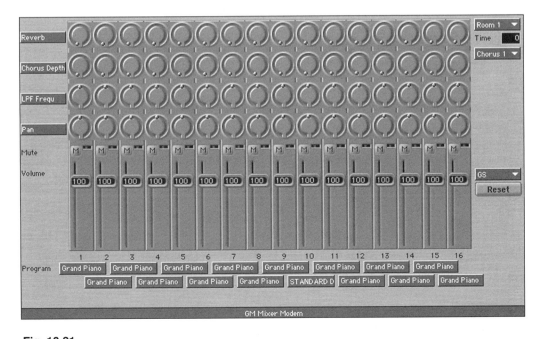

Fig. 10.21

MIDI mixing modules send control data, such as #7 (volume) and #10, pan, to MIDI devices.

You can blend the output from external MIDI instruments with your audio tracks by patching them, along with the output of your audio interface, into a physical mixer. You can also route them through auxiliary inputs in your software mixer.

Alternatively, you can "print" the audio output of your MIDI tracks to disk, creating an audio track to replace the MIDI track. This gives you the advantage of locking in the MIDI performance and freeing up the MIDI module for other tasks, as well as enabling you to add audio processing and effects on a permanent basis.

Software instruments (see Chapter 12) can actually be mixed in two ways. Because they're driven by MIDI data, they can respond to MIDI controls in the same way that external MIDI modules can. But because they're resident in your DAW and their sound is routed through your software's audio system, they can also be integrated into a mix and treated like regular audio tracks—which means they can be routed to the same effects buses, use the same plug-ins, and respond to the same automation data as your audio tracks.

TIP

Software instruments can use up a lot of computer processing power, and can therefore slow performance. To save computer resources, you can bounce the output of a software instrument to disk and import the resulting audio file into an audio track in your arrangement. You can then disable the software instrument, thereby freeing up resources. Another option is to use your DAW's "freeze" feature to temporarily lock the track into its current settings. A frozen track uses fewer resources, but cannot be edited. However, it can be unfrozen if you need to make changes.

■ Mixing from the Arrange/Edit Window

Software mixers are designed to look and work like hardware mixing consoles—that's why they sport user interfaces complete with faders and knobs. But the hardware model isn't always the most efficient way to work with computer-based tracks. After all, the hardware mixer was designed for the rigid world of wires and electrical signals, not the free-flowing world of the desktop studio.

Recently, software developers have started to move beyond the limitations imposed by physical recorders and mixers by integrating mixing tools into the editing and arranging sections of their software.

The editing process itself is a form of mixing. By dividing a track into regions, you can delete or mute parts within the arrangement independent of mixer settings. **Fig. 10.22** shows an example of a track with muted regions.

You can also use waveform-editing tools to create fades, change the level of audio files by normalizing and adjusting gain, or apply effects directly to the audio file by making destructive edits. Refer to Chapter 6 for more on these techniques.

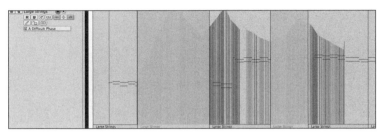

Fig. 10.22

A DAW's edit/arrange features can be used as part of a mix. Here, some parts of a MIDI track are muted (lighter gray).

In addition to performing these basic editing operations, many applications let you control your mixer directly from the Arrange/Edit window. Settings you make in this way are reflected in the Mixer window's controls. **Fig. 10.23** shows the Pro Tools edit screen with mix controls enabled.

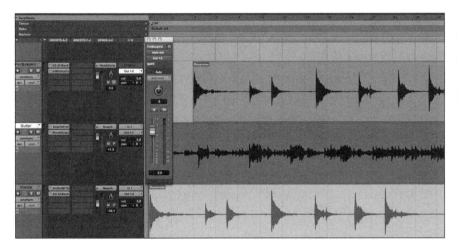

Fig. 10.23

Accessing mix controls directly from Pro Tools LE's Edit window.

DRAWING A MIX

If you want to move beyond the world of faders and pots, you can use your software's edit features to draw mix parameters onscreen. This can be done both to make changes to automation you generated in real time with the mixer's controls and to create new automation from scratch.

Before you edit mix data, you must be able to see it. Generally, a DAW will show data for any parameters that have been automated, but will only let you access one parameter at a time. Typically, a mini-menu associated with each track will allow you to choose what, if any, automation data is available for graphic editing. You can display parameters such as volume, pan, mute status, and plug-in and bus settings. **Fig. 10.24** shows a few automated tracks in Logic. Note that not all channels are displaying the same parameters. Because the mix data is superimposed over the audio waveform display, you can see how the parameters relate to the arrangement. And you can also use the Arrange window's locating tools to move quickly through a mix.

The drawing method doesn't give you the auditory feedback you get when you're moving faders, but it does make it easier to make precise moves. For example, it can be way easier to

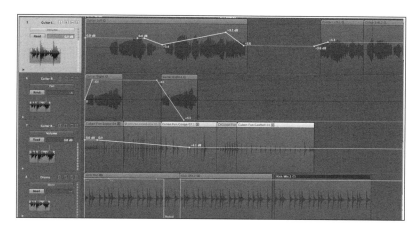

Fig. 10.24

Logic's track automation data on display. As with other DAWs, it lets you record and edit virtually every setting and move you make in a mix for perfect playback every time.

create a smooth fadeout or toggle a mute on and off by drawing these moves in the Arrange/Edit window.

Automation data can be cut, copied, and pasted just like other data in an arrangement. So, for example, you can draw a mute on one drum track, and copy it to all the others.

DISABLING AUTOMATION

Even if you're happy with the way a mix sounds after it's been stored in automation, you may want to disable the automated playback and hear the tracks "raw." For example, you've muted the first half of a guitar track, but have decided to add a new organ part and use the guitar for reference. Instead of erasing the automation data and starting over, you can take that track out of automation mode completely. It won't read the automation that's stored with it, and it won't overwrite the automation on playback. When you're ready, you can turn the track automation back on.

KEEPING ALTERNATIVE MIXES

Mixing is an art form, and like other arts, it is a combination of subjective judgment and objective skill. It's always good to listen to your mixes away from your studio on as many different playback systems as you can. It's also helpful to take a break from the mix, and to compare different versions.

You can keep alternative mixes by saving a new project file for each version of the mix, taking care not to overwrite the file containing a potential keeper. The disadvantage of this is that you have to reload the file every time you want to hear an alternative mix.

Some DAWs allow you to store more than one version of an automated mix similarly to the way you might have more than one take of a track. Refer to your software's documentation to see if and how it implements this useful feature.

SNAPSHOT AUTOMATION

Snapshot automation takes a complete picture of every setting on a mixer at a particular time. The term comes from the days of analog mixing, when engineers took actual photographs of the mixer to remember where they set the controls. Some DAWs include snapshot automation, but it's used less often than the dynamic automation described above.

SAVING MIXER SETTINGS FOR LATER RECALL

Many DAWs let you save complete mixer and channel settings and store them as a preset, similarly to the way a synthesizer or effects device can store a patch. These presets can then be recalled in any project opened by the software. For example, Logic (see **Fig. 10.25**) can store all a channel's settings, including the plug-ins inserted into the channel strip, how the controls on the plug-ins are set, which sends are enabled, etc. On software instrument tracks, these presets will also include the software instrument assigned to the track and the sound patch loaded into the instrument at the time it was saved.

Fig. 10.25

Storing all of a channel's settings for later recall.

As you can imagine, this is very handy for channel settings you use often, especially when they include more than one plug-in. If you always like to use a certain compressor or EQ on your vocal, or like to play guitar through a specific digital amp simulation, or favor a particular drum kit in your sampler, you can save tons of time when starting a new song by storing these preferences as presets.

■ HARDWARE CONTROLS FOR SOFTWARE MIXERS

Software mixers are powerful, but there's one thing about them that's almost universally despised: having to mix with a mouse. If you've had any experience with a traditional mixing console, you may find the mouse especially confining.

Hardware **control surfaces** put your software's faders, transport, and other controls under your fingertips. They can range in price from a few hundred to several thousand dollars, and in size from that of a notebook to that of a full-fledged mixing console.

Control surfaces fall into several categories. Pure control devices such as the Euphonix MC Control (see **Fig. 10.26**) and the Mackie Control have no (or few) audio features, and require a separate audio interface. However, these units can work with a wide range of software applications (yet because there's no standard for support, the performance may be more elegant with some software/control surface combinations than others).

These higher-end control surfaces boast motorized faders that move automatically to reflect the current settings in the software—an important feature if you want the control surface to behave like a traditional mixer. While a control surface is no requirement for computer-based mixing, it can speed the process greatly. Once you've worked with one, it's hard to go back to mixing with a mouse.

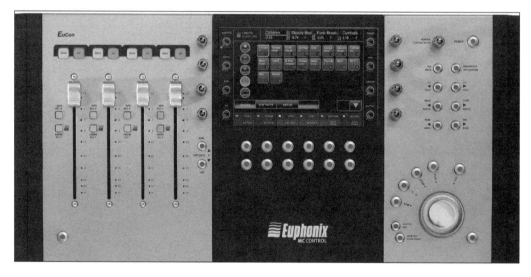

Fig. 10.26

Euphonix MC Control

Some control surfaces are designed for specific applications. Steinberg's CC121 (see **Fig. 10.27**) and Digidesign's Command|8 are two examples. The advantage of these units is that they can access a greater range of features from their respective applications, and also enjoy direct support from the software developers.

Other control devices include remote fader/transport units such as Novation's Remote Zero SL, CME's Bitstream 3D, and Korg's compact nanoKontrol (see **Fig. 10.28**), which is about the size of a QWERTY keyboard. These can be programmed to control specific functions on a software mixer (as well as other devices in your system, such as MIDI synthesizers). While these units lack the motorized faders of more elaborate motorized units, they can be cost-effective tools that you can use to free yourself from the limits of mixing with a mouse.

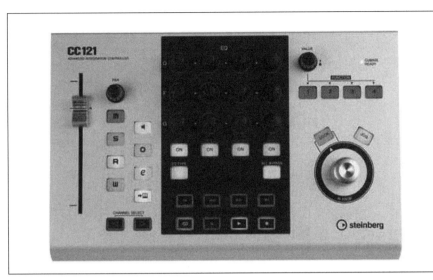

Fig. 10.27

Steinberg
CC121

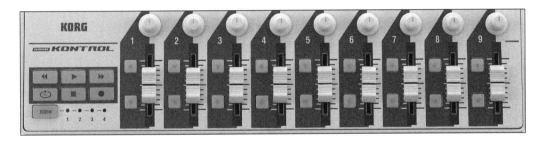

Fig. 10.28

Korg nanoKontrol

INTERFACE/CONTROL SURFACES

Some products combine an audio and MIDI interface with a control surface. Examples include Digidesign's popular 003 (see **Fig. 10.29**), M-Audio's ProjectMix I/O, Alesis's MasterControl, Yamaha's n12, and Cakewalk's Sonar V-Studio 700 (see **Fig. 10.30**). Some interface/control surfaces, like the Digidesign, M-Audio, and Cakewalk products, are designed for specific software, but can be used with other programs as well. Others, like the MasterControl and Tascam's FW-1884, are designed to be universal.

By mating control features with audio and MIDI I/O, these units centralize three important elements in your desktop studio. Their portability makes them ideal for laptop users.

The last category doesn't include control surfaces at all, but is composed of physical mixers, such as the Yamaha 01V96CM and Tascam DM-3200. In addition to offering full-featured audio mixing independent of the computer, these devices can transmit MIDI control messages to your software mixer.

Fig. 10.29

Digidesign 003

Fig. 10.30

Sonar V-Studio 700

Then there are consoles like PreSonus's Studio|Live 16.4.2, which are designed to act as stand-alone mixers but which also include FireWire data output as either a standard or optional feature, allowing them to double as interfaces.

To take full advantage of a control surface, your application must have the appropriate driver to map the controller's messages to the software's functions. If your software doesn't directly support your control surface, you may be able to program, or map, your control surface commands to specific software features. Most applications can assign remote MIDI messages to a variety of commands.

As control surfaces have become more plentiful, they have also become more affordable. The key to choosing one is to learn as much as possible about how it works with the software you have. Can all the controls on the control surface be used with your DAW? How easy is it to access secondary parameters, such as plug-in settings? Can the control surface be used for editing and transport? If so, how flexibly? Does the display show what's on your tracks? Can you navigate through different windows and access menus, or will you still need to make frequent use of the mouse and keyboard? If the control surface has motorized faders, how durable is its engine? If it includes an audio interface, how good are its A/D converters, how flexible is its routing, and how stable are its drivers?

If possible, physically test the control surface the same way you would an instrument. Go on user groups and ask around. Because of their complexity, you may not have a real picture of how well a control surface works for you until you've owned it a while, so every bit of pre-purchase research helps.

FINAL OUTPUT

The ultimate goal of producing audio in the multitrack environment is to create a work that you can distribute to your friends, fans, and clients. This final distillation of your work is called the mix, or **master**.

There are two ways to create a final master: 1) by printing to an external recorder, called a mixdown deck; or 2) by recording the mix internally to disk. The latter is also known as *bouncing*. In either case, your first step is to prepare the mix by setting levels, adding effects, and if necessary, automating your moves until the mix is exactly as you want it. If you wish to create several mixes for the same project, you can save each version individually.

PRINTING YOUR MIX TO AN EXTERNAL RECORDER

If you're using an external mastering deck, you must route the output of your audio interface (as well as any outboard instruments and processors that are part of your project) to the input of the mixdown deck. The ideal way to do this is to use a hardware mixer that consolidates signal from your audio interface, outboard effects, sound modules, etc. Some producers will "print" their final mix to analog tape using this method.

PRINTING YOUR MIX TO DISK (BOUNCING)

You don't need an outboard mastering deck to print a finished mix. By bouncing your mix to disk, you can create an audio file that will serve as your master. This audio file encompasses all the mixing moves you've created. You can create this audio file in a number of formats—including MP3—for distribution.

Typical bounce parameters include:

File Type: The format of the audio file(s) to be generated. Typically, it will be in AIFF, WAV, or MP3 format, but other formats may be supported as well.

Resolution: The bit depth of the output file; typically for AIFFs and WAVs, you'll be choosing between 24 and 16 bits.

Sample Rate: If you're bouncing mixes for CD, export to 44.1 kHz (16-bit). Otherwise, the sample rate is up to you. Remember, a higher bit depth and sample rate generally yield better sound, but use up more disk space.

Range: The parts of the project that will be included in the bounce. Check this setting carefully: sometimes the software will automatically set the bounce range to the loop/cycle range you have active. Of course, if that's the part you want to bounce, then that's a good thing.

Channels: Typical options include stereo interleaved (one file with two channels); stereo dual mono (two related mono files, each containing one side of the stereo mix); surround (separate files for each channel in the surround format you've chosen); and mono.

Destination: Where the bounce file will be written.

After you've bounced the mix, give it a listen. Be sure that there's no clipping, that all of the edits you've made sound clean, and that all of the mix moves sound smooth. From here, these mix files can be further edited (if necessary), mastered, burned onto CD (see Chapter 13), prepared for Internet distribution, and even imported back into your project.

BOUNCING TO STEMS

In some professional situations, a client may want the option of adjusting specific parts of a mix after you've finished it. They may ask you to provide *stems*, or individual tracks from the mix, each bounced to its own file. You may be asked to create one stem for each track, or to only deliver stems for specific groups of instruments.

To create a stem, solo the track or tracks you want to include in the stem (or mute the tracks you *don't* want in the stem) and bounce as you would a complete mix. Take some extra time to clearly name each file to show both the song title and the tracks contained in the stem.

TIP

Always include a complete mix of the song along with the stems. Store all the stems, and the complete mix, together in one folder.

▨ MOVING ON

Mixing in the software environment is just another step in the desktop production process and involves elements of arranging, editing, sound design, and mastering. As you build your mix, you'll be calling on the techniques we discussed in Chapters 5, 6, and 9. To learn more about polishing your masters, see Chapter 13. Next, however, we're going to look at some tools for bringing your audio tracks to life: plug-ins.

CHAPTER 11:   SOFTWARE SIGNAL PROCESSORS

A *plug-in* is a helper application that enhances the performance of a larger software program, or **host**. Think of it as a modification; like adding extra horsepower to your sports car. In fact, plug-ins are common in all types of software. Your Internet browser, for example, uses plug-ins to help it read multimedia files.

▨ PLUG-INS AND AUDIO

In audio circles, the term *plug-in* is often used as a synonym for "effect" or "signal processor." In the hardware world, a **signal processor** is a device that alters an audio signal in real time. Just as a virtual mixer is a software version of a hardware mixer, a plug-in is a software version of a hardware effects device.

In this chapter, we'll focus on plug-ins that are used to provide effects such as reverb, delay, dynamics processing, EQ, and others. Another category of plug-ins, software instruments, is covered in Chapter 12.

A set of basic effects is often included with DAWs, 2-track editors, and loop construction applications. In fact, these days even notation software, such as Sibelius 5, can include some onboard audio processing. Some software instruments also include "internal" effects processing, such as reverb, chorus, or delay, which can be used to "sweeten" the sounds the instrument produces.

NATIVE PLUG-INS

A *native* plug-in is powered by a computer's internal processor and can work independently of external hardware. Its performance is affected by the speed of your computer. Common native formats include Steinberg's cross-platform **VST** (Virtual Studio Technology); Apple's Audio Units, or AU (compatible with a range of Mac OS X applications); Microsoft's **DirectX** (for Windows; DXi is the software instrument version); MOTU's **MAS** (MOTU Audio System for Mac OS); and Digidesign's **RTAS** (Real Time Audio Suite, for Windows and Macs running Pro Tools). Linux users can find some VST support, as well as the LV2 format.

Many applications also provide what one might consider to be "internal" plug-ins: effects that will only run within that application. Logic, for example, comes with a wide range of audio effects and instruments that will only run in that application. Similarly, Live, Digital Performer, Pro Tools, and Cubase include a series of effects that will only run within their respective programs.

DSP-BASED PLUG-INS

DSP, which is short for *digital signal processing*, actually has two meanings when it comes to plug-ins. The first is self-explanatory—every plug-in is in itself a digital signal processor. The second meaning refers to the hardware technology used to drive the plug-in. DSP plug-in formats do not use the computer's native processor, but instead utilize digital signal processors contained on an expansion unit attached to the computer. The most popular example is Digidesign's **Pro Tools HD** format, which will only run on specific Digidesign hardware. Unlike native plug-ins, DSP plug-in performance is less dependent on the computer's processor.

NATIVE POWERED PLUG-INS

Powered plug-ins offer a compromise between native and hardware DSP systems. A powered plug-in uses external DSP hardware to process effects—but operates in a native environment, such as VST, AU, RTAS, and DirectX.

The external device can be connected to the computer via FireWire or an expansion card. Examples include TC Electronic's PowerCore family (see **Fig. 11.1**), Universal Audio's UAD series, and Solid State Logic's Duende series. Each of these products comes in a range of FireWire and PCI/PCIe formats and includes special versions of native plug-ins that can run within any compatible host software.

Currently, these devices will only run effects that are specifically written for them. In other words, you can run TC Electronic's Mega Reverb on the PowerCore from within Logic, Cubase, Live, and so on. But you can't use the PowerCore with, say, Logic's native Platinum Reverb.

Fig. 11.1

TC Electronic's PowerCore Compact is an example of a "powered" plug-in platform (repeat 10x fast).

Note: Some third-party developers do write plug-ins for these powered formats. Sonox, for example, offers a range of high-end processors for PowerCore.

PLUG-IN HOSTING HARDWARE

Another type of hardware support comes with devices like the Muse Receptor 2 (see **Fig. 11.2**), which can host and operate compatible VST plug-ins (including both signal processors and instruments) without a computer. Think of it as a multichannel rack effects device that you can customize by adding effects modularly. The Receptor can be connected to other gear via analog or digital audio cables, and can also be connected to a computer via an Ethernet network cable; in this configuration, it is designed to integrate directly into a DAW.

Fig. 11.2

The Muse Receptor 2 can host VST plug-ins without a computer.

In addition to including some plug-ins with the device, Muse offers an application that allows users to install VST plug-ins they already own and run them from Receptor.

SM Pro Audio's V-Machines come in compact tabletop, rack, and guitar pedalboard versions, and can also host Windows-based VST effects and instrument plug-ins for use away from the computer.

■ REAL-TIME VS. OFFLINE

Most plug-ins can work in two ways. In *real time*, they function the same way as a conventional hardware signal processor—the plug-in is applied to the signal as it plays back *without* changing the actual audio data. With a real-time plug-in, you're free to make adjustments at any time. You activate real-time plug-ins by "instantiating" them into a mixer channel or effects bus by using the respective channel's insert slots (see Chapter 10).

The disadvantage of using a real-time plug-in is that it taxes the computer's processor (or, in the case of a DSP-based plug-in, the DSP resources). The more real-time plug-ins you activate at one time, the more strain you'll put on your system.

Offline plug-ins permanently alter the audio file. Because this process is done in the background, an offline plug-in uses much less processing headroom than a real-time plug-in. You can preview the sound and make adjustments before committing it to disk. Most offline plug-ins automatically make backups of your original, "clean" audio data, allowing you to return to the source if you don't want to keep the newly processed version. Some software multitracks let you apply plug-ins in both real time and offline.

TIP
Freezing Real-Time Plug-ins

DAWs that offer a "freeze" feature can help you save computer resources while allowing the flexibility inherent in real-time processing. When you're happy with the plug-in's settings, freeze the track. The computer will make a temporary audio file reflecting the effects settings, and use that for playback. This frees up the processing resources that would have been used on that channel's plug-ins. If you want to make changes, unfreeze the track. Refer to Chapter 10 for more on freezing.

■ CHOOSING A PLUG-IN FORMAT

Choosing the correct plug-in format is usually done by default—any format that's compatible with your host software will work.

One of the great things about plug-ins is their versatility. Most can be used in a number of situations. For example, the same DirectX plug-ins that work in a loop-production/sequencing program such as Cakewalk's Sonar will also work in Sony's Vegas Video A/V production package, as well as Steinberg's WaveLab digital waveform editor.

Today, many developers offer their products in all native formats at once. So you can install a reverb you bought in RTAS format for Pro Tools LE, but the AU version (usable in Live, Logic, and others) and the VST version for Cubase are also included in the same installer.

PLUG-INS AND SYSTEM PERFORMANCE

No single element in your desktop studio taxes your system resources as much as real-time plug-ins. In general, the faster your computer's processor, the better real-time performance you'll get from native plug-ins. Hardware-based plug-ins are less dependent upon CPU power, but they do require an additional investment. If you have a slower machine and are on a budget, you can get by with offline plug-ins.

Some effects use more processing power than others. A complex reverb plug-in will tax your system more heavily than a simple stereo delay. The key to getting the best performance out of your system is to know how much of a drain each plug-in puts on your CPU, and to use the hogs sparingly. Your software's system performance meter will tell you how your computer is holding up (see **Fig. 11.3**).

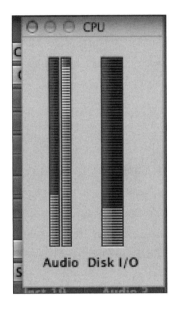

Fig. 11.3

A DAW's performance meter keeps you apprised of available system resources.

INSTALLING PLUG-INS

Because plug-ins are designed to work within the host software, they must reside within the same folder or directory as your audio software, or inside your system folder (as shown in **Fig. 11.4**), unless otherwise specified by the manufacturer.

▼ Library	Feb 22, 2009, 4:55 PM	--	Folder	
▶ Address Book Plug-Ins	Nov 8, 2008, 10:09 PM	--	Folder	
▶ Application Support	Yesterday, 11:38 PM	--	Folder	
▼ Audio	Apr 14, 2009, 11:37 PM	--	Folder	
▶ Apple Loops	Jun 21, 2007, 1:30 AM	--	Folder	
▶ Apple Loops Index	Feb 3, 2008, 11:56 PM	--	Folder	
▶ Impulse Responses	Apr 3, 2007, 3:44 AM	--	Folder	
▶ MIDI Configurations	Oct 11, 2007, 11:36 PM	--	Folder	
▶ MIDI Devices	Mar 29, 2009, 1:09 PM	--	Folder	
▶ MIDI Drivers	Apr 14, 2009, 11:37 PM	--	Folder	
▶ MIDI Patch Names	Jul 8, 2008, 1:05 PM	--	Folder	
▼ Plug-Ins	Apr 14, 2009, 11:37 PM	--	Folder	
▼ Components	Today, 1:14 AM	--	Folder	
247C Limiting Amplifier Mono.component	Feb 8, 2008, 2:48 AM	3.5 MB	Pro Tools Plug-In	
247C Limiting Amplifier.component	Feb 8, 2008, 2:48 AM	3.5 MB	Pro Tools Plug-In	
Absynth 3.component	Jan 20, 2008, 11:26 AM	11.4 MB	Pro Tools Plug-In	
Absynth 4.component	Mar 22, 2008, 1:33 PM	48.2 MB	Pro Tools Plug-In	
AkoustikPiano.component	Mar 22, 2008, 1:35 PM	52.2 MB	Pro Tools Plug-In	

Fig. 11.4

Plug-ins in Mac OS X's Library folder.

You add new plug-ins to your studio by placing them in this plug-ins folder. In the old days, you'd have to repeat this process for every host application, but today's operating systems do a better job of collecting plug-ins and making them available to all compatible hosts on your computer. This is especially helpful when you're adding or upgrading a host program such as a DAW; it will find the existing plug-ins in your system.

You can organize your effects by creating subfolders based on brand, effects type, or any other criteria you find useful. Some plug-ins, such as the Waves bundle, operate under a *shell*—a software bridge between your host software and the plug-ins themselves. The company feels the shell allows it to build more efficient plug-ins. You install the shell into your plug-ins folder, and the shell accesses the actual processors that reside in a separate folder in your system. This makes it easier to share them among a number of applications.

LAUNCHING OR INSTANTIATING PLUG-INS

If you've had any experience patching together audio equipment, then you already understand the concept of patching an outboard processor into a signal path. To use a real-time plug-in, you must first assign it to a track's insert or to an effects bus. (See Chapter 10 for a description of tracks, inserts, and buses.)

Your software looks in the plug-ins folder for all the available choices. Simply select the one you want, and you're ready to get started. **Fig. 11.5** shows an effects insert menu; as you can see, a wide array of choices are available. Selecting the plug-in by name places it in the insert slot and turns it on.

Fig. 11.5
Logic's effects insert menu.

PLUG-INS AS BUS EFFECTS

When you want to assign a plug-in—such as reverb—to a number of different channels, you should use an effects bus, as described in Chapter 10. **Fig. 11.6** shows a typical effects bus.

When you're working with a bus effect like reverb, you should set the effects mix to 100 percent effect (or "wet"). You can control the amount of effect applied to each track with the send control; the fader on the auxiliary bus determines the effect's output level.

PLUG-INS AS INSERT EFFECTS

Reverb and delay work well as bus effects, but other signal processors, like compression and EQ, are better employed as inserts on individual channels (see **Fig. 11.7**). In addition to the typical insert applications we just mentioned, you can also use channel inserts to add ambient and spatial effects; in this case, you must adjust the effects mix within the plug-in.

Fig. 11.6 (far left)

An effects bus in Pro Tools LE.

Fig. 11.7

Compression and EQ are commonly inserted into the channel strips of individual tracks (Logic Pro shown).

CHAINING EFFECTS TOGETHER

Because software mixers usually have four or more inserts available per channel, you can chain plug-in effects together to create more complex sounds. For example, you might add EQ, compression, and pitch correction to a vocal channel; or a gate, EQ, and limiter to a drum channel. You might create a bus effect with delay, reverb, chorus, and compression, all in a series.

Note that you can insert any plug-in into any available slot; you don't need to start with the top one. Why does this matter? Some effects work better early in the signal chain, others later. You might want to add a compressor, for example, in the second slot and leave the first one free in case you want to insert an EQ later.

You can also move effects in the chain after they've been inserted. Some DAWs allow you to store effects chains as mixer channel presets. These presets can be used to instantly load the effects chain on other channels within the current project, or to load it into the mix of another project. Refer to Chapter 10 for more on mixer presets.

ADDING EFFECTS "OFFLINE"

Offline plug-ins can accomplish many of the same audio tasks as real-time plug-ins, without using as much computing power. Offline processing is a good choice when you're sure about the sound you want from an effect, because there's no disadvantage to making the effect permanent. You can also use offline processing to apply an effect to a specific region within a track without touching the others, as shown in **Fig. 11.8**. This can sometimes be more efficient than using mix automation to accomplish a similar goal.

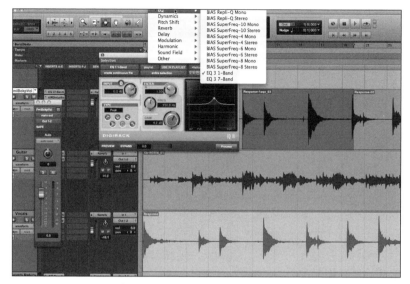

Fig. 11.8

Adding an effect offline creates a new version of the audio region with the effect permanently in place. This lets you save system resources and apply processing only to specific parts of a track or region.

TYPES OF SIGNAL PROCESSORS

While there are literally hundreds of plug-ins on the market, most of them fall into common audio-processing categories. Here's a brief rundown of the most common processors and what they're used for.

DYNAMIC EFFECTS

Dynamics processors include compressors, limiters, gates, and expanders. They're usually used as insert effects to process one track at a time at 100 percent wet.

COMPRESSORS AND LIMITERS

A compressor reduces the dynamic range (the difference between loud and soft signals) by attenuating (making quieter) any signal that exceeds a threshold. **Compression** is one of the most important processors in audio production, and can be used on almost any source during tracking and mixdown.

Limiting is similar to compression, but reduces the dynamic range by stopping the signal from exceeding a specific level. Limiters are used in mastering, on mix outputs, and on individual tracks.

Multiband compressor/limiters divide an audio signal into *bands* based on frequency range, and allow you to set the processing for each. You can, for example, apply more compression to the midrange than to the bass and treble. Multiband processors are most commonly used in mastering or on the main output of a mixer prior to bouncing/mixdown.

Important parameters include:

Threshold: Sets the signal level that will trigger the processor. Any signal that's above the threshold gets attenuated; anything quieter than the threshold level is untouched.

Ratio: Governs the amount of attenuation in the signal above the threshold. The higher the ratio, the more pronounced the compression.

Knee: Determines how pronounced the compressor's effect will be. Soft knee is gentler than hard knee.

Attack and Release Time: Determine how quickly the compressor will engage (attack) and how long it will remain in effect (release, or hold) when the signal crosses the threshold.

Gain: Input gain controls the level of the signal fed to the circuit; output gain controls the final level after processing.

GATES AND EXPANDERS

While compressors and limiters reduce the level of signal *above* a set threshold, a **gate** (or **noise gate**) mutes any signal that falls below a set threshold. Gates can be used to eliminate unwanted low-level noises, and to create special effects, such as gated reverb. An **expander** increases the dynamic range by reducing the level of any signal that falls below the threshold, while leaving signal above the threshold intact.

Like compressors and limiters, gates and expanders let you fine-tune their response by adjusting the attack and release times. Many digital gates have a "look ahead" feature that lets them anticipate attacks that cross the threshold for more accurate response.

EQUALIZATION AND FILTER EFFECTS

Equalization is a fancy way of saying "tone control." You'll find many types of equalization, or **EQ**, in the digital world. "Filtering" is another way of saying EQ.

GRAPHIC EQ

In a graphic equalizer, a slider controls each area of the frequency spectrum. With a standard graphic EQ, the frequencies are fixed, but with most software versions, you can set the bands to any value that fits the current application.

PARAMETRIC EQ

Each band of a parametric EQ (see **Fig. 11.9**) gives you control over three parameters: the center frequency, bandwidth, and boost/cut level. Bandwidth or "Q" determines how frequencies near the center are affected. A wider bandwidth affects a larger frequency range; a narrow bandwidth focuses more closely on the center frequency. Narrow-bandwidth frequency control (especially attenuation) is sometimes called notch filtering.

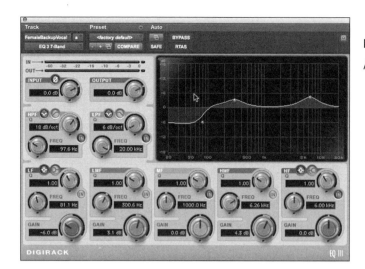

Fig. 11.9

A parametric EQ

SHELVING, BAND-PASS, AND OTHER EQS

Graphic and parametric EQs are versatile tools, but other types of EQs and filters can be simpler to use, and may better suit your application. **Shelving EQ** affects signal above or below a specific frequency, or hinge point. A typical example would be the high band of a mixer's three-band EQ section.

A *low-pass* (or hi-cut) *filter* attenuates frequencies *above* the specified hinge point. Lower frequencies pass through—hence the name. A *high-pass* (or lo-cut) *filter* attenuates frequencies *below* the hinge point.

A *band-pass filter* processes frequencies above and below the specified frequency range.

An *auto filter* is an EQ that changes over time. You can use an auto filter to create wah-like effects.

GAIN EFFECTS

Gain effects control the loudness of an input signal; at they're simplest, they can be used to make a quiet track sound louder with no other changes.

But gain effects can also be used for audio coloration. Distortion units, overdrives, and fuzz boxes—all of which boost gain to cause audio overload—are essential items for electric guitarists, and can also be used on bass, keyboards, synthesizers, and even vocals. Their main parameters are gain, which governs how much distortion the effect will produce, tone (or EQ) to adjust the frequency balance of the sound, and level, which determines how loud the post-distortion signal will be.

MODULATION EFFECTS

Modulation effects include chorus, flanger, phaser, rotary speaker, tremolo, and vibrato. Modulation effects are used for sweetening—adding a little bit of flavor to an otherwise static sound. These types of effects are most commonly used on electric guitar, bass, and keyboard instruments, though they can also be effective on vocals, acoustic guitars, and even drums.

They're called modulation effects because they alter some element of the sound—such as its pitch, amplitude, or frequency response—over time, usually in a cyclical manner. Parameters include the speed, or rate, of the modulation; the depth, or intensity, of the effect; and the mix between the effected and dry signals.

Modulation can also be applied to spatial effects; some reverb and delay plug-ins have modulation parameters built in.

PITCH SHIFTING

As the name suggests, *pitch shifting* is used to change the pitch of an incoming signal. A basic pitch shifter can transpose a mono voice up or down by a specific interval. When transposing, pitch shifters raise and lower pitch in half-step increments. This signal can be mixed with the original to create a harmony, or be used on its own to transpose the melody. While basic pitch shifters transpose a signal by a fixed interval, *intelligent pitch shifters* can create diatonic harmonies by adjusting the interval to match a given scale.

Pitch shifters can also work in subdivisions of a half step, called *cents* (there are 100 cents in a half step). Altering the pitch by a few cents and mixing it with the original can yield a chorus-like effect that can be used similarly to other modulation effects.

Pitch shifting, when it's applied to vocals, can take a voice outside of its natural range. A feature call *formant shifting* can change the quality of the vocal sound, for example, making a male voice sound female, and vice versa. This allows you to generate a multi-voice background part from one source track.

PITCH CORRECTION

One of the most popular effects in the desktop studio (and, many would argue, the most abused) is *pitch correction*. This technology was pioneered by Antares with Auto-Tune (see **Fig. 11.10**)—"auto-tuning" has become sort of a generic term for pitch correction—but is

Fig. 11.10

Antares Auto-Tune

now available from a number of developers and is included with such programs as Cubase and Logic Pro.

Pitch correction software can analyze an incoming signal and "quantize" it to conform to a preset scale, which can be chromatic, diatonic, or customized. Even some non-Western scales are supported. The processor can be set to operate on all pitches passing through it or only on notes that you find particularly problematic. Other controls determine the speed at which the processor operates (slower speeds allow for more variation leading up to a note; fast speeds can produce a robot-like effect) and how much human variation will remain intact.

While some pitch correctors work only as real-time processors, Auto-Tune can also operate in a graphical mode that allows you to draw in the desired pitch correction (see **Fig. 11.11**).

As of this writing, Auto-Tune and similar programs are designed to operate on monophonic material—such as a voice, violin, or horn—producing one note at a time. They are not effective on chords.

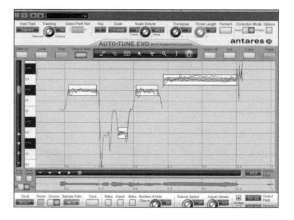

Fig. 11.11

Auto-Tune's graphics mode lets users "draw" in the correct pitches for errant notes.

Celemony's Melodyne offers another approach to graphical pitch editing/correction, in which pitches are treated like MIDI notes, which can be both corrected and transposed. Melodyne can work as a stand-alone application or as a plug-in via the Melodyne Bridge. At press time, a version of Melodyne capable of processing polyphonic material—chords—was about to become available.

Cubase 5's VariAudio feature, which is part of its Sample Editor section, also offers MIDI-like pitch editing.

DELAY

You can use delay, or echo (see **Fig. 11.12**), to create doubling effects (short delay), slap-back effects (medium delay), or long, repeating echoes (long delay). Combined with modulation effects, delay can be used to paint lush audio landscapes. It can be applied to everything from guitars to synths to vocals. Even some drum tracks can sound good running through a delay.

Parameters include delay time, which controls the amount of time between the initial signal and the repeats; **feedback**, which controls the number of repeats; and **mix**. Many plug-in delays can be set to play in sync with your tracks, automatically setting the delay interval to a musical value such as a quarter note or dotted 16th note.

Fig. 11.12

A delay processor can be used to create echo effects and more.

There are several different types of delay. *Mono delay* sends the original and delayed signals through the same output. *Stereo delay* lets you set separate delay times for each channel. *Ping-pong delay* bounces the delayed signal between the left and right channels. *Panning delay* gradually pans the delay across the stereo spectrum. *Tape delay* and *modulation delay* process the delayed signal to simulate the sound of a tape-based delay device. *Multitap delay* lets you set up a number of different delay intervals to create a more complex sound.

Reverb is probably the most widely used effect in recording. It creates a dimensional space around the input signal. Different reverb types, or **algorithms**, simulate different spaces, such as **rooms**, **halls**, and **chambers**, as well as "artificial" types of reverb, like **plates** and **spring** units.

Reverb parameters include **predelay**, which controls the amount of time it takes before the reverberant signal is heard; **reverb time**, which determines the length of the reverb's decay; **early reflections**, which set the delay time and loudness of the first echoes in a reverberant sound; gate, which can be used to abruptly cut off the reverb's decay; and **EQ**, or **frequency adjust**, which determines how the reverb will respond to specific frequencies.

Convolution reverbs (see **Fig. 11.13**) are designed to simulate the acoustical characteristics of a specific space. Instead of using basic algorithms, they base their sound on a short sample,

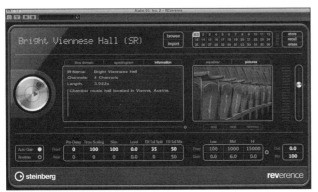

Fig. 11.13

Convolution reverbs emulate the ambience of actual physical spaces.

called an *impulse*, that is used to create a sonic footprint, which is then applied to a new sound. In a way, it's like sampling: an impulse taken from a famous concert hall would replicate that space's acoustics.

AMP SIMULATORS

Amp simulators are designed to emulate all of the parts of a guitar or bass player's setup, including the amplifier, speakers, and effects. In their complexity, they're almost like software instruments, because each amp simulator program involves many sub-processes at the same time. Like software instruments, most amp simulators can be used both as plug-ins and as stand-alone processors. The latter feature allows them to be used in live performance without a DAW host.

An amp simulator's main job is to imitate, or *model*, the sound of a real tube or solid-state amplifier. Most programs come with algorithms designed to model a range of classic and new models from a variety of amp manufacturers. The available controls change, depending on the amp being modeled, and are usually designed to be as close to the original as possible.

Some versions of this modeling software specialize in the sound of a particular manufacturer's amps (for example, IK Multimedia's AmpliTube Fender, designed with Fender's input, only offers Fender amp models), or specialize in a specific genre. But most of the time they try to be as comprehensive as possible.

In addition to amps, these modeling plug-ins simulate speaker cabinets, stompbox-type effects, rack-type effects, built-in tuners, and other processors that guitarists and bassists might find useful, such as tape loop simulators, phrase trainers, and so on.

Some of the most popular products include Native Instruments' Guitar Rig (see **Fig. 11.14**), IK Multimedia's AmpliTube, Line 6's POD Farm, Peavey Electronics' ReValver, and Waves' GTR3.

Fig. 11.14

Native Instruments' Guitar Rig 3

Fig. 11.15

Native Instruments'
Guitar Rig controller
(top) and IK
Multimedia's Stomp I/O
(bottom) offer pedal-
board-like control over
their respective virtual
amps and double as
audio routers.

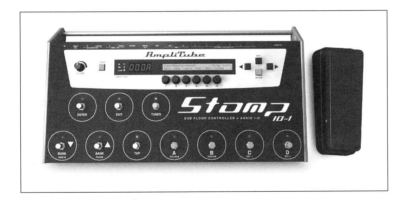

Amp simulators can be mated to special foot controllers (see **Fig. 11.15**) that allow guitarists and bassists the kind of control they get from their hardware pedalboards. These devices, which typically connect to the computer via USB, often include audio interface functions as well.

You can custom-build an effects chain within the plug-in; for example, you can use a fuzztone and wah-wah pedal to feed an amp, use that amp's controls to add reverb, send the amp to a speaker cabinet with a virtual mic of your choosing, and then run the mic through a studio compressor and delay. This frees you from having to insert these effects after the amp simulator in your DAW, but it's also one reason why amp simulators are especially greedy when it comes to CPU resources.

USING EXTERNAL CONTROLLERS

Control surfaces can make editing plug-ins much easier than having to use a mouse. Often, getting the right setting on an audio effect involves changing a number of parameters, which interact to produce the final result. Being able to grab a knob and adjust more than one of these parameters at once can save you a lot of time.

Many plug-ins also respond to MIDI messages generated by keyboard controllers and other MIDI devices. You can often assign a controller to change a specific parameter or range of parameters within a plug-in. While this may take a little more preparation than using a control surface, it's a useful alternative when a control surface is not available.

WORKING WITH PRESETS

Plug-ins—like the hardware processors they emulate—offer a dizzying array of parameters. But computers, being the data-storing powerhouses that they are, are good at keeping track of those parameters.

Most plug-in interfaces allow you to store presets for later recall. This is a great way to share plug-in settings between projects or tracks within a project. For example, I've set up some specific compressor and EQ plug-ins that seem to work well on my electric bass. Whenever I work on a new bass track, I start with one of those presets. I usually need to tweak it a bit to fit the project, but having a starting point saves me time.

TIP

Storing a preset within a plug-in, as opposed to saving the channel strip configuration as outlined previously, has one advantage: if the plug-in works with more than one host in your system, the preset will be available on all of them. Of course, you can do both—save your plug-in presets and save your channel strips. That will make you impressively organized.

AUTOMATING PLUG-INS

Like other components in your computer mixing system, plug-in parameters can be automated (for more on automation, see Chapter 10). This allows you to make dynamic changes in your sound as the music plays back.

One of the simplest and most effective ways to use plug-in automation is to toggle the effect between active and bypass status. For example, you might activate a delay effect during a guitar solo, but leave it off when the guitar is playing the verses.

More complex operations, like changing the wet/dry mix, delay time, or modulation speed, can also work well, though sometimes there can be some weird audio artifacts as the changes take place.

As with other mix parameters, effects automation can be entered in real time or graphically (see **Fig. 11.16**).

BOUNCING TO DISK

Earlier in this chapter we discussed the toll that some plug-ins can take on your computer's processor. The truth is, no matter how powerful your system is, you'll find yourself running

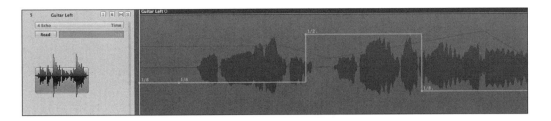

Fig. 11.16

Like other mixer parameters, effects settings can be automated to change as the mix plays back. Here, delay time is changed from an eighth note to a half note and back

up against your CPU's limitations more often than you would like. We discussed the use of offline processors as a way of getting more out of slower computers. Another solution is to bounce down the output from effects plug-ins to audio tracks.

First, set up the tracks you want to bounce with all their processing in place. Assign them to an output on your software mixer. You can send them to a bus, or to the main outputs. If you choose the main outs, make sure no other tracks are playing back during the bounce process—otherwise, they'll be recorded along with the intended tracks.

Next, use your audio production software's Bounce command to record a new audio file. You can have the software automatically add the bounced file to your project's audio pool or bin, making it easy to find and drag into your arrangement. (Otherwise, you will have to search for the file on disk and import it into the project—an extra step or two.)

Start the bounce. With some software, you'll hear the audio file play back as the bounce occurs. Other programs do the bounce offline. When the bounce is complete, you can import the new file in place of the old, removing the plug-ins from the corresponding tracks. The original file is untouched; if you don't like the results of the bounce, you can go back and try it again.

LATENCY AND PLUG-INS

Audio plug-ins—especially those that use hardware processing—can introduce latency into the audio signal chain. This can be subtle or very audible, especially when powered plug-ins are applied to input channels.

Some DAWs can compensate for this problem automatically (look for a setting such as "plug-in delay compensation"). But you may need to manually compensate for the latency by delaying by a few milliseconds the tracks that are *not* using the offending plug-ins. This is an evolving issue that has many variables (e.g., the plug-in platform, the host software, the computer's capabilities, etc.), so there's no one correct way to address it. But you should consider how to resolve this issue in relation to your own setup.

■ Moving On

We're almost at the end of our production process. Once you record and edit your tracks, apply effects, and mix them down, you're ready to go on to mastering. But first, there's one other software area that links audio and MIDI technology: the software instrument, coming up in Chapter 12.

CHAPTER 12:   SOFTWARE INSTRUMENTS

IN THIS CHAPTER
- ▓ SOFTWARE INSTRUMENT FORMATS
- ▓ LAUNCHING A SOFTWARE INSTRUMENT
- ▓ AUDIO ROUTING FOR SOFTWARE INSTRUMENTS
- ▓ TYPES OF SOFTWARE INSTRUMENTS
- ▓ BUILDING AND MANAGING SOUND LIBRARIES
- ▓ MIXING STRATEGIES

Since the early days of computer-based audio, the marketing folks responsible for driving software off the shelves have called the computer a "musical instrument." The scary thing is that these days, they're right. Software can be used to emulate the performance of hardware instruments such as synthesizers, drum machines, samplers, organs, and pianos.

But like plug-in effects—which aren't constrained by the hardware limitations imposed on conventional signal processors—software instruments can give you capabilities that outstrip the original devices they're modeled after.

▓ SOFTWARE INSTRUMENT FORMATS

Software instruments come in a number of formats, which basically correspond to those used for audio plug-ins, such as VST, AU, RTAS, and DXi. A **software instrument** can run as a stand-alone application—interfacing directly with a MIDI controller—or as a proprietary plug-in that will only work with specific host software. Like audio plug-ins, many of the most popular software instruments can work in a number of formats, insuring compatibility with a range of popular applications.

Increasingly, however, DAWs have been including software instruments in their feature sets; these resident instruments are usually only accessible through the host DAW. For example, the ES1 synthesizer included with Logic will not play in Cubase or Pro Tools.

SOFTWARE INSTRUMENT SUITES

Some programs combine software instruments into a *suite* that's the computer equivalent of a rack full of gear. The most popular of these are Propellerhead's Reason (see **Fig. 12.1**), Cakewalk's Project 5, and Image Line's FL Studio.

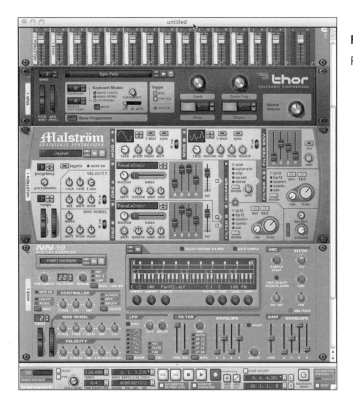

Fig. 12.1

Propellerhead's Reason

These suites offer a complete electronic music environment, and include a range of instruments such as modeled synthesizers, drum machines, and digital samplers, as well as mixers, audio effects, and sequencers that allow you to record performances. They can work as stand-alone programs or be integrated into a DAW environment via ReWire, which we'll come back to shortly.

■ LAUNCHING A SOFTWARE INSTRUMENT

There are two ways to play a software instrument: 1) as a stand-alone application, or 2) as a plug-in operating within a sequencer.

STAND-ALONE OPERATION

When a software instrument operates as a stand-alone device (see **Fig. 12.2**), it uses its own audio engine and MIDI input routing. Stand-alone mode works well when you want to play the instrument in real time (such as during a live performance) or if the instrument, like

Fig. 12.2

Native Instrument's Absynth operating in its "standalone" mode.

Reason, provides its own set of recording and playback features. Because there's no DAW or other host software open, your computer can devote all of its resources to the instrument.

In stand-alone mode, you must set the instrument up to access your audio and MIDI interfaces directly (see **Fig. 12.3**) (we discuss how this is done in Chapters 5 and 8). If you plan to open more than one instrument, or are using a software instrument while another audio application is running, you must make sure that there are no conflicts in accessing the audio hardware. This can occur when two or more applications are trying to access the same audio interface at the same time. (This doesn't happen when you're using the instrument as a

Fig. 12.3

Setting up a stand-alone software instrument.

plug-in or through ReWire, because the software instrument is routed through the host application, which in turn addresses the audio interface.)

Latency, the delay that occurs in an audio signal as it travels through your computer's audio system, is as much an issue with software instruments as it is with audio recording. High-latency systems can cause an audible delay between the time you trigger a note on your MIDI controller and the time you hear the note come back through your speakers. As is the case with audio recording, lower buffer settings produce lower latency, but also require more CPU resources.

PLUG-IN OPERATION

You can also access software instruments from within your DAW/sequencer software. This is the best choice when you want to incorporate the software instrument into a larger mix, and take advantage of the audio/MIDI recording and processing features of the host application. Your sequencer will treat the instruments like other audio tracks—allowing you to route them through plug-ins, automate their mix levels, and bounce them to disk to free up system resources.

When you're working with a DAW, adding a software instrument is done in two basic steps: 1) load the instrument, and 2) create a track to feed MIDI data to the instrument. The specific procedure varies depending on the software. In Logic, GarageBand, and versions of Digital Performer from 6 on, you first create an instrument track, which is automatically designated to record and play MIDI. From there, you insert the instrument as the track's input (see **Fig. 12.4**).

Fig. 12.4

A software instrument track in Logic Pro.

In Cubase and Pro Tools, you load the software instrument into an audio channel or special audio bus, and then route a MIDI channel to that bus (see **Fig. 12.5**).

Fig. 12.5

To add a software instrument in Cubase, you must first create a channel for the instrument (a), assign an instrument to the track 9b) and assign a MIDI track to that audio channel (c).

a.

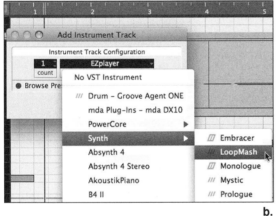

b.

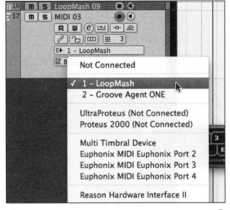

c.

In either case, the application will treat the software instrument as it would an outboard MIDI device.

DAW LATENCY AND SOFTWARE INSTRUMENTS

Latency can be even more of a problem when playing software instruments from within a DAW than when working in the stand-alone mode described above, simply because the computer has more to process in a typical DAW mix. Low buffer sizes, which produce the lowest latency, may not be possible if you're using a lot of software instruments at one time, because the low buffer setting and the amount of processing power required to run the synths may cause the software to hang or crash. But higher latency can make an instrument seem slow and unresponsive. When that happens, bounce or freeze any instruments you're not playing. Also, disable any processor-hungry audio effects while you're tracking the software instrument; you can re-enable them at mix time.

WORKING WITH MULTITIMBRAL INSTRUMENTS

By default, software instruments are stereo devices that play one sound at a time. But some, such as Native Instruments' Kontakt sampler (see **Fig. 12.6**), are capable of loading multiple sounds, which can be layered together and played from one MIDI channel, or separated so that each is triggered by its own MIDI channel. This is known as *multitimbral* operation. For multitimbral operation, you'll need to create a separate MIDI track for each MIDI channel, and then route it to the corresponding sound on the instrument. Your assignments might look like this:

MIDI track 1: Piano > Instrument 1: Kontakt > MIDI channel 1

MIDI track 2: Drums > Instrument 1: Kontakt > MIDI channel 2

MIDI track 3: Bass > Instrument 1: Kontakt > MIDI channel 3,… etc.

When working in multitimbral mode, make sure that each sound loaded into the software instrument is assigned to its own MIDI channel. Often, the sounds default to channel 1 or Omni, and must be adjusted after loading.

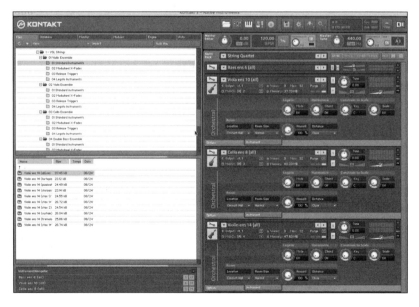

Fig. 12.6

Native Instruments' Kontakt sampler

ADDING SOFTWARE INSTRUMENTS VIA REWIRE

Software suites such as Reason and Project 5, as well as devices like the drum track program DrumCore, are designed to work as stand-alone musical tools; their individual components cannot be launched as plug-ins directly within a DAW. However, the suite *can* be integrated into a DAW mix with the ReWire internal connection protocol, which routes audio and MIDI data between two applications. The DAW serves as the host, and the program providing the sound serves as the slave.

ReWire routing involves the following basic steps:

1. Launch the host. The host DAW should be open before you launch the slave application.

2. Launch the slave. Because the host is already open, the slave will probably default to ReWire routing mode. At this point, you may want to load some sounds into the slave, just so you can test the system.

3. Create a ReWire channel in your DAW. This is usually a separate procedure from creating a standard audio or software instrument channel. Often, you'll need to create a special auxiliary channel. Make sure this track is turned on and assigned to an output that leads to your audio interface.

4. Assign the ReWire channel to the slave's outputs. If you have more than one ReWire-capable program, you'll see a set of choices. In **Fig. 12.7**, we've chosen Reason's stereo output.

5. Generate sound with the slave. Switch to the slave and use its controls to make some kind of noise. If you have a drum machine or other self-playing device loaded in the slave, start it and let it run. Hopefully, you hear audio coming through the DAW!

If you *don't* hear audio, try the following troubleshooting steps:

1. Make sure that the slave is generating signal by checking its internal mixer.

2. Make sure the slave is set to send that signal to the same outputs you've chosen as the input in your DAW.

3. Make sure the DAW input is in fact assigned to the right ReWire source.

4. Make sure the DAW channel is assigned to an output.

5. If none of the above works, save the settings in the slave, quit the slave, then the DAW, reopen the slave in stand-alone mode, and see if the settings you just saved generate audio. Once that's working, quit, relaunch the DAW, then the slave, and try ReWire again.

ReWire also lets you connect individual outputs from the slave device (assuming the slave itself allows for multiple outs). So you can have a stereo track for the overall mix, or individual mono or stereo tracks for

Fig. 12.7

Selecting a ReWire device from a list.

any device generating sounds in the slave. This allows you to route, say, a Reason sampler to one DAW input, a synthesizer to another, and the individual outputs from a drum machine to four more, as shown in **Fig. 12.8**.

MIDI AND REWIRE

Once the audio is working, you have two options: 1) Use the slave's internal tools to trigger sounds; or 2) Route MIDI from the DAW and control the sounds that way.

The first option works if you want to play back existing performances in the slave's memory. For example, let's say you're using Reason's internal drum machine and step sequencer to play a number of pre-programmed patterns. Because Reason is connected to the DAW via ReWire, these patterns will play in sync with your DAW project. All you have to do is hit Play on either the DAW or Reason and everything locks in.

The second option lets you record and edit performance data within your DAW, which may be a good choice if you're using, say, a modeled analog synthesizer generated by Reason, because the performance will be stored with the DAW project—and is therefore available if you want to replace the Reason synth with some other MIDI instrument.

To route MIDI from the DAW to the slave:

1. Create a MIDI track.

Fig. 12.8

Routing individual channels from Reason via ReWire.

2. Assign the MIDI track's output to the appropriate MIDI input on the slave.

One important difference between using a software instrument suite via ReWire and launching one of the DAW's resident instrument plug-ins is that the DAW *does not store any of the sound settings you make in the ReWire slave*. In a way, it's just like sending MIDI to an external instrument via a hardware interface. You'll need to save the sounds in the slave separately, and reload them every time you reopen the project in the DAW.

TIP

Once you have recorded and edited your software instrument tracks the way you want them, you can bounce the audio from the slave application and add it to your project. This can be done by assigning the audio from the ReWire channel to an audio track, or by generating an audio bounce directly from within the slave program. If using the latter option, be sure the slave's tempo matches your project.

VIRTUAL "WORKSTATIONS" AND SOUND COLLECTIONS

Another recent development has been the emergence of software and hardware that can organize a range of different instruments into one central interface, such as Native Instruments' Kore 2 (see **Fig. 12.9**) and Apple's MainStage. This software acts as a shell that can load a range of VST and AU instruments and effects independently of a DAW—which makes them useful for live performance. Users can then mix and match and process these modules as a group to create unique sounds. Kore comes with a special hardware controller to allow hands-on access to the sounds.

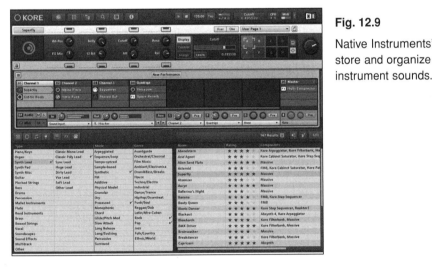

Fig. 12.9

Native Instruments' Kore 2 can store and organize many software instrument sounds.

■ AUDIO ROUTING FOR SOFTWARE INSTRUMENTS

One of the nice things about working with software instruments in a DAW environment is that the instrument is automatically part of the project each time you launch it. For those of us who worked with outboard MIDI gear, which often had to be reconfigured every time we called up a new track, this is a joy. In a DAW, all your software instrument settings will be saved with the project file.

Typically, you'll load a software instrument into either a mono or stereo track that runs alongside the other audio tracks in your mix. You can add plug-in effects to your software instrument channel as inserts or sends, as you would with any other audio channel. And like audio tracks, software instrument channels can be automated, with the added bonus that you can even make automated changes to the instrument's parameters.

WORKING WITH MULTIPLE AUDIO OUTPUTS

Adding another variation to the "one instrument, one channel" theme are instruments that are capable of sending more than the standard mono or stereo audio signals through your host software's mixer. This type of *multichannel operation* allows you to separate individual sounds for processing.

This can be useful in the multitimbral example we discussed in the previous section—where you send the piano and drums to independent stereo channels in your software's mixer, and route the bass to its own mono channel (see **Fig. 12.10**).

Multichannel operation can also be useful when you're working with a single MIDI channel/part, but want more control over individual sounds. The most common example would be when working with a sampled drum kit. The kit may receive MIDI data all on one channel, but the ability to separate individual instruments such as the kick, snare, toms, cymbals, etc., and route each to its own MIDI channel (see **Fig. 12.11**) offers you more control over your mix than you would have if all the drums were coming through the same stereo channel.

PRE-MIXING SOFTWARE INSTRUMENTS

While some software instruments offer little in the way of audio processing beyond their core sounds, others include built-in mixers and audio effects that let you fine-tune their sound before feeding it back to your mixer.

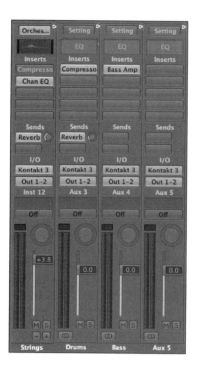

Fig. 12.10

Routing a multitimbral software instrument's sounds to individual audio channels allows each to be processed independently in a DAW's mixer.

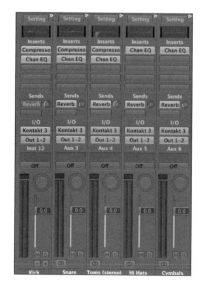

Fig. 12.11

Individual sounds within one Kontakt drum patch have been separated into independent audio streams, each routed to its own mixer channel.

This feature is more likely to be included in a multitimbral instrument or sampler, as well as specialized instruments such as Toontrack's Superior Drummer 2, which offers an extensive internal mixing environment (see **Fig. 12.12**). Suites such as Reason and Project 5 also include robust and flexible mixers and effects. In the above case, the internal mixer can combine its output into a stereo feed and go to a stereo channel on your DAW's mixer, or can be split into independent virtual outputs and feed individual mono or stereo channels on the DAW.

Fig. 12.12

Toontrack's Superior Drummer 2

■ Types of Software Instruments

All software instruments are digital in nature, even if their features mimic those of analog instruments from the past. Though there are many types of digital sound production (including FM synthesis and subtractive synthesis), the two most important technologies for software instruments these days are *sampling* and *modeling*.

A *sampler* creates sound by playing back short recordings, called *samples,* which we discussed in Chapters 5, 6, and 7. Samples can be used to produce the natural acoustic sound of instruments like drums, piano, strings, etc. They can also be used to play short snippets of music, or loops, which we discussed at length in Chapter 7.

Instead of playing back a recording of a source instrument the way a sampler does, digital *modeling* technology emulates the performance of that instrument by using digital technology to create a virtual version of the real circuitry. This same principle is used on the amplifier emulators we discussed in Chapter 10. Modeling is used to emulate electronic instruments (such as analog synths, vintage organs, and electric pianos) as well as to replicate the sounds produced by acoustic instruments. But where a sampler might reproduce a flute sound by playing back recordings of a flute, a modeler would use software to create a virtual pipe and send virtual air across its mouthpiece.

MODELING INSTRUMENTS

Ironically, modeling technology came about as a means of preserving old sounds. As vintage analog synths, organs, electric pianos, and other instruments became scarce, their sound became more popular. Finding a vintage instrument in working order became a matter of luck—and an expensive piece of luck at that.

A **modeled** instrument is a software rendition of a physical device. The most popular instrument modeling software emulates classic synthesizers, drum machines, and keyboards, like the Hammond B3 organ (see **Fig. 12.13**).

Fig. 12.13
Native Instruments' B4 emulates the Hammond B3 organ.

Modeled instruments offer an almost limitless variety of features and interface styles. Some models are designed to be as faithful as possible to the original, while others are designed to produce unique sounds. Here are just a few of the categories you're likely to find, with a brief explanation of their hardware counterparts.

ANALOG SYNTHESIS

The first synthesizers were *analog* devices, which used electrical signals and oscillators to generate sounds. Once vast machines that could take up entire rooms, these devices allowed various parts to be connected via cables called "patch cords"—which is why a stored sound is called a *patch* to this day. The first models were *monophonic*—capable of producing only one note at a time. Eventually, analog synths got small enough to be portable and included built-in keyboard controllers. *Polyphonic* instruments capable of producing more than one note were then developed.

Basic features on an analog synth include the *oscillators* that generate the sounds, or *waveforms*; the *filters* that shape the tone of the sound generated by the oscillators; and the *envelopes*, which modulate the behavior of the filters over time. There's lots of variation within these few components, and one of the cool things about using analog synths is that their simplicity makes them easy to control.

Important analog synths that are often emulated today include devices by Moog, ARP, Roland, Yamaha, and Sequential Circuits (see **Fig. 12.14**); like the guitar amp simulators discussed in Chapter 11, manufacturers try to recreate the circuitry of these devices using software. But software designers also create analog-type synths that, instead of emulating some classic hardware of yesteryear, are designed to create unique sounds.

Fig. 12.14

Native Instruments' Pro-53 emulates Sequential Circuits' Prophet 5 analog synth.

Whether you're using a new or emulated analog synth, analog synths are a good place to start learning about synthesis, because the controls are easy to understand. Analog synths are especially popular for generating bass sounds, pads, fat lead sounds (similar to a distorted guitar), and synthetic strings.

FM SYNTHESIS

Frequency modulation, or FM, synthesis is a powerful method of generating sounds, though FM synths are more complex to program than analog synths. The Yamaha DX7, emulated today by devices like Native Instruments' FM8 (see **Fig. 12.15**), is a classic example. Here, *operators* are used to both generate waveforms and to modify the sound of other operators. Four-operator FM synths are simpler than six-operator devices like the DX7. With clever programming, FM is capable of a very wide array of sounds, but is best known for producing glassy textures, the bell-like electric piano sound that became a staple of 1980s ballads, and fat basses. Notoriously hard to program on those early hardware devices, software makes it much easier to create FM synth sounds of your own.

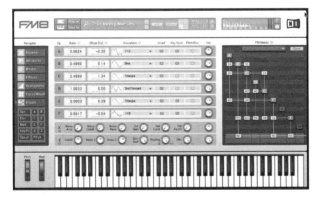

Fig. 12.15

Native Instruments' FM 8 emulates the Yamaha DX7 FM synthesizer.

WAVETABLE SYNTHESIS

Wavetable synths switch among a selection of waves that produce various harmonics to create sounds. The most famous model was the PPG Wave, but the technique was also adopted by Korg, Sequential Circuits, and others. An adaptation of the concept was later used in the development of sample-playback synths such as the Korg M1. Though never as popular as FM, wavetable synthesis is a compelling way to create unique tones and can be a component in many software synths, including MOTU's MX4 (see **Fig. 12.16**).

Fig. 12.16

MOTU's versatile MX4 includes wavetable synthesis among its features.

SAMPLE PLAYBACK

Sample playback synthesizers emerged in the late 1980s, and quickly became the industry standard. These devices used digital samples stored in permanent ROM memory as the basis for sounds, processing them through filters to produce both realistic emulations of acoustic instruments and more synthetic tones. The Korg M1 was the most popular early example, but the technology was used by Yamaha and Roland as well, and remains a central part of the keyboard workstations produced today. While not as versatile as pure samplers, the advantage of sample playback devices was their ability to access many sounds quickly from permanent memory. In a computer environment, the hard drive's ability to store samples means that you don't have to deal with the limits of ROM memory. You can find digital emulations of early sample-based devices like the Korg M1. Cakewalk's Dimension Pro (see **Fig. 12.17**) is a modern and more versatile take on the concept, giving you fast access to a range of sample-based and synthetic sounds (including loops).

Fig. 12.17

Cakewalk's Dimension Pro is a powerful virtual workstation that includes sample playback features.

ELECTRIC PIANOS, ORGANS, AND CLAVINETS

Modeling technology is also used to emulate the sound of early electronic keyboard instruments such as the electric piano, tonewheel/drawbar organ, and clavinet. Like analog synthesizer models, these are often patterned after specific hardware products, such as the Hammond B3 organ, the Rhodes Mk III electric piano, and others, with controls that emulate the originals in layout and functionality.

VOCODERS

A vocoder is something between a synthesizer and an audio effect. It uses a bank of filters to modify an input signal and generate a new one. What makes it an "instrument" is that you can use a controller to play a melody with this new signal. Vocoders are most commonly associated with the robot voices heard in electronic music.

HYBRID SYNTHESIS

Any synthesizer that uses more than one type of technology can be considered a hybrid. In the software realm, hybrids are common because designers aren't restricted by the costs associated with hardware technology. So you'll find synthesizers that use samples, FM, analog-type filters, and wavetables pretty regularly.

SAMPLERS

The development of the digital sampler back in the 1980s changed the face of music by letting people capture sounds and trigger them in their own music. While it was revolutionary at the time, today we take this technology for granted. Sampled sounds are found in everything from children's toys to cell phones.

You can use a sampler in two ways: 1) to play back short loops and other recordings; or 2) to imitate the sound of an acoustic instrument, such as a piano, violin, or drum set.

All things being equal, the more individual samples that you can assign to a sampler instrument, the more realistic that instrument will sound. The duration of each sample is another factor in sound quality: the longer the sampled note, the more natural it will sound while it sustains and decays. But since each sample is a digital audio recording, the greater the number and length of the samples, the more memory, or sample time, is required.

And therein lies the power of software samplers such as Garritan's GigaStudio, Logic's EXS24, Native Instrument's Kontakt, and Steinberg's HALion (see **Fig. 12.18**). Thanks to the memory and storage capabilities of computers, these software samplers can handle a large number of samples per instrument. This allows them to produce very complex and realistic sounds.

Fig. 12.18

Steinberg's HALion sampler

With a conventional hardware sampler, samples must be loaded into RAM in order to play back. The total sample time available is determined by the amount of onboard RAM in the sampler. Computer samplers also rely on RAM (and if you plan to use your computer for sampling, add as much RAM as you can afford). But in addition to using RAM as a holding place for sample data, most software samplers can play back, or stream, long samples directly from disk. Disk streaming allows you to play samples that would exceed the limit of your computer's RAM.

Computer-based samplers offer other advantages as well. A computer's graphical user interface can be a great aid when editing samples and sampler instruments. Sampling is a data-intensive technology—one instrument can consist of hundreds of small audio files. A computer's ability to store and organize data makes it easier to manage collections of sampled sounds.

You can import third-party sample libraries for use with your software sampler. Most software samplers can read the Akai format, and some developers also directly support popular soft samplers, such as HALion, GigaStudio, or the EXS24. The SoundFont format allows normal wave files to contain both sample and parameter data (similar to the type of controls you'd find in a hardware sample-playback synth). SoundFonts are compatible with a wide range of software instruments, including soft samplers and sample-playback synthesizers.

By working with a sampler from within a host audio application, you can take advantage of the host's audio-editing features. One of my favorite tricks is to import short audio regions, such as acoustic drum hits taken from a live track, into the sampler. I can then use the sampler to trigger new drum passages that sound like the originals.

Sample-playback devices, like IK Multimedia's SampleTank and Cakewalk's Dimension Pro, combine sampling and synthesis along the lines of the MIDI workstation keyboards that emerged in the early 1990s. These types of instruments have long been popular in hardware form because they give you quick access to a wide range of sounds (such as orchestral, brass, drums, bass, choir, etc.) with a minimum of fuss. They also allow synth-like processing of sampled sounds.

While most samplers are designed to produce a range of different sounds, some specialize in one type of instrument or style. IK Multimedia's Miroslav Philharmonik is a library of strings; FXpansion's BFD and Toontrack's Superior Drummer focus on drums. Spectrasonics' Stylus RMX focuses on loops. In these cases, the entire sound library included with the sampler is dedicated to one type of sound. This allows the developers to include many subtle variations within a given group of samples. Where a jack-of-all-trades sampler may feature four or five variations on a specific snare drum sound—say, one sample each for quiet, medium-quiet, medium, medium-loud, and loud hits—a dedicated drum program might have several dozen samples just for the medium hits on one snare drum!

HOW SAMPLERS PRODUCE SOUNDS

In a way, you can think of a sampler as a complex jukebox that lets you recall sounds from a vast menu with the touch of a button. Only here, the menu is made up of individual sounds, and the button is a key on your MIDI controller.

When you depress a key, you're essentially telling the sampler to "play Recording X." The sampler itself is oblivious: it doesn't care if "Recording X" is a one-second saxophone sample playing the note C, a single hit on a conga drum, a funky drum loop, or a sound effect guaranteed to produce a wacky sense of jocularity. You—or the programmer—have to tell the sampler which recording to play with each key, how long to hold it, whether to loop it or let it decay naturally, and how to process it.

The process of assigning a sample to a note—called *key mapping*—is the most basic part of creating a sampled instrument. In theory, any sample can be assigned to any key, but in practice, you usually want the key to be the same as the note's original pitch: The sax playing C should be assigned to the key C. But it doesn't have to be. If you're loading musical phrases that you intend to trigger or loop with a sampler, you must also assign these to one or more keys. When assigning an audio file to a key, you must tell the sampler the file's original pitch so that the sampler knows how to process the sample relative to the note used to trigger it. You can also tell the sampler to ignore the instrument's pitch and play the file as-is, no matter what key triggers it. This is common when working with drum samples and loops. But you don't have to do this. Letting a loop follow pitch, for example, can open up some interesting creative possibilities.

Samplers can play audio files in a number of different ways. You can tell the sampler to start the playback some time after the actual beginning of the file (attack time), to stop playback before the file ends (decay), repeat all or part of the file (loop), and even play the file backward (reverse). These settings can be made for each sample loaded into the instrument.

MULTISAMPLING

In the early days of sampling, when memory was at a premium, it was common to assign one sample to a range of keys. This range typically started at the sample's original pitch and went a few notes above and below it. The sound was a little unnatural, but it worked reasonably well.

Today, the opposite is often the case: a single key on a sampler may have a number of audio files assigned to it. For example, the middle C on a piano may have several samples, recorded at different dynamic levels. The sampler can then be programmed to select among these sounds based on the velocity of the note the controller or sequencer sends the sample. This technique, known as *velocity switching*, lets a soft sample play at low velocity, a hard sample play at high velocity, and so on. Today, one instrument like a piano or drum set can include hundreds of samples.

Velocity switching is only one of the ways a sampler can respond to performance input. MIDI controllers such as aftertouch, modulation, and others can be used to switch samples in a multisample layout. For example, a string library may switch from legato to staccato to pizzicato based on the positions of such controllers.

Samplers don't merely play the raw recordings back; they also process them using filters (see Chapter 10) and other sound-shaping tools, may of which are similar to the ones found on synthesizers. As with sample switching, a filter may respond to controller input and note velocity. For example, playing the keyboard harder may set the filter to allow more treble through; playing it softer may make the filter attenuate the treble for a mellower sound.

USING SOFTWARE INSTRUMENTS AS EFFECTS ON AUDIO TRACKS

Hardware synthesizers use filters and envelope generators to modify tones produced within the instruments themselves, but in the software world, these components can be "detached" and applied to audio tracks. When installing software instruments, an effects plug-in with some of those instruments' sound-shaping features is added to your system along with the instrument itself. You'll see them along with other audio effects, and can apply them to audio tracks, as shown in **Fig. 12.19**.

Fig. 12.19

The filters and other processors of some software instruments can be applied to other audio tracks. Here, Pro-53 has been added as an insert on a bass track.

▓ BUILDING AND MANAGING SOUND LIBRARIES

Samplers, whether they're hardware or software, are only as good as the sounds they play back. Collections of these sounds are called *libraries*.

A *sample library* includes two types of data: the audio files that contain the actual audio recordings—the raw samples—and the program file that tells the sampler what to do with that audio. The audio files may be in a common format (such as .wav files), and therefore they can be opened in any sampler or even loaded into a DAW or 2-track editor. But without the program data, none of the settings such as the key mapping, filters, loops, etc., that the sound designers made on the audio will be present. Conversely, if the audio data is not accessible when you load a program into the sampler, there will be no sound.

INSTRUMENTS THAT GO OUTSIDE THE BOX

As we mentioned above, a software instrument is not constrained by the physical limitations of a hardware device. Software manufacturers take advantage of this in a number of ways. One is to combine instruments with some kind of recording capability to create a hybrid—an interactive recorder that can be played like an instrument.

Ableton Live (see **Fig. 12.20**) is one example. It can load sampled loops and other audio files, and assign them to keys on your computer or MIDI keyboard. You can arrange the loops as you would with a standard loop-construction package, or you can trigger them in real time as the music plays. You can assign a key to play one loop or a string of loops, essentially allowing you to remix on the fly. Reason is a complete suite of electronic instruments—sort of like a synth rack in a box. It offers analog synth modeling, sampling, a step sequencer, a drum machine, and a special module for playing back ReCycle files (see Chapter 7). You can work in Reason as a stand-alone application, or mate it to an external sequencer via ReWire.

In addition to these hard-to-categorize tools, you'll find software that lets you assemble modular synths from scratch, and signal processors that mangle your audio so severely that they can be considered instruments in and of themselves. With software instruments, experimentation is the name of the game.

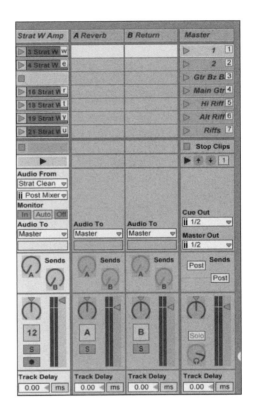

Fig. 12.20

Ableton Live can play loops in a sampler-like fashion.

MOVING ON

The ability to work with audio and video within a single environment is one of the most powerful (not to mention fun) features of the desktop studio, and there's no doubt that computers have revolutionized the audio-for-video industry. No less revolutionary is the technology that lets you create your own CDs (and other media) for distribution. Mastering and CD burning, which we explore in Chapter 13, are the final steps toward getting your work to your audience.

CHAPTER 13:   MASTERING, CD BURNING, AND MAKING MP3S

Mastering is the final stage in the production process. Here is where you prepare your audio files for final output to CD or another medium. CD burning — no, this isn't some form of ritualistic protest — is the process of writing data onto a compact disc. Since the two activities often go hand in hand, we'll cover them together.

■ TURNING MIXES INTO MASTERS

I like to think of the mastering process in three steps. Step 1 is preparing the individual audio file: cropping off the excess, checking for anomalies, normalizing, and adding some EQ and compression. Step 2 is assembling all of the files that will make up an "album" and comparing them. Do they work as a coherent whole? Some of the files may need level or EQ adjustments to make the entire project flow. Step 3 involves putting the material in order, checking transitions, and doing a test run to make sure the CD is up to spec. Then it's time to burn.

Much of the mastering process — editing the files, doing basic DSP and general cleanup — can be done with a waveform editor (see Chapter 6), which today is essentially designed to be a mastering tool. In fact, many waveform editors can burn CDs directly. Some programs, such as Apple's WaveBurner, offer less in the way of hardcore waveform editing, but streamline the process of assembling a CD. **Fig. 13.1** shows a typical suite of mastering tools.

Fig. 13.1

IK Multimedia's T-Racks mastering suite offers various compressors, limiters, and EQs optimized to work on final mixes.

MASTERING DEFINED

In the pro audio world, mastering engineers have traditionally stood apart from the multi-track production process. These specialists work almost exclusively with completed mixes, adding the final touches in EQ and dynamics processing that will turn them into masters suitable for mass reproduction and distribution. Think of the mastering studio as the finishing school for audio.

Hardware mastering tools are specialized and expensive; two reasons why few artists mastered their own work—until software got into the act. The availability of software mastering tools—combined with the affordability and ease of using CD burners—supplies you with the final link between concept and product.

You can prepare your own audio, save it in an uncompressed or compressed digital format, burn it onto CD or other medium, and send it off for duplication, or even, given some additional equipment, duplicate it yourself.

If you want to draw on the skills of a mastering expert, you can still prepare your audio by trimming the excess before sending it out.

SIGNAL PROCESSING

The art of mastering is delicate and subjective, but it boils down to bringing the best out of a mix via careful signal processing. The two most important tools are EQ (to balance a mix across the frequency spectrum) and dynamics control (to maximize the apparent loudness of your mix without causing digital overload). One of the most important mastering applications is a multiband compressor, which applies separate dynamics processing to different sections of the frequency spectrum (see **Fig. 13.2**).

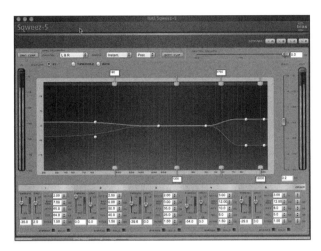

Fig. 13.2

Bias's Sqweez-5 multiband compressor

As with the plug-in processors we examined in Chapter 11, you can audition the sound of your mastering processors on the audio file. But unlike these real-time plug-ins, a mastering suite is designed to "print to disk," or create a new file.

You can apply processing to individual audio files or to an entire CD program. Some applications, such as Apple's WaveBurner Pro (see **Fig. 13.3**), allow you to assign plug-ins to individual regions or audio files in real time. Extensive real-time processing can affect the success of burning a CD, so if you're doing a lot of processing, you might want to bounce your edits down to a master file called a *disk image*.

Fig. 13.3

Apple's WaveBurner Pro

TIP

DAWs can also be used for mastering. Any mastering processors, such as final limiters, multiband compressors, and EQs, would be applied to the master bus, instead of to individual tracks. With a DAW, you have two options: 1) import previously bounced mixes and reprocess them through the mastering effects, or 2) apply these effects at the output of a multitrack project. The latter option allows you to make changes to individual tracks (for example, adjusting EQ on the bass guitar track, rather than adjusting the bass control on the master EQ)—yet another case where the desktop studio environment blurs the lines between the different areas of music creation and production.

FINALIZING THE MASTER

When you're mixing a song, you're usually focused on the details: the sound of individual tracks and how they fit together within the whole. Mastering is different—you're listening to how the complete mixes fit together.

It's always a good idea to listen in context. Compare the processed master with your original mix, with all the other songs in your project, and against other professionally mastered material.

You may be tempted to overprocess a mix in the mastering stage. This is especially dangerous if you're working on one of your own mixes, because you won't have the advantage of impartiality and distance from the original material. Mastering is about polishing something finished. If the track needs too much work, you may want to revisit the original mix.

LOUD VS. DYNAMIC

One of the most controversial issues with modern mastering is whether a track should be "loud" or should have a wide dynamic range. In the first school of thought, compression and limiting are driven to just below their absolute limits. Quiet passages sound hyped and loud passages are "squashed" to make them equal in audio level on playback. To get a sense of this, just turn on any FM rock station, where it's not uncommon for the station to add even more compression. You can often hear the music "pump and breathe" as the compressor kicks in.

Others feel that too much compression robs the music of not only dynamic range, but also any sense of acoustical space and dimension.

The right answer has as much to do with the style of music you play and with your personal taste than with any technical considerations. You should experiment and listen on a lot of different systems, as you would during the mixing stage. However, one thing I've observed is that the presets on many mastering plug-ins tend to favor the "squashed" approach of adding a lot of compression. And in areas where you're not an expert, it may be tempting to think it's "supposed" to sound that way. It's not. It *can,* but only if that's what you want.

The same is true of some mastering EQs that hype the treble and bass at the expense of the midrange. As soon as "mastering" sounds like it's messing with your original intention, remove it—or at least create a version without it.

CREATING A CD

If there's one area that illustrates the way desktop recording empowers you to get your music heard, it's CD writing, or "burning." At one time CD burners cost thousands of dollars; today, they're standard issue on a moderately equipped home computer, and outboard units can be had for a song.

ASSEMBLING THE TRACKS

Once you have your tracks mastered, there's nothing tricky about assembling tracks for the CD. You import your masters into a **track list**, where you can set their playback order and start ID number, and program the duration of the silence between tracks (two seconds is the standard).

For basic tasks like this, a program like Roxio's Toast (Mac) or Creator (Windows) should do the trick. "Lite" versions of these applications are usually thrown in when you buy a CD burner. In face, you don't even have to spend any money: freeware like Apple's iTunes, Windows Media Player, RealPlayer, and other software can assemble playlists and burn CDs.

But software that combines editing, mastering, and CD burning—such as Steinberg's WaveLab, Apple's WaveBurner Pro, Bias's Peak Pro, and Sony's Sound Forge—offers the advantage of letting you master individual tracks in the context of the complete CD.

These programs also let you perform nondestructive edits on individual regions (see **Fig. 13.4**). You can alter their boundaries, set up fades, adjust levels, and apply plug-in effects.

When setting a final signal level, be sure not to create digital overload. An **"over"** will ruin the CD. A good limiter is an especially valuable tool at the mastering stage. You can push your tracks close to digital zero (the limit before clipping), and the limiter can prevent them from going over. This can add some punch to your mixes and increase the apparent loudness of the material.

START IDS AND INDEX NUMBERS

Each track on a CD must have a **track start** ID, or index number, indicating where it begins. Otherwise, all of your audio would play back as one long track. A CD can contain up to 99 start IDs. Most of the time, you'll want to have a separate start ID for each audio in your program, as shown in **Fig. 13.5**.

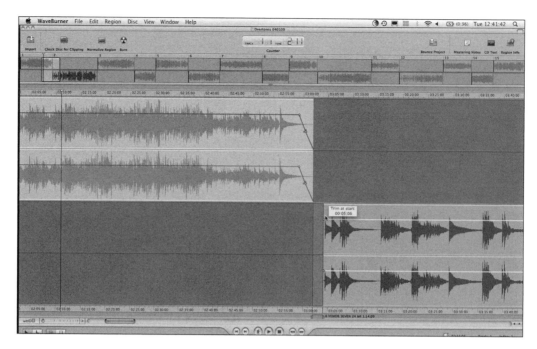

Fig. 13.4

Assembling a 15- track CD in WaveBurner. The overview at the top shows the entire CD. The detail shows the transition between track 1 (upper row) and 2. Note the fadeout at the end of the first track (indicated by the diagonal line). The shaded area shows the time gap between the end of track 1 and the start of track 2.

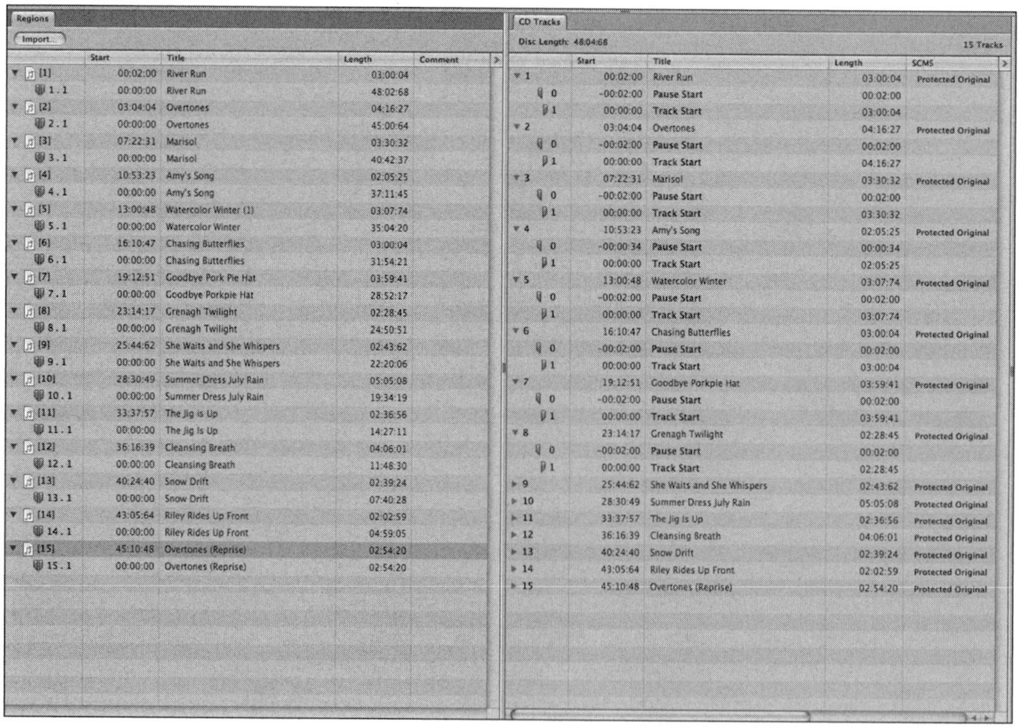

Fig. 13.5

Indexing a CD

SUB-INDEX

Sub-indexes (or sub-indices) are used to identify subsections of a track. You can have up to 98 sub-indexes per track. These are useful when your CD contains lots of short passages (such as a drum sample CD).

BURNING CDS

Audio CD burning was once a specialized process, but these days virtually all CD burners on the market are capable of burning audio CDs that will play back on any system.

CDs that are intended for audio playback are different from data CDs, which are used to store audio files. Audio going onto a CD for playback *must be at 16-bit, 44.1 kHz.* Files of different formats must be converted before burning. If your CD burning software can handle 24-bit audio files, you may be able to do the conversion as you're writing to disk. Otherwise, you'll need to create separate 16-bit versions of all of your mixes. Whenever you convert an audio file to a lower resolution (**downsampling**), you're degrading the audio signal. One way to mask some of the audible effect of this is to use a dithering plug-in.

DISC-AT-ONCE VS. TRACK-AT-ONCE

If your software and hardware support it, you'll most likely want to burn your CDs using **disc-at-once** mode. This creates the complete audio file that conforms to the **Red Book** standard, which you'll need for error-free replication. **Track-at-once** mode, which is supported by some older burner/software combinations, writes each track individually. With disc-at-once, you write a CD in one pass—you can't make any changes to the CD once it's burned. Track-at-once technology lets you add tracks incrementally, at different times, but the CD won't play back in a standard recorder until you complete the process by **finalizing** the disc.

■ MAKING DATA CDs AND DVDs

Audio is not the only data that you can burn to CD. Thanks to the storage capacity of CDs (more than 600 MB per disc), CD burners also make excellent archiving and backup tools. Unlike audio CDs, you don't need to master or convert your data files before writing them onto CD.

You can back up your work by simply copying the target files to the disc, uncompressed, or by using a backup application. Backup software compresses the files, which saves space on the CD. The drawback is that the files on the backup disc must be restored before your computer can read them again.

With the uncompressed approach, your files will take up more space on the disc, but they're also instantly accessible. I like to keep each project in its own folder, with the song file and the audio files grouped together. This way, I can copy the folder directly to disc. If my project exceeds the capacity of a single CD, I create subfolders within the main folder, keeping each subfolder within the storage capacity of one disc. I then copy each subfolder to its own disc.

TIP

If you plan to share data CDs across platforms, burn the discs in a Windows-friendly format. Macs can read data files from Windows discs without the use of additional conversion software.

MP3s and Compressed Formats

Thanks to the Internet and the advent of the portable MP3 player, you're not limited to the CD as a distribution medium for your work. You can upload audio files in a number of **compressed** formats suitable for sharing on the Internet.

The most popular of these formats is the MP3, which is really the first form of audio compression that doesn't completely rob a track of its original audio character. (Audiophiles will disagree, but for most of us, MP3s do a reasonable job.) An MP3 converter uses a special algorithm called *lossy compression* that removes the least important data from an audio file to reduce its size. A typical MP3 file is 1/10th the size of a 16-bit, 44.1 kHz audio file. So a three-minute stereo mix that is 30 MB at 16-bit, 44.1 kHz will be around 3 MB in MP3 form.

Note: Lossy compression is not the same as audio compression. "Lossy" refers to the data compression of the file; audio compression refers to a reduction in dynamic range between loud and soft sounds.

Other compressed formats include Advanced Audio Encoding (AAC), which is part of the MP4 spec and generally offers slightly better fidelity than standard MP3s, and Apple Lossless Encoding. Both are used by iTunes; MP4/ACC is also used by the Sony Playstation 3 and others.

You can convert uncompressed audio files into MP3s (and other compressed formats) by using a waveform editor, or with any number of readily available free programs like iTunes. Many DAWs now allow you to bounce mixes directly to a compressed format.

TIP

Some engineers create a separate master for compressed files to help compensate for the audio differences between these and their uncompressed counterparts. As an experiment, you might want to buy commercially prepared compressed versions of songs you also have on CD and A/B them; then, using your own software, create a compressed file from the same CD. Compare your and the commercial product to see how well they match.

NAMING AND TAGGING MP3S

When you generate an MP3, you'll typically name the file with the song's title. If it's part of an album, it's common practice to put a two-digit number before the title to indicate its order in the playlist; e.g., 01 First Song.mp3; 02 Second Song.mp3; etc.

Use two digits—even for numbers 1–9—because computer operating systems sort file names based on the first character, not on a numerical value, even when the name includes numbers; files starting with 10, 11, and 12 would come *before* a file starting with number 2, but *after* one starting with 02.

TIP

If you plan to upload the MP3s to a website, you may want to add a character such as an underscore between the words in the file name. Not all web software supports spaces in file names elegantly, so adding the underscore—to create a name like 01_First_Song.mp3—can ensure compatibility across the board.

In addition to the file name, you add metadata, or *tags* (similar to those discussed in Chapter 7) that tell listeners about the file (see **Fig. 13.6**). Typically, this information includes the artist's name, the name of the album, the composer's name, the year of release, and the genre. You can even add an album cover graphic if you want. Music players such as iPods, as well as music player software like iTunes, use these tags to help users search for and organize files.

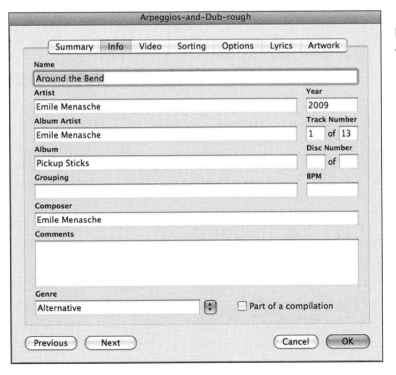

Fig. 13.6

Tagging an MP3

Moving On

With its ability to burn CDs and generate MP3s, the computer gives you a means to deliver music to fans and clients instantaneously. You really can create and deliver an entire professional-quality production without ever leaving the computer environment. But there are also times when you'll want to expand your horizons by operating your computer in sync with other recording tools, such as outboard sequencers, video machines, and tape recorders. Synchronization and video are next, in Chapter 14.

CHAPTER 14: SYNCHRONIZATION AND WORKING WITH VIDEO

Although your desktop studio can function as a self-contained production system, you may find some situations where you'll want to link your software to other recording and playback equipment, such as multitrack tape recorders, video decks, drum machines, and even other software applications. But before we talk about this, let's look at how digital audio devices themselves synchronize.

WORD CLOCK

Whenever you link two digital devices together using a digital connection (as opposed to connecting analog devices by plugging the analog outputs of one into the analog inputs of another), you are in essence synchronizing them. As we discussed in Chapters 2 and 5, every digital audio device runs on a clock, which controls its sample rate. If you interconnect devices using digital audio connections, one device must act as the *clock master*, and the other(s) as the *clock slave*(s). For example, if you connect your digital mixer to your audio interface, you could designate the mixer as the clock master. In this case, you'd set your audio interface to get its timing from an external clock source, which would make the audio interface the slave. This way, the two digital clocks will remain in sync. If both devices were left to run on their own internal clocks, the sample rates—even though they're set to the same value—would drift out of sync, causing distortion, a variation in timing known as *jitter*, and other audible audio problems.

Word clock is a means of synchronizing these devices. Supplied over direct digital connections, word clock provides a master digital clock that allows digital devices, such as mixers, effects, and audio recorders, to stay in digital sync.

The simple master/slave configuration works fine if you're dealing with only two devices. But whenever you've got more than two—for example, an audio interface, a digital mixer, and an outboard A/D converter—it's better to have a word-clock generator that can act as the master for *all* devices. You connect each device to the word-clock generator via special word-clock input jacks. All audio devices would then operate in slave mode.

Unfortunately, though it's a feature commonly found on pro-level digital audio gear, many of the more affordable audio mixers and interfaces lack the ability to sync to an external clock other than the one feeding its digital inputs. One way around this is to use a word clock generator that's also capable of converting and outputting multiple digital audio formats (such as Apogee's Big Ben; see **Fig. 14.1**). This type of device can accept a word-clock input and route a corresponding master clock to ADAT and AES/EBU digital outputs.

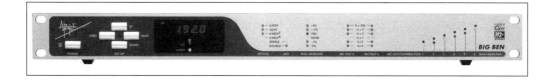

Fig. 14.1

Apogee's Big Ben

Synchronization Options

A DAW is a self-contained system, but what if you want to add another playback or recording device to your setup? In almost every case in which two playback devices are used simultaneously in one system, you'll want them to lock up, or *synchronize*, so that they play back as one unit.

You do this via *time code*, a special signal that indicates the movement of time, irrespective of the audio. No matter how many devices you synchronize, one device acts as the master, or controlling device, and the others act as slaves, which follow, or **chase**, the master. The master keeps track of the time and controls the transport of the slaves, which follow along for the ride.

There are several different ways to synchronize devices, and each has a separate function in a

desktop environment.

MIDI CLOCK

MIDI clock—though technically not a time code because it expresses synchronization information in bars and beats relative to tempo, as opposed to in minutes and seconds—lets multiple devices lock together in a musically useful way. With MIDI clock, the slave automatically follows the tempo map of the master. *Song position pointer* (**SPP**) works alongside MIDI clock to allow the slave(s) to chase the master according to the master's position (measure/beat) in an arrangement. If you start the master in the middle of, say, measure 30, the slave will go there (chase) too. Without SPP, the slave would start at the beginning of its cycle, no matter the position of the master.

You can also use MIDI clock to synchronize effects to your project, where it can control LFO, delay time, filter sweep, or other parameters.

SMPTE

SMPTE time code is named after the Society of Motion Picture and Television Engineers, so as you might guess, it has its origins in film and video production. SMPTE comes in several different formats. The most common for audio is LTC (longitudinal time code, called "lit-see" which is an audio signal that can be recorded to tape. When the tape isn't rolling, no LTC signal is sent from the master to the slave.

VITC (vertical interval time code, "called vit-see") is embedded into the video file itself and is output even when the video is stopped.

Because it is the standard for film and television production, SMPTE is often offered as a timing reference on DAWs, even when there's no need to sync to an external device (see **Fig. 14.2**).

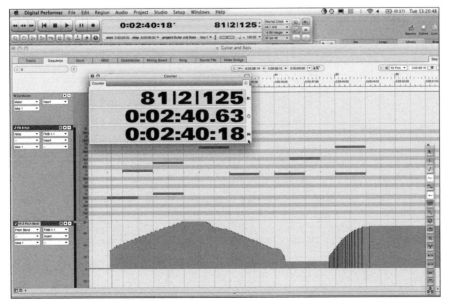

Fig. 14.2

SMPTE (the bottom row of numbers) is commonly used by DAWs such as Digital Performer.

SMPTE expresses time in hours:minutes:seconds:frames. No tempo information is inherent in the time code, so you must manually set the tempo in the slave application.

In the desktop studio, SMPTE is most often used to lock tape machines (either audio or video) to your software (see **Fig. 14.3**). Time code is recorded, or *striped*, onto a tape track and then fed through a **synchronizer** into the computer, where it is converted to a format that the software can read, such as MIDI Time Code (MTC).

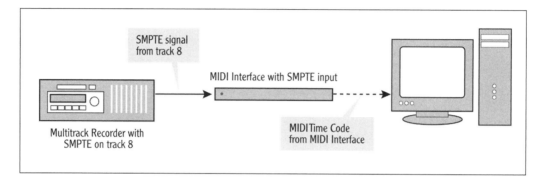

Fig. 14.3

The SMPTE reader on a MIDI interface can convert audio time code to MIDI time code (MTC).

There are several SMPTE formats. These are distinguished by **frame rate**—the number of frames per second (fps). When you're working with audio tape, 30 fps is common. Other formats include 30 fps drop frame and 29.97 fps (used in pro video), and 24 fps (used in film). Many synchronizers can automatically detect the incoming frame rate, but for others, you must specify the frame rate. If there's a mismatch between the master and slave, the two will go out of sync. If you're receiving a SMPTE-encoded tape from a third party, it pays to find out the frame rate before you begin work.

MIDI TIME CODE

MIDI Time Code (**MTC**) is a MIDI synchronization protocol that measures time linearly, using the same time divisions as SMPTE. A **SMPTE-to-MIDI** converter can translate a SMPTE signal from tape into a MIDI format that can be interpreted by most sequencers, allowing the sequencer to chase, or follow, the tape.

MIDI MACHINE CONTROL

MIDI Machine Control (**MMC**) is a two-way communications protocol that allows one device to control the transport and track-arming features of another. The master and slave lock together via MTC, but in addition to controlling the playback of the slave, the master can also arm tracks, put the machine into record mode, set up auto punches, and more.

MMC is especially useful when you want to control a tape deck or other recording device from your computer. Conversely, you can also use your software as an MMC slave; many digital mixers offer MMC features that let you operate your software from the hardware mixer's control panel.

SYNCING TWO APPLICATIONS WITHIN ONE COMPUTER

Synchronization is not just useful for locking outboard gear to your software. You can also use it to connect two pieces of software *within* your computer.

ReWire provides an audio and synchronization link between two ReWire-compatible applications (see Chapters 10 and 12). This link is automatically enabled when you follow the ReWire start sequence. Like MIDI clock, it follows your song's bars and beats.

When interconnecting applications that support the ReWire 2.0 specification, *either* application can act as the master at any time. For example, let's say you are using Cubase as the host for Reason (which features a built-in sequencer that operates on its own software instruments). You can use either program's transport controls to initiate playback, and the audio output of both will go through Cubase's audio engine. This is especially handy because it lets you create and edit parts in the Reason program and audition them without having to go back to Cubase.

You can also transmit MIDI clock or MTC through any internal MIDI stream that's recognized by both the master and slave software. This feature was more important a few years ago, when fewer programs were ReWire capable (and DAWs like Pro Tools had fewer MIDI features).

▧ SETTING UP SYNC

As mentioned earlier, in order to synchronize two or more devices, one must act as the master, the others as the slaves. As master, your sequencer will transmit time code to the slaves. You can specify which types of time code your sequencer will transmit, and through which MIDI connections they will travel.

Setting up a slave is a little more complicated. You must specify the following parameters:

- **Type of incoming time code:** This will be either MIDI clock or MTC.

- **Source of incoming time code:** Specify which MIDI connection will provide sync information.

If you're dealing with MIDI clock, that's all you need to do. The master will provide the tempo and song-position information. With MTC, you'll need to set up a few other parameters.

- **Frame rate:** This should be the same as the SMPTE or MTC format of the master. If your software can automatically detect frame rate, you don't need to worry about this one.

- **Offset:** Determines the sequencer's start position in relation to the incoming time code. Calculating *SMPTE offset* can be tricky to set up, because sometimes you have to subtract back from zero on the time code's scheme of hours:minutes:seconds:frames.

- **Fly Wheeling:** SMPTE time code can be subject to errors called dropouts, so *fly wheeling* allows the sequencer to continue playback despite short dropouts. When the signal resumes, the sequencer should still be locked to the master.

KEEPING AUDIO IN SYNC

MIDI Time Code provides very reliable sync for MIDI data, but can present problems when working with hard disk audio files. The reason for this has to do with the way sequencers trigger audio data. When a sequencer plays back a region, it's triggering the file once—in the same way it might trigger a long MIDI event. After that, the audio file plays back on its own until the sequencer stops. It's a little like sending a kid down a slide—she doesn't stop until she gets to the end.

This isn't generally a problem when you're dealing with a sequencer's internal clock, because the clock is stable and consistent. However, when you introduce external time code—especially time code that's coming from a tape track—you might run into problems. Any variations in speed, or drift, can cause the audio tracks to fall slightly out of sync.

There are two solutions to this problem. Word clock can provide a more stable master. Many basic audio interfaces, however, don't support word clock—it's one of those expensive features found on professional gear. Another solution is to chop up long audio files into shorter regions. With short regions, there's less possibility of drift. And even if there *is* some drift, when each new region in a track is triggered at its own precise start time, this retriggering will bring the audio track back into line.

▦ WORKING WITH DIGITAL VIDEO

If you're planning to use your computer to produce music or sound effects for motion pictures, you can eliminate a lot of synchronization hassles by digitizing the video and importing it into your production software. Today, this is by far the most common way to both edit video and produce audio for picture. If you're working on a production for a video producer, you'll often be supplied with a video in a digital format that you can directly import into your DAW.

Digital video is even more data-intensive than audio. You'll need a fast computer with a large, fast hard drive, and plenty of RAM. If you're digitizing the video yourself, you'll need a video I/O interface that can bring video signal into your computer. Many modern video cameras can do this directly over built-in FireWire or USB connections. External video interfaces, which can convert the output of analog video decks, are also available.

CAPTURING VIDEO

Before you can import video into a sequencer, you must first record, or *capture*, it into the computer. If the video is in an analog format, this is sometimes referred to as *digitizing*. Basic capture and editing software is usually bundled with a video interface or may even come with your computer (as iMovie does with Macs). These programs are fine for digitizing and can also be used for some editing.

For more involved work, you can upgrade to a more feature-laden digital video editing application, such as Apple's Final Cut Pro or Sony's Vegas (see **Fig. 14.4**). These offer a digital editing environment that's similar to the audio editing environment of a DAW, letting you mix multiple tracks, add effects, and more. Knowing your way around such a program can be an asset if you're planning to do post-production work that involves mixing music, dialog, and effects, or if you plan to produce your own music videos, etc.

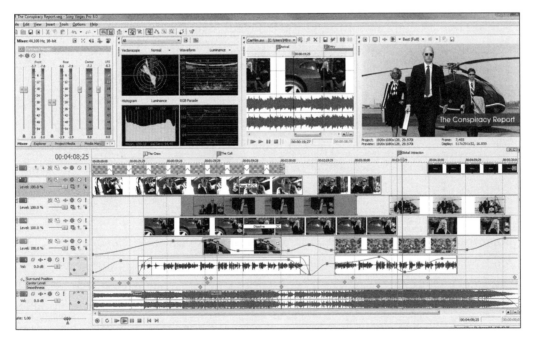

Fig. 14.4

Sony Vegas video editor

No matter what software or hardware you're using, capturing video is much like recording audio. You connect the output of the video device to the input of the computer, launch the software, set a destination for the video file on your hard drive (make sure the drive has enough room to store the file — they get pretty big!), and enable *import* or recording (see **Fig. 14.5**). Check both the video and audio signals to make sure the computer is seeing them.

Fig. 14.5

Importing video in iMovie.

Start the recorder and start the tape playback. If you're connecting a camcorder via FireWire, the capture software may actually be able to control the camera's transport, so when you hit Record in the software, the camcorder begins playback automatically.

CHOOSING A VIDEO FILE FORMAT

When you import a file into the computer, you may be given a set of options about the video's dimensions (usually expressed in pixels, as in 640 x 480 pixels), audio quality, and file format. If you have the disk space, import the video at as high a resolution as you can; you can always convert it to a smaller format later.

In order to play back the video file, your computer needs the appropriate software, called a coder/decoder, or **codec**, for your video file format. Popular video file formats include digital video (.dv); QuickTime (.mov); MPEG (.mpeg or .mpg); Audio Video Interleave (.avi); Windows Media Video (.wmv); Flash (.flv); and Real Movie (.rm); but there are many others. Within these formats, you will find videos of various compression ratios, pixel dimensions, etc. As with audio, higher resolutions can produce larger files; uncompressed .dv files can run into multiple gigabytes. You'll probably want to convert any uncompressed files to a compressed format that offers reasonable video quality without being so big that they bog down your system. You would import this compressed file into your DAW.

Not all systems can (natively) read all formats. Mac users may have trouble with AVI and WMV files, and PC users with QuickTime files, unless they download the appropriate codec software, which is often available for free or at minimal cost online. In addition, not all formats can work in a DAW. Streaming formats like .rm and .flv can't usually be imported directly, but must be converted to another format first.

Check the documentation for your DAW and operating system to learn the appropriate video format.

LOCKING UP AUDIO AND VIDEO

Most DAWs can open a digital video file and import it into an audio project (see **Fig. 14.6**). As with SMPTE or MTC sync, you must set your project's start time (or offset) so that it lines up with the video.

Fig. 14.6

Most DAWs can import and display video files.

Using digitized video (as opposed to video that's on a VHS tape or an outboard deck) is a major time saver. Your sequencer's transport controls will play back the video, and as you navigate through your project, the video will follow. You can set markers to the exact frame location for your intended audio cues and use your sequencer's spotting, step-edit, and snap-to features to line them up exactly.

There are two ways to view video on a DAW: in a separate video window like the one in **Fig. 14.6**, or on a timeline (see **Fig. 14.7**). The timeline lets you see how various segments of the video file relate to the audio regions. Some DAW programs can automatically look for "cuts," or scene changes, in the video. You can use markers to make note of these points on the timeline, making it easier to find important cues in an audio project.

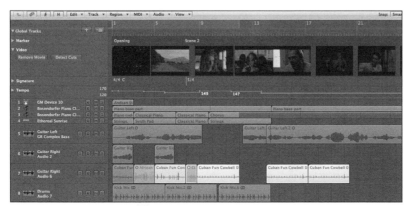

Fig. 14.7

Viewing video on a timeline.

TIP

Ask the video producer or editor to include an onscreen time code display, called a *window burn*, in your video. A window burn shows SMPTE timecode onscreen as the video plays. This will give you a reference when setting your DAW's time code offset.

WORKING WITH THE AUDIO ON THE VIDEO

If the video you've imported into your project includes audio (such as dialog and effects), you'll probably need to hear it as you create additional audio (like a musical score) to go along with it. Depending on the DAW, you have two options:

1. *Monitor the audio via the video player.* Many DAWs use a video player that has its own separate audio track, which does not send any signal through the DAW's mixer. When this is the case, the video player will have its own audio control, which lets you hear or mute the video's existing soundtrack. Often, this audio is routed through the computer's built-in audio, so you won't hear it through your audio interface, but rather on the computer's internal speakers.

2. *Import the video's audio as a track in your DAW project.* This lets you edit the audio and incorporate it into your mix, which can give more control as you work—even if you're only monitoring the original audio for reference. This audio track can be edited like any other track.

If you choose to import the video's audio into your project, be sure its track is muted when you bounce your mix (unless, of course, you *intend* to include the video's audio in your mix).

TIP

If the video has a *temp music* track—music that the video producer and editor used for reference but do not intend to keep—ask for a version without it. If the producer wants you to hear it for your own reference, ask that the temp track be placed on one channel of a stereo mix, with the dialog and effects on the other. Then import the video's audio into your project and use the mixer to control how much if any of the temp track you hear.

TEMPO AND VIDEO

When working with video projects that require more than one piece of music, one of the biggest challenges is matching the video's time to musical time. Let's say you have two important musical cues, 2 minutes and 45 seconds apart. The first cue calls for a moderate-tempo piece at 146 bpm; the second cue, a slow ballad at 80 bpm. Not only will the tempo of the two pitches be different, requiring a tempo map (see Chapter 8) switching from 146 to 80 bpm, but the start time of the second section, at least if you calculate from 146 bpm, won't fall at the beginning of a measure, but instead on the third 16th note of the second beat.

To account for this, you'll need to adjust the tempo in between the end of the first cue and the start of the second so that the latter starts on a downbeat. This can be done with a tempo curve, though it may take some manual calculation.

Another option is to create a separate project file for each cue, and use SMPTE offset to set the start of each cue to match the desired point in the video.

MOTU's Digital Performer is especially adept at music for video, and one reason why is that it lets you work with *chunks*, which are like files within a file. Each chunk can have its own tempo and SMPTE start time.

MIXING AND EXPORTING AUDIO FILES TO VIDEO

Mixing audio for video is not that different from mixing music for CD or MP3. If you're working on a film/video score, you may need to consider additional factors, such as where the sound effects and dialog will be heard in relation to your music. Always check the music you're working on against any existing audio on the video.

Once you're satisfied with your audio, you can bounce your mix to disk and import the results into a video file. If your video card can output a video signal in real time, you can opt to print your mix to videotape.

In addition to standard stereo tracks, some video producers will ask for mixes in a surround format, or ask for some elements to be exported as stems (see Chapter 10).

TIP

When collecting mixes for a video producer, make note of the SMPTE start time of each cue.

COMBINING AUDIO AND VIDEO EDITING

Digital video editing applications allow you to fine-tune your video clips, add audio, and *export*, or render, the final master to disk or to an outboard video recorder.

If you're familiar with the nonlinear editing techniques we've discussed throughout this book, you'll be right at home with a **video editor**. Most programs feature multitrack audio in one form or another, with random-access editing, automated mixing, and plenty of signal processing. You can import audio files (such as completed mixes) or record directly into the video editor.

In the future, expect to see more direct video editing support from audio production software. Some programs, such as Sony's Vegas and Magix's Samplitude, already blur the line between multitrack audio and video production. These programs allow you to record, mix, and edit video and audio in one streamlined platform, and to render a finished video file or audio file of the results.

Video software programs, such as Final Cut Pro, also allow you to export and open XML (Extensible Markup Language) files. This allows for file exchange between the video editor and a compatible DAW, such as Logic Pro or Digital Performer 6 (see **Fig. 14.8**) and later (DP even allows direct linkage between it and Final Cut Pro when both are open on the same computer).

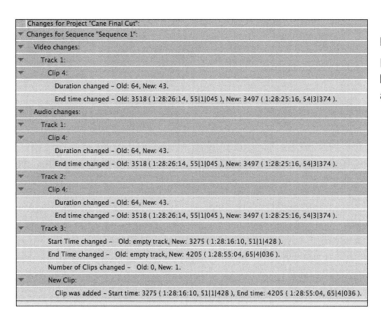

Fig. 14.8

Exchanging information between video editing files and Digital Performer.

▪ MOVING ON

Not long ago, audio CDs and video soundtracks were the two primary media outlets for a desktop music producer. But a third medium has recently invaded our culture, one that can't be avoided by musicians: the Internet. By allowing music files to travel through cyberspace and reside on the Web, the Internet has completely changed the way we hear—and distribute—music. Chapter 15 introduces you to some basics about creating audio for the Internet.

CHAPTER 15:   YOUR MUSIC AND THE INTERNET

The Internet is a gateway for all computer users, but it's an especially fertile resource for musicians and other audio folks. You can find sounds, share your music, download applications, keep your software up to date, and tap into the knowledge of other users. As long as you're online, you're never alone.

INTERNET RESOURCES

The Internet offers a direct link between your desktop studio and the software and hardware vendors who power it. Manufacturers' websites (see Appendix 2) offer a wealth of information about upcoming releases, bug fixes, tips, and more. I make it a habit to log on to key sites about once a week. On more than one occasion, I've found an update online that hadn't yet been announced in the press.

UPDATES

Major software upgrades may require a fee, but vendors regularly make incremental updates available to registered users free of charge. These updates can add new features—such as additional plug-ins, or compatibility with a new piece of hardware—or they can simply fix bugs or keep the software current with your computer's operating system.

It might not get a lot of media attention, but the functional difference between a 3.0 and a 3.01 version can be staggering. Most websites post Read Me files that detail the changes made in each version of the software.

If you don't want to subscribe to an email list or surf to every site to keep up to date on updates, a Web resource such as Versiontracker.com can give you the news on current versions for many applications.

You can also keep informed by subscribing to an online newsletter. Most vendors distribute free e-letters that inform you of updates, turn you on to tips, answer technical questions, and offer current information on drivers and operating system issues.

Vendor sites aren't the only places to find information. Musician sites such as Harmony-Central.com and Synthzone.com are full of useful links and information. Use these sites to link to user groups (for particular applications or more general topics), manufacturer sites, and unofficial sites that are devoted to the gear that make up your production arsenal. Newsgroups such as rec.audio.pro are also a good source of chat.

SHAREWARE, FREEWARE, AND OTHER RESOURCES

The Internet is also a great place to explore new software. *Shareware* is software that's developed by independent vendors and costs a fraction of the price of commercial software. The world of shareware is almost limitless. You'll find utilities (such as simple wave editors

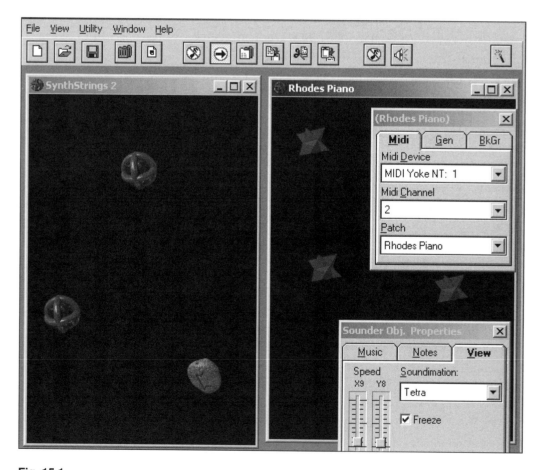

Fig. 15.1

Sounder is an example of the interesting shareware to be found on the Internet.

and MP3 players), as well as some full-featured programs like sequencers, software instruments, and effects. Sometimes, you'll find unique software that does things expensive applications can't, like Sounder (sounder.com), which lets you automatically generate ambient music (see **Fig. 15.1**).

Finding good shareware takes some research and a fondness for trial and error. There are some dogs out there, but you can also find some inexpensive gems online. Just be sure and support the folks who develop the software by registering and sending in the (often nominal) fee.

Freeware is like shareware—except, well, it's free. You can find free plug-ins and utilities on the Web. Some of my favorites are a little delay-time calculator called DelayCalc (see **Fig. 15.2**); Jack, a utility that lets you route audio between applications within one computer; and Audacity, a cross-platform audio editor that works for Mac, Windows, and Linux. Like shareware, finding the good stuff can take some digging, but it's also a lot of fun.

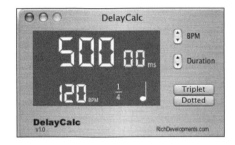

Fig. 15.2

DelayCalc

The Internet is also a great place to audition software and make purchases. You can download demos (usually with some features disabled) or trial versions (which are often full-featured, but will only work for a limited time, or may not allow you to save files). This is a great way to familiarize yourself with the vast array of options available.

THE ONLINE MUSIC COMMUNITY

In addition to keeping your computer as current as possible, the Internet is also a great way to share your creativity with other musicians, fans, and potential clients.

USER GROUPS, BLOGS, AND MESSAGE BOARDS

User groups and message boards can provide you with insights you won't find anywhere else. Because message boards are usually not affiliated with any manufacturer or publication (and proud of it!), you can get the unvarnished information—it's up to you whether or not to take it as gospel. The nice thing is that you can read about real-world experiences and share your own. You can also post questions (you may or may not get a helpful answer). Sometimes, in addition to average users, technicians from audio manufacturers may offer insights (or dispute criticisms!).

User groups and blogs are often "unfiltered," meaning that people can post whatever they want. *Moderated* groups, where there's some control over posts, tend to be a little more structured. If you're seeking advice, check out as many groups as possible—it's sort of like getting a second opinion for a medical problem.

COLLABORATING ONLINE

One of the most exciting developments in desktop production is online collaboration, which provides an Internet link between your computer and other musicians.

Sites like Kompoz.com, webjamming.com, musiccollaborate.com, and others let users upload tracks and invite collaborators to work on them—or vice versa. Some sponsor contests, such as indabamusic.com, which offers remix contests in addition to other collaboration opportunities.

Because audio files are large, a high-speed connection is virtually essential when you're collaborating over the Internet. Even with a fast connection, upload and download times can be long when you're working with large, uncompressed audio files.

INTERNET DISTRIBUTION AND PROMOTION

Internet distribution has become the primary way for musicians to get their music to fans. There are many avenues for musicians to explore, from free social networking sites to music networking sites to sites that allow you to sell CDs or downloads.

SOCIAL NETWORKING SITES

Social networking sites like MySpace and Facebook let musicians build networks of "friends" that include fans and associates in the industry. MySpace (see **Fig. 15.3**), which allows musicians to upload music for free, has launched quite a few careers in recent years, and is now used by new and established artists alike.

Fig. 15.3

MySpace is a popular site for musicians, and has helped launch some artists into the "big time."

Getting started is easy. You sign up for a free membership (on MySpace, you need to indicate that you're setting up a "band" site, even if you're a solo artist), describe your music, and upload MP3s and artwork. You need to have the rights to upload the songs (they don't allow cover songs). You then build your network by inviting friends (there's a verb for it: "friending"). Of course, with all the competition out there, it can be hard to get noticed. A good resource is *MySpace for Musicians*, by Fran Vincent.

Facebook is similar to MySpace, but is less focused on direct music sharing. However, Facebook users can set up the MyBand feature to create pages for their music and promote it, invite fans, and more. Facebook can also be a good tool for networking with other musicians in your area, or who share your interests. You'll find groups for instruments, genres, software, etc.

Twitter.com is an online community that asks users to answer one question: What are you doing? Users subscribe to these updates by "following" one another; your followers will see your updates, and you'll see the updates of the users you follow. Artists have been using this to let fans know about upcoming releases, tours, and other news.

If you're more interested in business and don't like the sometimes uncensored nature of the social networking sites, you might want to check out more professional networking sites such as LinkedIn.com. As with the social sites, you connect to other users, but here, you'll be posting your resume and seeking recommendations for your work. These sites also offer associations and groups that can help you meet others who share your professional interests.

Then there are customizable sites like ning.com, which let users create social networks of their own. In some ways the challenge isn't how many people you can reach—it's how to get and keep their attention when you do.

MUSICIAN NETWORKING SITES

Musician networking sites are more focused on musicians than the more general social networking sites. Most of these communities consist of musicians or others in the music industry, with a few hardcore music fans thrown in. These sites let you create artist pages, upload music, or submit it to contests for consideration and criticism. Basic membership is often free, but the contests, critiques, and A&R services usually cost a fee. Examples include GarageBand.com (which is owned by iLike.com, a site where fans can hear music), and Broadjam.com (see **Fig. 15.4**). As with the free sites, these sites usually require that you own the copyright to any music you upload.

Fig. 15.4

Broadjam.com

VIDEO HOSTING SITES

YouTube.com and other video hosting sites have become another way for musicians to build a "viral" following. ("Viral" is the online equivalent of word-of-mouth.) Professional artists upload videos to them, but so do average folks, and sometimes, their videos catch on. Often, these videos have some hook: perhaps a dazzling instrumental performance, or an arrangement of a well-known song using an unusual instrument. People use YouTube to teach lessons, show off live performances, display their composer's reels, and more.

SELLING MUSIC ONLINE

In some ways, the Internet is one big shopping mall; you may even have bought this book online. It can also be an avenue for you to sell your work, either on CD or via download.

CDBaby.com has become a popular site for independent musicians. Its premise is simple: you set up an account, describe your music, and send in some copies of your CD. CD Baby takes a percentage of the sale of each one, but charges no other fees. Optionally, you can allow the company to set up distribution through online partners such as iTunes.

These sites ask you to describe your music, and use tags from this description to let visitors know they might like your work, but they do no other promotion. Ultimately, your success in selling music on them comes down to your own promotional abilities.

ONLINE RADIO AND PODCASTS

Online radio stations and podcasts are another opportunity for independent musicians to be heard. Stations like Pandora.com and Slacker.com let users create custom channels based on an artist, song, or style they like; the station's software then chooses other music that they think the user will like. Often, you'll hear a mix of well-known and independent artists. Contact the stations for their submission guidelines.

Podcasts can run the gamut, from professional productions to homebrewed shows by independent hosts. The PodSafe Music Network (music.podshow.com) puts musicians/labels together with podcasters; artists who own all the rights to their works can upload tracks in MP3 format, which podcasters can then use in their programs.

■ BUYING AND SELLING GEAR ONLINE

The Internet is a great resource when you're assembling a music rig or studio because you can find just about anything you're interested in online. Reputable retailers like Sweetwater.com, Musiciansfriend.com, and Guitarcenter.com not only carry a lot of gear, but they often have online or phone tech support that can help answer your questions. Sites like CNET.com can be useful for reviews and comparison shopping. Even Amazon.com, known primarily for selling books and CDs, can be a good resource for musical gear.

Most software manufacturers, and many hardware manufacturers, also allow users to purchase goods directly from their sites. (In the case of software, this can often be via download.) One of the most innovative examples of this is Digidesign's DigiDelivery service, where users can log in and create download sessions that allow for massive files to be transferred online.

AUCTION AND CLASSIFIEDS SITES

Bargain hunters and those looking to buy or sell used gear often turn to auction sites like eBay.com and classifieds sites like Craigslist.com (the latter also offers community classifieds that can help you find gigs and other musicians).

While both can be valuable resources, you must be cautious with each. I've personally had some great experiences—and have a few horror stories. The bottom line: if a price seems too good to be true, it probably is. Be especially cautious when buying software from one of these sites. Software developers grant user licenses that are usually not transferable, which means you may be buying something that the seller has no legal right to sell. Aside from the moral issues involved in using pirated software, you won't be able to upgrade or get support for it. When in doubt, check with the manufacturer.

Moving On

It's interesting to note that many of the websites I've mentioned above didn't even exist when the first edition of this book was published in 2002—and many of the sites I mentioned in that volume were gone by the time I finished this chapter in early 2009. In fact, in the time it took to write the book, Twitter went from something only a few people knew about to a ubiquitous networking tool.

Perhaps in the future, higher-speed Internet connections—and increased capacity for portable music players—will mean that uncompressed audio will return to the fore. Perhaps online collaboration will become even more viable, and users will be able to share a single audio file in real time. We're still so early in the development of both computer-aided music and software (think of the auto industry circa 1915).

Google and other search engines may be your most important resource of all, because they'll help you find the next wave of websites, whatever that turns out to be.

APPENDICES

APPENDIX 1:   SURVIVAL TIPS

◼ READ THE MANUAL

This goes for all the software and hardware in your studio. It may sound obvious, but you'd be surprised how many people feel intimidated by the depth of their software. Don't be. Not only will knowledge help you avoid problems, you'll also learn some inside moves that will help you in your work.

◼ FOLLOW THE INSTALLATION INSTRUCTIONS

Every piece of hardware and software in your studio comes with a set of installation instructions. It's tempting to just plug things in or slap in an install CD, but a quick look at the installation Read Me file may alert you to some important requirements—such as system settings, memory requirements, etc.—that you may otherwise miss. Paying careful attention to installation procedures may also alert you to potential conflicts between your new music software (or hardware) and other applications that are already in your system.

◼ BEWARE OF CONFLICTS

Here's an ironic note: As I was preparing the screenshots that appeared in the first edition of this book, I ran into a problem that made my copy of Pro Tools LE crash consistently. I went through a whole range of utilities to fix the problem, but to no avail. Just as I was beginning to worry that my system memory or hard disk had developed a physical problem, I discovered the cause of my crashes. It was the screen-capture utility.

◼ REGISTER YOUR SOFTWARE

If you're online, it's so easy to register your software that you really have no excuse not to. Registered users have access to customer support and are usually alerted whenever there's an update available.

INVEST IN AN UNINTERRUPTIBLE POWER SUPPLY

Computers like clean and steady power. Blackouts and brownouts can cause crashes or worse—you can lose your work in the middle of a session, and your hard disk can become corrupted. In the event of power loss, a UPS can keep you running long enough to save your work and shut your computer down properly.

BACK UP OFTEN

You never know when disaster will strike, but you can count on two things: it will, and it will happen at the worst possible time. Backing up can be a pain, but it's essential.

SAVE OFTEN

There's nothing worse than losing creative work that you can't recapture. Saving your work will save you from disaster. If you're making major changes to a project and want to keep the original intact, use the Save As command to make an alternate version. If your software has an auto-save feature, enable it.

DON'T PANIC

When things go wrong, take the time to read through your troubleshooting guides. Sometimes problems can be more easily solved than you realize.

KEEP YOUR SYSTEM HEALTHY

Little problems, like excess junk on your hard disk and fragmented files, can slow your system and cause crashes. Maintain your system regularly.

PREPARE BEFORE CALLING CUSTOMER SUPPORT

Users often complain about customer support, but it's a two-sided coin. Customer support people aren't in the room with you, so they only know what you tell them. Write down the conditions that caused your problem in as much detail as you can. And don't forget to include vital stats such as your system, processor type, software version, the type of audio interface, other software, etc. Also, before you call or write to your vendor, check the manual and the vendor's online support pages. You may find your answers without ever picking up the phone.

▓ INVEST IN GOOD SPEAKERS

This book is focused on computer-based recording, so I've purposely avoided making recommendations about other gear in your studio. But good speaker monitors are essential if you want to create recordings that will sound good outside your own room. Powered monitors (which have a power amp built into the speaker cabinet) are ideal for a desktop studio.

▓ PRACTICE

Wait a minute—we're talking about working with a computer, not playing a guitar, aren't we? Computers may do a lot of the work for us, but to take real advantage of a computer studio, you need the same intimate knowledge as you would to sing or play the guitar, piano, or Sousaphone. Whenever I get a new piece of software, I start a project called Test and use it as a training ground. I like to experiment, so I just load up some audio files and start playing around with the features. If you like a more ordered approach, you can use the tutorial files supplied with most software.

▓ LEARN TO SHARE

You can share elements between applications in a number of ways. You can export Standard MIDI Files (SMF) from one sequencer to another. This is a great way of sharing arrangement ideas. On the audio side, there is XML and OMF (Open Media Framework), which allow you to export audio files, regions, and edit positions from one project to another.

▓ USE KEY COMMANDS

Unless you have some sort of addiction to rolling a mouse around a table, you're going to find the menu-jockeying that's inherent in desktop production to be a bit of a drag (no pun intended). Key commands make life so much easier. I know it takes time to learn them, and it requires a lot of memorizing, and that's not why you got into music in the first place, but it's still worth it. If you don't feel like you can remember all the obscure key commands in your software, invest in a keyboard template program like Power Keys. Or record key commands on a flat-file, nonvolatile data medium (you know, a piece of paper) and post it on the wall above your keyboard.

APPENDIX 2:   WEBSITES

■ SELECTED MANUFACTURERS

KEY

1   Internal audio interfaces
2   FireWire, USB, and PCMCIA audio interfaces
3   MIDI interfaces
4   Multitrack audio/MIDI software
5   2-track recorder/editors
6   Plug-in audio effects
7   Software instruments
8   Universal MIDI editor/librarians
9   CD burning, mastering, and format conversion
10   DSP hardware
11   Control surfaces
12   Digital audio mixers
13   Hardware synthesizers, samplers, and MIDI controllers
14   Outboard digital recorders
15   Outboard A/D converters
16   Synchronizers
17   Sound libraries
18   Computer systems and peripherals

Aardvark www.aardvarkaudio.com (1, 2, 3)

Ableton www.ableton.com (4)

Akai Professional www.akaipro.com (13,14)

Alesis www.alesis.com (1, 13, 14, 15, 16)

Antares www.antarestech.com (6)

Apogee www.apogeedigital.com (1, 2, 15)

Apple www.apple.com (4, 18)

Behringer www.behringer.com (12)

Bias Inc. www.bias-inc.com (4, 5, 6)

Cakewalk www.cakewalk.com (2, 4, 6, 7, 11)

CM Labs www.cmlabs.net (11)

Creamware www.creamware.com (1, 6, 7, 10)

Cycling '74 www.cycling74.com (6, 7)

Digidesign www.digidesign.com (1, 2, 3, 4, 6, 8, 10, 11, 16)

DUY www.duy.com (6)

E-Mu www.emu.com (1, 4, 7, 13)

Frontier Design Group www.frontierdesign.com (1)

IK Multimedia www.ikmultimedia.com (6, 7, 9)

JL Cooper Electronics www.jlcooper.com (11)

Korg www.korg.com (1, 7, 13, 14)

Line 6 www.line6.com (2, 6)

Mackie www.mackie.com (1, 4, 11, 12, 14)

Magix www.magix.com (4, 9)

MOTU www.motu.com (1, 2, 3, 4, 8, 11, 16)

Microsoft www.microsoft.com

M-Audio m-audio.com (1, 2, 3, 4, 7, 13)

Native Instruments www.nativeinstruments.com (2, 6, 7)

Panasonic www.panasonic.com (12, 14)

Peavey Electronics www.peavey.com (6)

Propellerhead www.propellerheads.se (6, 7)

Presonus www.presonus.com (1, 2, 11, 12, 15)

Radikal Technologies www.radikaltechnologies.com (11)

RME Audio www.rme-audio.com (1)

Roland www.rolandus.com (1, 2, 3, 12, 13, 14)

Sony www.sonycreativesoftware.com (5, 12, 14)

Steinberg www.steinberg.net (1, 3, 4, 5, 6, 7, 9, 11)

Tascam www.tascam.com (1, 2, 3, 7, 11, 14)

TC Electronic www.tcelectronic.com (5, 6, 7, 10)

Terratec www.terratec.com (1, 16)

Wave Mechanics www.wavemechanics.com (6)

Waves www.waves.com (6)

Yamaha www.yamaha.com (12, 13, 14)

▓ PUBLICATIONS

Computer Music www.computermusic.co.uk

Electronic Musician Magazine www.emusician.com

Future Music www.futuremusic.com

Keyboard Magazine www.keyboardonline.com

Mac Life www.maclife.com

Macworld www.macworld.com

Mix Magazine www.mixonline.com

PC Magazine www.pcmag.com

PC World www.pcworld.com

Sound on Sound www.sospubs.co.uk

Tape Op tapeop.com

▓ COMMUNITY AND INDUSTRY SITES

www.craigslist.org

www.facebook.com

www.garageband.com

www.harmony-central.com

www.synthzone.com

www.shareware.com

www.musicplayer.com

www.broadjam.com

www.myspace.com

www.reverbnation.com

www.twitter.com

APPENDIX 3: GLOSSARY

In an effort to provide a more helpful comprehensive resource, the glossary includes some terms that do not appear in the text.

Aftertouch: A MIDI control signal that generates a message based on the pressure exerted on a MIDI key.

A/D (Analog-to-digital) conversion: The process by which analog audio signals are converted to digital audio data.

Absolute time: Format that measures time in hours, minutes, seconds, and milliseconds.

Acidizing: Encoding process that stamps an audio file with time and pitch information, allowing these characteristics to be manipulated in real time by software such as ASCI and SONAR.

ADAT: **(1)** An eight-track digital tape recorder developed by Alesis Corporation. **(2)** A widely used type of multichannel digital audio connection that streams eight channels of audio on one optical cable. Also known as Lightpipe.

AIFF (Audio Interchange File Format): Uncompressed audio file format compatible with a wide variety of software.

Algorithm: A formula used by a sound module or effects device for generating sound.

Amplitude: The loudness of an audio signal, illustrated by the height of the waveform.

Analog input: A connection for analog audio signals.

Anchor: See **Sync point**.

Arm: See **Record-enable**.

Arpeggiator: Device for creating automatic arpeggios (chord-based musical patterns) based on notes input from a controller.

Arrange window: The main edit screen of multitrack audio and MIDI software (variously referred to as the Edit, Tracks, or Project window).

ASIO: (Audio Streaming Input Output): Native audio system developed by Steinberg (and adopted by other manufacturers) that can access a variety of audio interfaces.

Attenuate: Decrease in level, or make quieter.

Audio connections: Any physical or computer-based routing that traffics audio signal from one destination to another.

Audio Interface: Any device that can route audio to and from a computer. Types of audio interfaces include sound cards, USB interfaces, FireWire interfaces, and internal (built-in) audio.

Auto-punch: A type of recording where the beginning and end of the section are predefined; the recorder is then programmed to automatically begin recording at the "punch-in" and end recording at the "punch out" points.

Automation: The recording and playback of controller information; e.g., mixer setting.

Auxiliary bus: A bus, or path, that receives signal from an auxiliary send.

Auxiliary send: A secondary mixer channel output that routes signal to an independent destination in parallel to the channel's main output.

Balance: Stereo mixer channel control that determines a signal's position in the stereo field.

Bank: A group of patches or settings, as in a synthesizer or effects device.

Beat mapping: Analyzing an audio file for tempo information.

Beat-matching: Technique for making two or more audio files of different tempos play in sync with one another.

Bit depth: The number of bits used to represent a single sample in an audio file.

Bit-depth conversion: Changing a sound file's format from 24 bit to 16 bit, or vice versa. Necessary when recording at one bit depth (24 bit) and then burning commercial CDs (which are 16 bit).

Boot drive: See **System drive**.

Bounce: To record all or part of a mix to one or more audio channels.

Breakout box: An external device that houses connections for an interface. Most commonly used to connect audio to a PCI card interface.

Buffer: A temporary holding place for data on its way to a final destination. Buffers are used to ensure smooth audio recording or playback. RAM is often used to buffer audio being recorded to hard disk.

Built-in: The computer's internal sound-generating circuitry, in contrast with external or added hardware or software.

Bus: On a software mixer, a common path that signals share to reach a single destination point. Examples include outputs, master outputs, internal effects sends, and groups.

Cache: A high-speed memory-storage buffer that can speed computer operation by storing common software routines and commands.

Capture: The recording of audio or video into a computer.

CD Burner: Any unit that can write data to CD-R and CD-RW.

Channel: (1) A path through which audio signal travels. (2) A signal path for MIDI data.

Channel strip: A set of controls for a mixer channel.

Chase: To follow in sync with a master device via time code.

Chord generator: MIDI processor that can generate automatic chords based on the input of single notes.

Class compliant: A computer peripheral that requires no additional drivers to be recognized by the operating system.

Click or **Click track**: A sound used to indicate the tempo; in desktop audio parlance, the track containing a click that acts as a metronome.

Clip: (1) n. An audio region. (2) v. To distort, or overload, audio.

Clipping: Condition where the amplitude of a wave exceeds the maximum allowed recording level, chopping off (or clipping) the waveform.

Clock speed: The speed at which the CPU processes instructions, measured in MHz and GHz.

Codec (Coder/decoder): Software used for compressing and decompressing audio and video files.

Compression or **Compressor**: (1) When referring to audio file data, compression reduces the size of an audio file by eliminating some of the audio data while recording (also known as lossy compression). MP3s are an example of a compressed format. (2) Dynamics processing or processor that reduces dynamic range by quieting any signal exceeding a specified amount (the threshold) by a given ratio.

Control surface: Mixer-like device that offers physical control of a software-mixing environment.

Controller: (1) Device used to transmit MIDI messages; e.g., a MIDI keyboard. (2) MIDI message used to control parameters in real time; e.g., MIDI volume and pitch bend commands.

Controller editor: MIDI editor that can access controller information.

Controller pane: Window within a MIDI note editor that can access controller information.

CPU: Central Processing Unit, this is the processor that drives the computer.

Crop: Elimination of the *unselected* area of an audio file. Also known as **trim**.

Crossfade: Technique for blending elements of audio files or regions to create a seamless edit. Small amounts of data taken from before and after the edit point are mixed together to make the edit seem more natural.

Cross-platform: A computer application or peripheral that is compatible with more than one operating system.

Cycle: To **loop** a section of an arrangement during playback or recording.

DAT (Digital Audio Tape): Cassette format for recording and playing back stereo digital audio signals.

Data connections: Any physical or computer-based routing that sends digital information from one device or module to another.

DAW (Digital Audio Workstation): Device that combines multitrack audio recording, editing, and mixing. The term is often used to describe a **digital audio sequencer**.

DC offset: Condition where a piece of hardware adds DC current to an audio signal, pushing the waveform of a digital audio file off of the baseline. Though normally inaudible, DC offset can chew up headroom and cause problems when processing the audio.

Decibel (dB): Unit of measure for audio level.

Destructive edits: Permanent changes to a data file.

Digital audio sequencer: Software that combines multitrack digital recording, multitrack MIDI recording, mixing, and editing.

Digital Input: A connection for digital audio signals.

Direct monitoring: Technology that routes the inputs of the audio interface directly to its outputs, bypassing the software audio engine. Direct monitoring is used to improve monitoring latency on some native audio systems.

DirectConnect: Digidesign's interconnection format that can be used to route third-party applications through a Pro Tools audio system.

DirectSound: Audio driver architecture developed by Microsoft.

DirectX: Multimedia technology developed by Microsoft that allows Windows software to share multimedia resources. DirectX plug-ins (a subset of the DirectX specification) are compatible with a wide variety of Windows applications.

Disc-at-once: A method for writing all the data to the CD in one pass. This is the best method for creating audio masters to be used for duplication.

Disk image: A copy of the complete CD file that is stored onto hard disk.

Display filter: A feature in a MIDI editor that can select which categories of events are available for editing.

Dithering: Process used to mask sonic artifacts that occur when reducing the bit depth of an audio file.

Dongle: See **Hardware key**.

Down sampling: Reducing the sample and or bit rate of an audio file.

Download: **(1)** Process of transferring patches and parameter information to a sound module. **(2)** Process for copying files onto your computer from an online source, such as a website.

Driver: An application that allows software and hardware to communicate.

Drum editor: Multichannel MIDI editor designed to work with rhythm parts.

DSP (Digital Signal Processor): **(1)** Any device that's used to process digital audio. **(2)** Hardware-based signal processor.

Dual mono: Two separate mono audio files that are linked together to represent a single stereo recording.

Dual processor: A computer with two CPUs.

Dump: To upload data into the computer; e.g., **SysEx** from a synthesizer to a sequencer.

DXi (DX instrument): A software instrument that runs under the DirectX plug-in format.

Dynamics: Quality describing the loudness of a performance.

Dynamics Processor: A device that can automatically control the loudness of an audio signal.

EASI (Enhanced Audio Streaming Interface): Native audio driver developed by Emagic capable of addressing a range of audio interfaces.

Editor/librarian: Software that lets you edit and store MIDI System Exclusive data.

Effect: See **Signal processor**.

Embedded loop: A small repeating section of MIDI or audio that occurs within a larger repeating section.

EQ: **(1)** Equalization, or tone control. **(2)** Equalizer; a device that allows you to alter the frequency response of a signal in order to control its tone.

Ethernet: High-speed data connection that can be used to create a computer network, access the Internet, and transfer data between a computer and compatible audio hardware.

Event: Any MIDI or audio occurrence or change, such as a note on or continuous controller change.

Event list: A MIDI editor that shows MIDI messages in a chronological list.

Expander: A dynamics processor that reduces, by varying amounts, the level of an incoming signal that falls below a user-defined threshold.

Expansion slot: Section of a computer motherboard that interfaces with peripherals, such as sound cards.

Export: To output data from one application for use in another; e.g., exporting audio files for from a multitrack to a waveform editor.

Fade: Gradual change in audio level.

Fader: Linear control used to set signal level.

Fast Fourier Transform (FFT) Analysis: A method for analyzing the audio spectrum of a wave file.

Feedback: **(1)** Condition where signal at an input is looped through an output and back to the input; e.g., a microphone feeding a speaker output and the speaker feeding the microphone. This can happen to both audio and MIDI signals. In both cases, it can cause problems, such as howling (with audio) or a hanging note or buffer overload (with MIDI). **(2)** A feature of delay and echo effects in which some of the delayed signal is routed back to the input (and back through the delay line). Increasing feedback increases the number of repeats in the delay.

Finalizing: preparing a mix for mastering.

FireWire (IEEE 1394): High-speed interface protocol used for connecting peripherals such as disk drives, CD burners, and audio interfaces.

Fly wheeling: A SMPTE mode that allows the slave module to generate its own SMPTE signal for short periods of dropout from the master source.

Format: **(1)** n. Type of data file; e.g., **wave** file, or **AIFF** file. **(2)** v. To prepare a hard disk for data by wiping its memory clean.

Fragmentation: A condition in which files on the hard drive are broken up into separate pockets of data. Fragmentation can slow the drive and hamper audio performance.

Frame: A time division representing one section of film or video.

Frame rate: The number of frames per second; used to distinguish **SMPTE** formats.

Full duplex: Feature on an audio interface that allows it to record an audio track while another one plays back.

Full-frame: Video signal that preserves the frame rate of the original source.

Gain: Expression of signal level.

Gain adjust: Change the loudness of an audio file by a fixed amount.

Ghost copy or **Alias**: A copy of a region that is linked to an original region; when you edit the original, the alias changes as well.

Graphical editor: **(1)** Any editor that uses a visual interface to represent audio information. **(2)** A MIDI **key editor**.

Grid: A method for defining the layout of an arrangement as it occurs over time, and the basis of time-based editing operations, such as **quantization**. Grids can be set to musical values (bars and beats), real time (hours, minutes, seconds, and milliseconds), **SMPTE** values (hours, minutes, seconds, and frames), or user defined values (such as markers).

Groove quantize: A type of **quantization** that conforms MIDI messages and regions to a custom grid.

Group: **(1)** To operate two or more audio **channels** with one control. **(2)** A **bus** that routes signal from several channels to a common destination.

Hard disk recording: Recoding audio data onto a hard drive.

Hardware key (a.k.a. Dongle): A device used for software copy protection that connects to the computer. If the hardware key is missing, the software will not run.

Host: Application from which **plug-ins** are launched.

Hot: Describes the loudness of an audio signal; to say a signal is "too hot" means that it is too loud, and may cause distortion.

Hot key: See **Key equivalent**.

Hot-swap: Connect or disconnect a peripheral (such as an external hard drive) while the computer is running.

Hub: A peripheral that allows you to expand the number of available connections in your system.

Hybrid systems: computer audio systems that combine native audio processing with additional DSP hardware, such as devices used for powered plug-ins.

Import: To open an existing file from within an application; e.g., importing an audio file created in a **multitrack** into a **waveform editor**.

Inline: A type of connection that interrupts the flow of a signal path; e.g., an insert.

Input: Any connection that enables signal to enter a circuit or signal path. Examples include audio interface inputs, track inputs, and effects inputs.

Input-processing: Signal processing performed on audio as it comes into the recorder.

Input-quantizing: Quantizing feature that conforms incoming MIDI data to a specified grid.

Insert: **(1)** v. To create an event, object, or region (e.g., inserting a MIDI note into an arrangement). **(2)** n. Section in a channel strip that routes signal to an audio processor in series with the channel's signal flow.

Interface: A device that routes signal to and from the computer; e.g., audio interface; **MIDI interface**.

ISA: A type of expansion slot found on some Windows-compatible computers. Not recommended for critical audio applications.

Jumpers: Short audio connectors used to connect modules on an analog synthesizer.

Key editor: Software window that display MIDI information on a **grid**.

Key equivalent: A keyboard key used to initiate a software command. Many audio applications let programs customize key equivalents.

Latch: **Automation** mode in which changes are recorded from the time you touch a control until the time you stop playback.

Latency: The delay between input and output of a signal as it travels through the audio system.

Library: A system for organizing samples, sounds, or patches into categories.

Lightpipe: See **ADAT**.

Limiting: Dynamics processing that stops any signal from exceeding a threshold.

Linear time code: See **SMPTE**.

Link: To connect two or more software applications.

location points: Predefined positions on a recorder's timeline used to set the start of playback, define loops, etc.

Locator: A **marker** that can be used to move to a specific position in an arrangement.

Logical editor: MIDI editor that can automatically select and edit material based on preset criteria.

Loop construction: Production method that utilizes repeating regions, called loops, to build an arrangement.

Loop (cycle) recording: Technique in which the same section of music is recorded repeatedly; each loop is stored separately, without erasing the others. In MIDI, this loop can layer data.

Loop: **(1)** v. To repeat (see **Cycle**). **(2)** n. Section of audio or MIDI that repeats within an arrangement. **(3)** n. A portion of an audio **sample** that, when repeated, allows the sample to sustain beyond its original duration.

Lossy Compression: See **Compression**.

Main bus: See **Master Bus**.

manual punch: Recording technique where, while the music plays, the user physically triggers the beginning and end of the recording.

Marker: A user defined pointer that identifies a location in a track or arrangement.

MAS (MOTU Audio System): A native audio system supported by MOTU Digital Performer and a number of third-party plug-in developers.

Master bus: The main output **bus** on a mixer.

Mastering: Process for preparing an audio file for output to a playback medium.

Matrix editor: See **Graphical editor**.

Merge: (**1**) v. To combine two or more regions into one. (**2**). Method of MIDI recording that combines new events with those previously recorded into a common track or region.

MIDI (Musical instrument Digital Interface): Protocol for sending control signals between compatible devices.

MIDI clock: MIDI **Synchronization** signal that follows bars and beats.

MIDI Machine Control (MMC): A two-way communications message that allows one device to control the transport of another.

MIDI message: See **Event**.

MIDI port: A MIDI connection that can send or receive 16 MIDI channels.

MIDI port: DIN-type connector that allows for the transmission of MIDI data. See MIDI In, MIDI Out and MIDI Thru

MIDI Time Code (MTC): MIDI **synchronization** signal that follows hours, minutes, seconds, and frames.

Mix: (**1**) v. To blend multiple signals for final output; e.g., mixing a multitrack arrangement to a stereo format. (**2**) n. An audio master recording created from a multitrack arrangement.

MME (Multi Media Extensions): Windows audio **driver** used to communicate with audio interfaces from a variety of manufacturers.

Modeling: Digital technology that creates sound by emulating the performance of another device; e.g., a modeling instrument based on an analog synthesizer; a modeling signal processor based on a tube guitar amp.

Modular: Any device that is made up of a group of smaller components.

Modulation: (**1**) Type of audio effect that uses delay and pitch to alter the sound over time. Examples include chorus and flanger. (**2**) MIDI continuous **controller** message that can be used to alter the sound of a MIDI note; e.g., adding vibrato.

Monitor: (**1**) v. To listen. (**2**) n. Playback system used to listen to audio.

Motherboard: Central foundation of the computer. The motherboard houses or connects to all the elements of the computer, including the **CPU**, disk drives, **expansion slots**, and communications ports.

MPEG (*.mpg; *.mpeg): Compressed digital video format.

M-Points (Cubase): Peaks in an audio file that can be used to create slice-like divisions. See ReCycle.

Multiband processor: A signal processor that divides the audio signal into sections, or bands, based on frequency, and processes them independently.

Multiport MIDI Interface: A device that offers multiple independent MIDI connections, each capable of transmitting or receiving sixteen MIDI channels.

Multitimbral: In a MIDI instrument, capable of responding to more than one MIDI channel at a time.

Multitrack: A device capable of recording and playing back more than two tracks of audio.

Mute: **(1)** v. To silence a signal. **(2)** n. A switch on a mixer that silences the output of a channel or bus.

Native: An audio system that utilizes a computer's internal processor for signal processing.

Noise gate: Dynamics processor that attenuates any signal that falls below a threshold.

Nonlinear: A recording and production technique in which the elements of an arrangement can be manipulated independent of the order in which they were recorded.

Normalize: Set the **peak** of an audio file to a maximum level.

Note: MIDI message that triggers a sound in a MIDI device.

Nudge: To move an **event** or **region** by a predetermined value.

Offline: **(1)** Audio processing that occurs in the background, not during playback; usually writes a new file to disk. **(2)** Any device or track that is not active.

Output: Connection or bus by which signal is sent to a destination.

Over: A signal that exceeds the amplitude limit of a digital signal path, causing distortion.

Overdub: To record new material in parallel with previously recorded material.

Overview: A display showing an entire project, arrangement, or audio file.

Painting: Editing technique whereby dragging the cursor across an area track fills that area with events.

Pan: Control for positioning a signal in the stereo (or surround-sound) field.

Parallel: Drawing the signal from a channel without interrupting the signal flow, as with an effects send.

Parallel port: A PC interface used for connecting printers; sometimes used to connect **hardware keys** for software.

Parameter: Any element in a device that can be controlled.

Partition: To divide a hard drive into separate sections, or volumes.

Patch: **(1)** n. A collection of settings that can be stored for later recall. **(2)** v. To connect two signals or devices together; e.g., patching an effect into an insert.

Pause: **(1)** v. To temporarily stop playback. **(2)** n. A section of silence that separates audio tracks on a CD.

PCI slot: High-speed expansion slot on a computer motherboard.

PCMCIA slot: **Expansion slot** found on laptop computers.

Peak: Maximum **amplitude**, or loudness, of a **waveform**.

Physical input: An input connection on an **audio interface**.

Physical output: An output connection on an **audio interface**.

Piano roll: See **Key editor**.

Pitch bend: MIDI continuous **controller** message that's used to change the pitch of a note over a specified range.

Pitch correction: **Signal processing** that conforms an audio file's pitch to a preset scale.

Playlist: A collection of **regions** designated for playback.

Plug-in: Software that extends the capabilities of a **host**. Most commonly refers to audio effects processors and **software instruments**.

Pool: A software window for storing and organizing audio files and regions.

PPQ (Pulses Per Quarter note): A measure of MIDI resolution.

Pre-allocate: To reserve space on a hard disk for recording.

Pre-quantize: To conform a performance to a **grid** as it's being recorded.

Pre-roll/Post-roll: A user-defined playback time that exceeds the boundaries of a selection or region.

Profile: A template used by software to communicate with a device such as a **control surface** or synthesizer.

Program: **(1)** n. A software application. **(2)** n. A memory location for storing instrument parameters; e.g., a synthesizer patch or effects setting. **(3)** v. To edit or create a sound or a part on a synthesizer, sequence, or effects device.

Punch points: Boundaries that indicate the beginning and end of a punch-in recording.

Punch-in: A type of recording in which new material is inserted into a previously recorded track.

Punch-out: To end punch-in recording.

Quantize: To conform MIDI or audio events to a pre-defined **grid**.

QuickTime: Apple multimedia file format.

RAID (Redundant Array of Independent Drives): A system of hard disks that act as one storage unit.

RAM: Random Access Memory.

Read: **(1)** To play back mix **automation** data. **(2)** To access data from a storage medium such as a hard disk.

Real Media G2 (*.rm): **Streaming** video format from RealMedia.

Real-time processing: **Signal processing** that's applied to a source as the source plays.

Record-enable: To make a track ready for recording (see **Arm**).

Red Book: Specifications developed by Philips/Sony for creating audio CDs.

Region: A section of an audio file, audio track, or MIDI track.

Render: Print to disk for final output.

Resolution: The number of subdivisions in a given time format. MIDI resolution measures the number of pulses per quarter note (**PPQ**). Audio resolution measures the number of **samples** per second (see **Sample rate**).

Return: An **input** that routes signal from an external source or internal bus into the main mix; e.g., effects return.

ReWire: A software routing protocol that's used to connect audio and MIDI between compatible applications.

REX file: A file format created by ReCycle (and supported by many third-party vendors) used for **beat mapping** audio files.

Reverse: Playing a sample or loop from back to front.

Rip: To extract audio files from an audio CD.

RTAS (Real Time Audio Suite): A **native** audio format developed by Digidesign for Pro Tools LE and Pro Tools Free.

Sample: **(1)** The smallest unit in a digital audio recording. At a **sample rate** of 44.1 kHz, there are 44,100 samples per second of audio. **(2)** An audio recording that can be triggered in real time by a **sampler**.

Sample rate: The number of **samples** per second, expressed in Hertz.

Sample-rate conversion: Changing the **sample rate** of an audio file.

Sampler: An electronic instrument that can record and play back short audio files, called **samples**.

Scrub: To play audio back by moving the cursor across a region. Scrubbing is used to identify sections for editing.

SCSI (Small Computer System Interface): Interface used for connecting hard drives, CD burners, and other peripherals.

SD2 (Sound Designer 2, also SDII): Uncompressed audio file format used by Digidesign software, and compatible with most Mac OS audio software.

Segment: See **Region**.

Send: Mixer control that routes signal to an effects **bus**, **output**, or other destination.

Sequencer: Traditionally, a data recorder that stores MIDI commands, or events. Current usage also includes **DAWs**.

Serial: Audio connection in which a device interrupts the signal flow (see **Inline**).

Serial port: Communications interface used for connecting modems and MIDI interfaces. Sometimes used to connect **hardware keys**.

Shell: An application that serves as a gateway between a **host** application and a collection of **plug-ins**; e.g., WaveShell.

Shift: Editing command that moves events by a specified amount; e.g., *shifting* a region one measure later.

Signal flow: The path a source signal takes on its way to a destination. Also called **signal path**.

Signal level: The gain, or intensity, of an audio signal.

Signal processor: Any device that alters a signal. Most commonly refers to audio effects.

Silence: Editing command that reduces the amplitude of an audio file or region to zero.

Smart cursor: An editing tool that changes its functionality depending on the position of the mouse relative to the targeted edit object.

SMPTE: Linear time code used by the Society of Motion Picture and Television Engineers that expresses time in hours, minutes, seconds, and frames.

SMPTE-to-MIDI converter: Device that translates **SMPTE** time code to **MIDI Time Code (MTC)**.

Snap: When editing, to conform a region or event to a grid position.

Snapping: an edit to a zero crossing point can eliminate audible problems, such as pops and clicks.

Snapshot: A form of static **automation** that stores all current mixer settings for later recall.

Soft synth: See **Software instrument**.

Software instrument: A software emulation of a physical instrument, such as a **synthesizer**.

Solo: (**1**) v. To silence all but the selected mixer channel(s), track(s), or region(s). (**2**) n. Mixer control used to isolate the playback of a channel.

Song Position Pointer (SPP): See **MIDI clock**.

Sound card: A PCI-based audio interface.

Split: To divide a region into two or more sections.

Spot: To place an event or region by entering a specific location.

Stand-alone: Refers to any device or application that can function independently. For example, a stand-alone **software instrument** can operate without host software.

Step record: To enter MIDI information one event at a time.

Step sequencer: A recorder into which notes are entered manually (not in real time).

Stereo interleaved: A two-channel audio file that represents a stereo recording.

Stream: **(1)** To play a file (such as a video file) over the Internet. **(2)** To access data from disk in real time, as in a streaming **sampler**.

Stripe: To record **SMPTE** time code onto a tape.

Sub-Index: Marker used to identify subsections of a CD track.

Submix: A mix within a mix. See **Group**.

Sync: Synchronize.

Sync point: A marker within a region that can be used to position the region on a grid. Also known as an **anchor**.

Synchronize: To lock two devices so that they play back together.

Synthesizer: An instrument that produces sound by manipulating an electronic (or digital) signal. Synthesis techniques include additive synthesis, frequency modulation (FM), wavetable synthesis, digital modeling, and others.

System drive: A hard drive that contains system software. Also called a **boot drive**.

System Exclusive (SysEx): MIDI messages used for transmitting parameter data between devices.

TDM (Time Division Multiplexing): Proprietary Digidesign audio architecture for use with DSP-based Pro Tools TDM systems.

Template file: A data file that can be used by an application to set the basic parameters of a project. For example, a template file for a digital audio sequencer might include audio track assignments, MIDI track assignments, effects settings, etc.

Tempo map: A list of tempo changes that occur through an arrangement.

Throughput: Speed at which data travels through a device or data path.

Thru: Avenue for MIDI transmission that passes through a device on its way to another.

Time code: Signal that carries synchronization information.

Time compression and expansion: Process for changing the duration of an audio file, with or without changing its pitch. Time expansion makes an audio file longer; time compression makes it shorter.

Time stamp: An parameter that indicates the baseline tempo and pitch of an audio file. The software uses this information as a reference for time compression and pitch shifting.

Time stretching: See **Time expansion**

Timeline: An area in an edit window that indicates time on a horizontal axis.

Touch: **Automation** mode in which changes are recorded only while a control is being operated. When you let go of the control, the automation reverts to previously recorded automation information.

Track: **(1)** n. An independent channel of audio or MIDI. **(2)** v. To record.

Track-at-once: A method for recording data onto CD in which tracks are written one at a time. Additional tracks can be added to the disc at a later time.

Track list: The running order of an audio program as it will appear on the CD.

Track start: The ID indicating the beginning of an audio track.

Transport: A set of controls that lets you locate various points in a project. Common transport controls include rewind, fast forward, record, play, and stop.

Transpose: Change an event's pitch or key.

Trim: **(1)** Editing technique in which the boundaries of a region are altered without moving the region's contents (see **Crop**). **(2)** Hardware mixer control used to set the input level on a channel.

Ultra ATA: High-performance interface for internal hard disks

Universal editor/librarian: Application that can edit and store **MIDI System Exclusive** information for a variety of devices from different manufacturers.

Upload: To transfer to a computer.

USB (Universal Serial Bus): Interface used for connecting disk drives, CD burners, audio interfaces, MIDI interfaces, controllers, and other peripherals, such as keyboards and mice.

Velocity: A MIDI note parameter that measures the force with which a key is struck. Velocity is usually used to control dynamics, but can be mapped to other attributes, such as tone.

Velocity scaling: Editing technique that conforms the velocity of selected events to a preset range.

Video editor: Software that can record, process, edit, and render video files.

Video for Windows (*.avi): Windows digital video format.

Virtual memory: Technology that uses a portion of the hard disk to act as an extension of RAM. Virtual memory can be incompatible with most audio applications.

Virtual tracks: Audio data that occupies a track slot, but which is not heard on playback because other data is using that track's audio channel. If you picture each track as a deck of cards, the top card is the active track, the cards stacked underneath it are the virtual tracks. Reshuffling the deck makes a new virtual track active.

Volume: (1) Loudness of an audio signal (2) A partition on a hard drive. Every hard drive contains at least one volume.

VST (Virtual Studio Technology): A **native** audio **plug-in** format that's compatible with a wide variety of effects and host applications.

Wave (.wav): Uncompressed audio file format for Windows (but also compatible with most Mac OS audio software).

Waveform: A visual display of an audio file.

Waveform editor: Software that can record, process, edit, and rewrite audio files

WDM (Windows Driver Model): A low-latency audio **driver** for Windows that's compatible with a wide variety of software and audio interfaces.

Wide SCSI, Ultra SCSI, And Ultra-wide SCSI: High-speed versions of the **SCSI** spec.

Windows Media Format (*.asf): Streaming video standard from Microsoft.

Word clock: Digital clock format that can be used to **synchronize** a number of digital audio devices to one master clock.

Write: (1) To burn onto a CD. (2) To record automation data.

Write speed: The speed at which a **CD burner** can write data to disc. Expressed in multiples (as in 4x, 8x, 16x, etc.).

Zero crossing: Section of an audio file where the waveform has an **amplitude** of zero.

INDEX